EXPERT SYSTEMS
Principles and case studies

EXPERT SYSTEMS
Principles and case studies

EDITED BY

Richard Forsyth
Polytechnic of North London

LONDON   NEW YORK

Chapman and Hall

First published 1984 by
Chapman and Hall, Ltd
11 New Fetter Lane, London EC4P 4EE
Reprinted 1985
Published in the USA by
Chapman and Hall
29 West 35th Street, New York NY 10001

© 1984 Chapman and Hall
© 1984 Tom Stonier (Chapter 13)

Printed in Great Britain at the University Press, Cambridge

ISBN 0 412 26270 3 (hardback)
ISBN 0 412 26280 0 (paperback)

British Library Cataloguing in Publication Data

Expert systems.
  1. Expert systems (Computer science)
  I. Forsyth, Richard
  001.64   QA76.9.E96

  ISBN 0-412-26270-3
  ISBN 0-412-26280-0 (pbk.)

Library of Congress Cataloguing in Publication Data

Expert systems.

  Bibliography: p.
  Includes index.
        1. Expert systems (Computer science) I. Forsyth,
Richard.
QA76.9.E96E96 1984   001.64   84-15529
ISBN 0-412-26270-3
ISBN 0-412-26280-0 (pbk.)

Contents

Foreword

An expert system is a computer system that encapsulates specialist knowledge about a particular domain of expertise and is capable of making intelligent decisions within that domain. Areas successfully tackled so far within the expert systems framework include medical diagnosis, geological exploration, organic chemistry and fault-finding in electronic equipment.

Although expert systems typically focus on a very narrow domain, they have achieved dramatic success with real-life problems. This has excited widespread interest outside the research laboratories from which they emerged.

Expert systems have given rise to a set of 'knowledge engineering' methods constituting a new approach to the design of high-performance software systems. This new approach represents an evolutionary change with revolutionary consequences.

AIMS OF THE BOOK

Many people, whether they think of themselves as computer professionals or not, are aware that something momentous is taking place in the field of computing, and want to educate themselves to the point where they can evaluate and, if necessary, apply the new techniques.

This book serves that need by explaining the concepts behind expert systems to computer users unfamiliar with the latest research. It has been written as an introductory handbook for people who want to find out how expert systems work. It is not an academic text: it is a practical guide written by active practitioners in the field, designed to open your eyes to developments in a new and dynamic area of computer science. After reading it you should be able to begin work on practical knowledge engineering projects of your own.

PLAN OF THE BOOK

This is an introductory handbook for people who want to find out how expert systems work. It is divided into four sections.

The first section, Background, explains the ideas underlying knowledge-based systems and describes the anatomy of a typical expert system. It also sets expert systems in their historical context and considers the Japanese Fifth Generation computer project, as well as the urgent (some might say, frenzied) Western responses it has provoked.

Section 2 considers the problems of inference – how to use approximate reasoning strategies to arrive at a good estimate of the truth with uncertain data and imperfect rules. This is an area where expert systems designers have pioneered a breakthrough in computing practice: knowledge-based systems do not rely on zero-defect software engineering. Take away one rule at random from an expert system's knowledge base and its performance will (probably) be slightly degraded; take away one statement at random from a conventional program and . . . The mind shudders at such a thought!

Section 3 concentrates on knowledge engineering itself. Can expert knowledge be adequately represented inside a computer and, if so, how? Here we adopt a case-study approach, looking at the various ways in which three specific software tools make that task possible. The tools are PROLOG (a programming language based on predicate logic), Micro Expert (an expert system 'shell' providing a standard inference mechanism and a notation for encoding knowledge) and REVEAL (a general-purpose programming support environment with special features facilitating the construction of expert decision support systems).

The final section addresses the subject of machine learning, a hot topic of the 1950s which fell from favour until recently revived by the demands of expert systems. The performance of an expert system depends crucially on the quality and scope of its knowledge base. Yet knowledge does not fall from the sky; it must be laboriously coaxed out of human experts, or read from between the lines of a textbook. This is the 'knowledge acquisition' bottleneck. One way of bursting through this bottleneck promises to be the use of automatic induction programs that discover new concepts and rules themselves from a database of examples.

This leads to the notion of 'mass producing' knowledge in symbolic form. A whole industry is springing up concerned with knowledge as a valuable commodity. The last chapter, by Professor Stonier, examines the social and economic impact of such developments and asks: how can we control the industrialization of knowledge?

R. Forsyth

Notes on contributors

ANNIE G. BROOKING

Annie Brooking is the founder and director of the Knowledge Based Systems Centre at the Polytechnic of the South Bank, London. Her academic background is in the methodology of systems design. Over the past two years she has taken the Knowledge Based Systems Centre from an idea into a thriving research unit – one of Europe's leading centres of excellence in intelligent knowledge-based systems.

PHIL COX

Phil Cox has had a long and varied career in the data processing industry. He started programming in 1961 with Air Canada in Montreal. In the mid-1960s he worked on the Boadicea project at BOAC. Since then he has concentrated on real-time programming and operating systems. After leaving SPL in 1971 he teamed up with a colleague to form ISIS Systems, of which he is currently technical director. He designed the Micro Expert package, an expert systems shell which runs on small desktop computers. He has also written an intelligent document interpreting program for a West German football lottery.

RICHARD FORSYTH

Richard Forsyth has a B.A. in Psychology from Sheffield University (1970) and an M.Sc. in Computer Science from the City University (1980). From 1979 to 1984 he was a lecturer, latterly senior lecturer, in computing at the Polytechnic of North London. Recently he left the Polytechnic to set up his own business, Warm Boot Limited, which is a software house specializing in machine-intelligence applications; and to write books.

PETER LLEWELYN JONES

Peter Jones is a computer consultant who works on both sides of the Atlantic. He holds a B.Sc. (1967) from Imperial College, and worked in production management and as a management consultant for Unilever before specializing in computer-assisted planning and decision support systems in the early 1970s. In 1973 he became Managing Director of On-Line Decisions International, a consultancy specializing in the development of large scale computer based corporate modelling systems. Experience in the application of DSS techniques underlined the importance of incorporating knowledge and judgement in management support systems, and led to the development of the REVEAL system in 1981. REVEAL is now marketed world-wide by Tymshare.

CHRIS NAYLOR

Chris Naylor holds degrees in Pyschology and Philosophy from the University of Keele and in Mathematics and Statistics from the University of London. He is a member of the British Psychological Society, the Institute of Mathematics and its Applications, the Institute of Statisticians, the British Computer Society and several other learned societies. At present he is a full-time author, researcher and freelance journalist. His recent books include *Build Your Own Expert System* from Sigma Technical Press. He is also a regular contributor on artificial intelligence and allied topics to a number of publications, including Computer Talk, Practical Computing and the Times.

ROY RADA

Dr Roy Rada is Assistant Professor of Computer Science at Wayne State University, Detroit, Michigan. He obtained his B.A. in Psychology from Yale University in 1973, an M.S. in Computer Science from the University of Houston in 1976 and a Ph.D. in Computer Science from the University of Illinois in 1981. He is also qualified to practise medicine (M.D., Baylor College, Texas, 1977) and his special interest lies in the application of artificial intelligence techniques to medical problems. Since October 1983 he has been editor of the Newsletter of the ACM's Special Interest Group on Biomedical Computing.

STEPHEN F. SMITH

Dr Stephen Smith is a Research Scientist in the Intelligent Systems Laboratory of the Robotics Institute at Carnegie-Mellon University. He received his B.S. degree (1975) in Mathematics from Westminster College and his M.S. (1977) and Ph.D. (1980) degrees in Computer Science from the University of Pittsburgh. Prior to joining the faculty of the Robotics Institute in 1982, he was Assistant Professor of Computer Science at the University of Southern Maine. Dr Smith's research interests include machine learning, hierarchical and distributed problem-solving, knowledge-based systems, and the application of artificial intelligence to industrial tasks. He is currently involved in the design of systems that improve their performance over time through the use of adaptive learning techniques. Other current work focuses on the development of methods for reasoning effectively under a large and conflicting set of constraints.

ANTONY STEVENS

In 1979, after eight years of teaching computing, Antony Stevens left his position as senior lecturer at the City of London Polytechnic to run a small medical DP department at the London Hospital Medical College. In 1981 he set up as a consultant in software for medical research, trading as Green Valley Software. An offshoot of this work is the development of an expert system to give advice on statistics. He moved to Brazil in 1984 and is currently a freelance computer consultant based in Natal on the north-east coast.

TOM STONIER

Professor Stonier is the Head of the School of Science and Society at the University of Bradford, Yorkshire. He obtained his A.B. from Drew University in 1950 and his M.S. (1951) and Ph.D. (1955) from Yale University. A New Yorker, he is based in Britain and well known in the UK as an expert on the impact of technology on society. He is a prolific speaker and author, and one of his recent books, *The Wealth of Information*, is a detailed study of the economics of information.

MASOUD YAZDANI

Masoud Yazdani was born in Iran, but has lived in England since 1975. He obtained a B.Sc. (1978) at Essex University before moving on to do research in artificial intelligence at the University of Sussex. Since 1981 he has been a lecturer in the Computer Science department at Exeter University. His special interests include educational computing and computer creativity. He has presented papers at a large number of international conferences, including the 1982 European Conference on

Artificial Intelligence; and is well known as the author of *Start Programming with the Electron* which accompanies every Acorn Electron microcomputer.

BACKGROUND

1

The expert systems phenomenon

RICHARD FORSYTH

Expert systems have burst into the news lately. To some, they represent the 'great white hope' of information technology; to others, they are more like an updated version of the 'yellow peril', since the Japanese may get there before us. To others again, the whole idea is a gimmick – old wine in new bottles, and coarse plonk at that.

The aim of this introductory chapter is to say what expert systems are by setting them in their historical context. In order to understand the phenomenon of the expert system, we must step back and examine the soil from which they sprang – the fertile field of artificial intelligence, or AI for short.

AI has a long and chequered prehistory, stretching back at least as far as the legend of Pygmalion. Mankind's enduring fascination with intelligent artefacts is a long and sometimes blood-curdling tale of golems, talking heads and notably Frankenstein's monster. (See Aldiss, 1975; McCorduck, 1979.) We skip over the first 2000 years of AI and pick up the story in the 1950s, when the fantasy at last showed signs of becoming fact, thanks to the digital computer.

Table 1.1 is a brief synopsis of AI history in the computer age. I have boiled it down to four easy stages – one per decade – and therefore, of course, simplified it drastically. Nevertheless, it highlights the important milestones.

The column labeled 'Paradigm' is the answer you would have got if you had asked an AI worker of the time what AI research was all about. The column labeled 'Workers' identifies one or two key figures who seem to characterize the spirit of their times in AI. (Underneath the main worker or workers I have put, in brackets, the thinkers or theorists whose ideas laid the foundations for their work.) Finally, the column headed 'System' picks out one typical system (not necessarily the best) which exemplifies the underlying trend or fashion.

Table 1.1 A bottled history of AI

	Paradigm	Workers	System
1950s	Neural nets	Rosenblatt (Wiener, McCulloch)	PERCEPTRON
1960s	Heuristic search	Newell and Simon (Shannon, Turing)	GPS
1970s	Knowledge representation	Shortliffe (Minsky, McCarthy)	MYCIN
1980s	Machine learning	Lenat (Samuel, Holland)	EURISKO

1.1 NEURAL NETS

In the 1950s AI researchers tried to build intelligent machinery by imitating the brain. With hindsight we are not surprised that they failed: the hardware just was not up to the job, to say nothing of the software.

The key system I have picked out was PERCEPTRON (Rosenblatt, 1957). This was a self-organizing automaton which can be thought of as a crude model of the retina in the human eye. It could be taught to recognize patterns, but only a limited class of patterns as Minsky and Paper proved later (1969).

At the time, there was a good deal of enthusiasm for systems such as Rosenblatt's, based on the pioneering cybernetic ideas of Norbert Wiener and Warren McCulloch about abstract neural networks. It was felt that a richly interconnected system of simulated neurons could start off knowing nothing, be subjected to a training program of reward and punishment, and end up doing whatever its inventor wanted. The fact that the human brain contains 10 billion neurons, each as complex as, say, a transputer, was conveniently overlooked.

This false optimism had already evaporated even before Minsky and Papert did their comprehensive theoretical demolition job on the PERCEPTRON concept. The empirical results were simply not good enough, and so a new fad took hold on the imagination of AI workers.

1.2 HEURISTIC SEARCH

The trailblazers on this new frontier were Allen Newell and Herbert Simon at Carnegie-Mellon University; and their work culminated in GPS, the 'General Problem Solver' (Ernst and Newell, 1969).

Central to their approach was the notion of heuristic search. They believed that human thinking is accomplished by the coordination of simple symbol-manipulating tasks such as comparing, searching, modifying a symbol and the like – the kind of things a computer can do. They viewed problem solving as a search through a space of potential solutions, guided by heuristic rules which helped direct the search to its destination.

They threw out the neural-net model, pointing out that even to design an ant's nervous system, comprising fewer than one thousand neurons, was beyond the limits of current technology. (To be fair, McCulloch, the grandfather of neural-net theory (1943), worked on a limited problem – the frog's visual system – and made valuable contributions to neurophysiology in that area.)

Newell and Simon began with a theorem-proving program, and moved on to computer chess. Then they turned their attention to the formulation of general techniques which could be applied to a wide variety of problems and came up with GPS.

GPS was general in that it made 'no specific reference to the subject-matter of the problem'. The user had to define a 'task environment' in terms of objects and operators to apply to those objects.

But its generality was confined to a restricted domain of puzzles with a relatively small set of states and well-defined formal rules. Like most of its contemporaries GPS functioned in a formalized micro-world where the problems (e.g. the towers of Hanoi, the missionaries and the cannibals) are, in human terms, no problem.

From a technical standpoint, moreover, it can be said that the GPS procedure, known as depth-first search, of breaking down a problem repeatedly into pieces until a subproblem is reached small enough to be solved directly is inefficient, since many blind alleys are explored rather thoroughly. Later workers have devised more efficient 'best-first' search strategies. (Though blind depth-first search is alive and well and living inside innumerable PROLOG interpreters!)

Nevertheless, the GPS project stands out from the ruck. Its authors, too, fell victim to misplaced optimism, as when Herbert Simon predicted in 1957 that within ten years a computer would be world chess champion; but there is a place for overconfidence in science. And, paradoxically, by emphasizing that both minds and computers are examples of general-purpose symbol manipulating devices, they raised the status of people. After all, it is obvious that they are programmed very ingeniously.

1.3 KNOWLEDGE IS POWER

What GPS could not do was solve real-world problems. In the 1970s a team led by Edward Feigenbaum at Stanford began to remedy that deficiency. Instead of trying to discover a few very powerful and very general problem-solving heuristics, they narrowed their focus. What a human specialist seems to have is plenty of know-how – a large number of useful tricks or rules of thumb.

And so the expert system was born, almost as a caricature of the real human expert who is said to know more and more about less and less. The mass-spectrogram interpreter DENDRAL (Feigenbaum, 1971) was the prototype of them all. But I concentrate here on its immediate successor MYCIN (Shortliffe, 1976) which has been even more influential.

MYCIN is a computer system which diagnoses bacterial infections of the blood, and prescribes suitable drug therapy. It has spawned a whole series of medical-diagnostic 'clones', several of which are in routine clinical use. For instance, PUFF, a lung function diagnostic tool built on the MYCIN plan, is routinely used at the Pacific Medical Center near San Francisco.

MYCIN introduced several new features which have become the hallmarks of the expert system. Firstly, its 'knowledge' consists of hundreds of rules, such as the following.

A MYCIN inference rule:
>   IF   (1) the infection is primary-bacteremia, and
>   (2) the site of the culture is a sterile site, and
>   (3) the suspected portal of entry of the organism is the
>   gastro-intestinal tract
>   THEN there is suggestive evidence (0.7) that the identity of the
>   organism is bacteroides.

Secondly, these rules are probabilistic. Shortliffe devised a scheme based on 'certainty factors' (not, strictly speaking, probabilities) to allow the system to reach plausible conclusions from uncertain evidence. This is highly significant. MYCIN, and systems like it, are robust enough to arrive at correct conclusions even when some of the evidence is incomplete or incorrect. This is because they have methods for combining fragmentary and possibly inaccurate information to derive a good estimate of the truth – whether based on probabilities, 'fuzzy logic', certainty factors or some other calculus of likelihood.

Thirdly, MYCIN can explain its own reasoning processes. The user (a physician, not the patient) can interrogate it in various ways – by enquiring why it asked a particular question or how it reached an intermediate conclusion, for example. It was one of the first genuinely 'user-friendly' systems. This degree of user-friendliness was really a by-product of the rule-based approach to programming. Each rule is a semi-independent packet of knowledge: if the user wants to know why a certain question was asked, the system simply regurgitates a descriptive trace of the rules which led to the question.

Fourthly, and crucially, MYCIN actually works. It does a job that takes a human years of training. Actually, MYCIN is very limited in scope, even compared to your hard-pressed neighbourhood GP, but the point is that the big corporations (and the government, and the media) are getting interested.

There is the famous example of PROSPECTOR, another West Coast expert system, this time in Geology, which found a previously unknown deposit of the valuable mineral Molybdenum. It is early days yet, but business has pricked up its corporate nostrils at the sweet scent of money. AI is losing its innocence.

1.4 THE NEXT STEP

So where does that leave us? It leaves us in the middle of yet another bout of gung-ho enthusiasm, not just within the introverted world of AI research, but throughout computer science and the data processing community.

This time the magic ingredient is knowledge. It is the extent and quality of its 'knowledge base' which determines the success of an expert system. And this time the enthusiasts may be right. If they are, then knowledge (in computer-usable form) is the black gold of the 1990s. And if it is, then the people who are going to hit the biggest gusher are the first ones to mass produce it by machine.

This brings us to the fourth and final section of Table 1.1. Doug Lenat (also of Stanford) has created a machine learning system called EURISKO (Lenat, 1982) which improves and extends its own body of heuristic rules automatically. Apart from winning the 'Trillion Credit Squadron' naval wargame three years in succession (with the rules changed each time in an attempt to prevent it), EURISKO has made a breakthrough in VLSI (Very Large Scale Integration) design by inventing a 3-dimensional AND/OR gate.

There can be little doubt that automatic induction programs like EURISKO are the key AI development of the decade, and therefore that machine learning is the key to the future. So far, codifying an expert's skill has been a long and labour-intensive process. Knowledge is a valuable commodity: sooner or later it will be manufactured, in bulk. (See also Chapter 10 of this volume.)

Thus while expert systems are living off the intellectual capital of the 1970s, AI in the 1980s has moved on to focus on the problems of machine learning.

Which brings us full circle, or rather round one spiral in the staircase of AI development, because machine learning was precisely the problem that the cyberneticians like Wiener, McCulloch and others were attacking with different methods and more primitive technology in the 1950s.

REFERENCES

Aldiss, B. (1975) *Billion Year Spree*, Corgi, London.
Ernst, G. and Newell, A. (1969) *GPS: a Case Study in Generality and Problem Solving*, Academic Press, New York.
Feigenbaum, E. (1971) On generality and problem solving. *Machine Intelligence*, **6**.
Lenat, D. (1982) Eurisko: a program that learns new heuristics and domain concepts. *Artificial Intelligence*, **21**.
McCorduck, P. (1979) *Machines Who Think*, Freeman, San Francisco.
McCulloch, W. and Pitts, W. (1943) A logical calculus of ideas imminent in nervous activity. *Bulletin of Mathematical Biophysics*, **5**.
Minsky, M. and Papert, S. (1969) *PERCEPTRON; an Introduction to Computational Geometry*, MIT Press, Massachussetts.
Rosenblatt, F. (1957) *The PERCEPTRON: a Perceiving and Recognizing Automaton*, Cornell Aeronautical Lab, New York.
Shortliffe, E. (1976) *Computer Based Medical Consultations: MYCIN*, American Elsevier, New York.

2
The architecture of expert systems

RICHARD FORSYTH

The most significant thing about expert systems is that they are highly successful: already there are systems that can out-perform skilled humans at medical diagnosis, mass-spectrogram interpretation, predicting crop disease, prospecting for minerals and much else besides. Suddenly people and indeed large corporations are using AI programs to get rich. Expert systems have finally disposed of the old dictum: if it works, it's not AI!

An expert system is based on an extensive body of knowledge about a specific problem area. Characteristically this knowledge is organized as a collection of rules which allow the system to draw conclusions from given data or premises.

This knowledge-based approach to systems design represents an evolutionary change with revolutionary consequences; for it replaces the software tradition of

Data + Algorithm = Program

with a new architecture centred around a 'knowledge base' and an 'inference engine', so that now

Knowledge + Inference = System

which is clearly similar, but different enough to have profound consequences.

2.1 FEATURES OF EXPERT SYSTEMS

But what exactly is an expert system? The British Computer Society's Specialist Group on the subject has proposed a formal definition.

An expert system is regarded as the embodiment within a computer of a knowledge-based component, from an expert skill, in such a form that the system can offer intelligent advice or take an intelligent decision about a processing function. A desirable additional characteristic, which many would consider fundamental, is the capability of the system, on demand, to justify its own line of reasoning in a manner directly intelligible to the enquirer. The style adopted to attain these characteristics is rule-based programming.

That says it all, but personally I prefer an informal definition: 'An expert system is a piece of software that causes TV producers to lose all sense of proportion.'

In fact, you may find a list of distinctive features more useful:

(1) An expert system is limited to a specific domain of expertise.
(2) It can reason with uncertain data.
(3) It can explain its train of reasoning in a comprehensible way.
(4) Facts and inference mechanism are clearly separated. (Knowledge is NOT hard-coded into the deductive procedures.)
(5) It is designed to grow incrementally.
(6) It is typically rule-based.
(7) It delivers *advice* as its output – not tables of figures, nor pretty video screens but sound advice.
(8) It makes money. (This is a performance requirement.)

Up to now the biggest problem has been getting the knowledge from an expert into a machine-manipulable form.

2.2 COMPONENTS OF AN EXPERT SYSTEM

We have said that an expert system contains an inference engine and a knowledge base. There are in fact four essential components of a fully fledged expert system:

(1) The knowledge base.
(2) The inference engine.
(3) The knowledge-acquisition module.
(4) The explanatory interface.

All four modules shown in Fig. 2.1 are critical, and while a knowledge-based system may lack one or two of them, a truly 'expert' system should not. Let us look at each of them in turn.

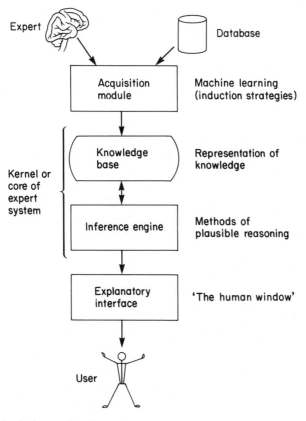

Fig. 2.1   A typical expert system

2.3 THE KNOWLEDGE BASE

A knowledge base contains facts (or assertions) and rules. Facts are short-term information that can change rapidly, e.g. during the course of a consultation. Rules are the longer-term information about how to generate new facts or hypotheses from what is presently known.

How does this approach differ from conventional database methodology? The major difference is that a knowledge base is more creative. Facts in a database are normally passive: they are either there or not there. A knowledge base, on the other hand, actively tries to fill in the missing information.

Production rules are a favourite means of encapsulating rule-of-thumb knowledge. These have a familiar IF–THEN format, for example:

Rule 99
IF   the home team lost their last home game, AND the away
        team won their last home game
THEN the likelihood of a draw is multiplied by 1.075; the
        likelihood of an away win is multiplied by 0.96.

But remember, these rules are not embedded in program code: they are data for a high-level interpreter, namely the inference engine.

Production rules are not the only way to represent knowledge. Other systems have used decision trees (e.g. ACLS), semantic nets (e.g. PROSPECTOR) and predicate calculus. Since one form of predicate calculus – 'Horn clauses' – is built into PROLOG together with a free theorem prover, this latter representation shows signs of gaining in popularity. At some very deep level all kinds of knowledge representation must be equivalent, but they are not all equally convenient. When in doubt, the best plan is to choose the simplest you can get away with.

2.4 THE INFERENCE ENGINE

There is some controversy in the field between supporters of 'forward chaining' versus 'backward chaining' as overall inference strategies. Broadly speaking, forward chaining involves reasoning from data to hypotheses, while backward chaining attempts to find data to prove, or disprove, a hypothesis. Pure forward chaining leads to unfocused questioning in a dialog-mode system, whereas pure backward chaining tends to be rather relentless in its goal-directed questioning.

Therefore most successful systems use a mixture of both, and Chris Naylor (1983) has recently described a method known as the Rule Value approach which combines some of the merits of both strategies. I call it 'sideways chaining'. (See also Chapter 6 of this volume.)

Whether your inferencing procedure works primarily backwards or forwards, it will have to deal with uncertain data and this is where things start to get interesting. For too long computer specialists have tried to force the soft edges of the world we actually inhabit (and understand well enough) into the rigid confines of hard-edged computer storage. It has never been a comfortable fit. Now we have means of dealing with uncertainty, in other words with the real world rather than some idealized abstraction that our data-system forces us to believe in.

Indeed, we have too many ways of dealing with uncertainty! There is fuzzy logic, Bayesian logic, multi-valued logic and certainty factors, to name only four. All sorts of schemes have been tried, and the odd thing is that most of them seem to work.

My explanation for this state of affairs is that the organization of knowledge matters more than the numeric values attached to it. Most knowledge bases incorporate redundancy to allow the expert system to reach correct conclusions by several different routes. The numbers measuring degree of belief are primarily for fine-tuning.

Hence, within reason, you are free to pick the measure of certainty that suits you best. (See also Chapters 5 and 6 in this volume.)

Let us move on to the question of knowledge acquisition.

2.5 INDUCTION STRATEGIES

Knowledge is a scarce and costly resource. How do we get hold of it?

Up to now the main bottleneck in the development of expert systems has been acquiring the knowledge in computer-usable form. Experts are notorious for not being able to explain how they make decisions, and the explanations they do give often turn out to be mere window-dressing. How then can we formalize their expertise?

The traditional way has been to closet a highly paid 'domain expert' (or two) with a highly paid 'knowledge engineer' for a period of months, during which time they effectively negotiate a codified version of what the expert knows. This process takes time and, obviously, money.

So there is a keenly felt need to automate the knowledge acquisition process. In my opinion Doug Lenat's EURISKO program (1982) is the forerunner of a new generation of machine-learning systems.

Lenat is not the only worker active in this field. Michalski (1980) has designed a system which learned to classify soya-bean diseases. Quinlan (1979) devised a concept-learning algorithm that grows its own decision trees by looking at a database of examples. I myself wrote a program (Forsyth, 1981) that uses a Darwinian scheme, termed 'naturalistic selection', to create and amend classification rules. It is called BEAGLE (Biological Evolutionary Algorithm Generating Logical Expressions).

But the striking thing about EURISKO is that its description language (the notation in which it stores rules and concepts) is expressive enough to allow it a rudimentary self-consciousness, in the form of 'meta-rules'. It is rather an introspective system, and spends a lot of time monitoring its own performance, recording its findings as rules that apply to itself.

One of its discoveries had an ironic twist. It noticed that human rules tended to be better than its own, so it came up with the heuristic:

      IF   a rule is machine-made,
      THEN delete it.

Luckily the first machine-generated rule that EURISKO erased was that one!

(Knowledge acquisition and refining is dealt with more fully in Chapters 10, 11 and 12 of this volume.)

2.6 THE HUMAN WINDOW

The fourth main component of a true expert system is the explanatory interface.

One of the best things about the classic expert systems like MYCIN is the care exercised over the user interface. At any time the enquirer can ask the system why it made a given deduction or asked a particular question. Rule-based systems generally reply by retracing the reasoning steps that led to the question or conclusion. The ease of doing this is a point in favour of rule-based programming.

The explanation facility should not be regarded as an optional extra. Donald Michie (1982) and others have warned about the dire consequences of systems which do not operate within the 'human cognitive window', i.e. whose actions are opaque and inexplicable.

If we are to avoid a succession of Three-Mile-Island-type disasters or worse, then our expert systems must be open to interrogation and inspection. In short, a reasoning method that cannot be explained to a person is unsatisfactory, *even if it performs better than a human expert.*

2.7 WHO NEEDS EXPERT SYSTEMS?

At this point the reader may be asking: Do I need an expert system? The answer depends on the kind of problem you want to solve. Table 2.1 is a checklist of features that affect the suitability of the knowledge-based approach.

Table 2.1

Suitable	vs.	Unsuitable
Diagnostic		Calculative
No established theory		Magic formula exists
Human expertise scarce		Human experts are two-a-penny
Data is 'noisy'		Facts are known precisely

If your intended application falls more on the left than on the right, you should seriously consider an expert system.

By a diagnostic problem we do not mean just medical diagnosis, but include any area where there are several possible answers and the difficulty is selecting the right one, or at least filtering out the improbable ones. Many categorization and prediction tasks fall into this framework, e.g. computer fault diagnosis. Once you know that it is the disc interface rather than the main memory that is playing up, the hard part is (or should be) over: the repair is a matter of routine board swapping.

By a domain where no established theory exists we mean topics like tax law, motor repair, weather forecasting and indeed most branches of medicine. There are too many variables for a complete and consistent theory, so skilled practitioners rely on knowledge and 'intuition'. We exclude, by contrast, problems where you can plug in a formula, crank a handle, and out comes the answer – for example, planetary motion, where Newton's laws are good enough for spacecraft guidance.

An area where human experts are scarce is easily recognized by the telltale symptoms of high salaries, job hopping and queues for vocational training courses. It is clearly cost-effective to try to computerize skills that are in demand (such as oil-well log interpretation) before more commonplace ones like image recognition which even pigeons can do, and which often turn out to be much harder to computerize than so-called intellectual skills.

Finally, if your information is reliable and clear-cut, an expert system is not particularly recommended. If on the other hand your data is 'dirty', it may be just what you need. Then fuzzy, fizzy, fudgy or some other funny logic can really come into its own.

2.8 LANGUAGE ISSUES

There is a widespread misconception that all expert systems have to be written in LISP or PROLOG.

LISP has proved its worth over 25 years of AI research but it is no accident that it has not caught on commercially. It thrives in academic hotbeds like MIT, Stanford and Carnegie-Mellon University, because it provides a medium for the interchange of ideas. You can take Joe Hacker's pattern-matcher, add Mike McQwerty's theorem-prover and bolt on young Carl Whizzkid's natural language parser. By that time you're more than half way there (as long as they speak to each other).

But once outside the AI sub-culture, you are on your own. LISP itself is hardly more than CAR, CDR, COND and CONS (plus EVAL). All the interesting bits are accretions which follow the LISP philosophy but which are in essence additional software packages. They are not standardized, and in the UK most of them are not even available. So just getting LISP really does not get you very far.

As for PROLOG, my advice is to forget it. PROLOG is a much-touted logic programming language heralded by some as the dawn of a new era in software development. If the Japanese do adopt it without radical modification (and the signs are that they will not), the West can relax till the end of the century. Perhaps the kindest thing to say about PROLOG is that it is ahead of its time. Now let's say some unkind things about it.

(1) PROLOG has very little error-protection against minor misspellings and so forth, which merely lead to bizarre unintended effects.
(2) The user must understand the implementation details of the backtracking mechanism to write code – i.e. it is not true 'logic programming'.
(3) The order of clauses is crucial to their meaning – again, this is contrary to the spirit of logic programming.
(4) Many built-in predicates have side-effects, rendering PROLOG unsuitable for efficient parallel execution.
(5) PROLOG provides a relational database for free – a big bonus, but the trouble is that it resides in main memory, and is consequently very greedy on storage.
(6) Everything in the database is global: there are no local facts or modules in the accepted sense.
(7) Depth-first search is done for you – whether you want it or not. If you want something more sophisticated, you have to 'cut' your way out of the jungle by hacking branches off the search tree.
(8) PROLOG is already riddled with non standard 'enhancements'.

In short, PROLOG is a hacker's delight, since only a dedicated elite can master its elegant intricacies. The claim that it is a logic programming language simply will not bear serious scrutiny. Some of my best friends use PROLOG, but I wouldn't touch it with a keyboard. When you hear of schoolchildren using it fluently you can be sure that they are being taught a subset which leaves out the 'knobbly bits' (and therefore would not suffice for serious software development).

As Feigenbaum and McCorduck (1983) put it: 'The last thing a knowledge engineer wants is to abdicate control to an "automatic" theorem-proving process that conducts massive searches without step-by-step control exerted by knowledge in the knowledge base.'

If you must use PROLOG, wait until it has been digested by BASIC. BASIC is like a ravenous python, devouring all that lies in its path. It has just finished swallowing PASCAL with all its control structures. After a short pause and a few burps it will be ready to gobble up PROLOG, and we shall see BASICs that offer built-in resolution theorem-proving. Then it will be time to consider switching to PROLOG. (But see also Chapter 7, of this volume.)

2.9 DO IT YOURSELF

The best plan is to use the language you know on the machine you have. One relatively cheap solution is to purchase an expert system shell (e.g.

Micro Expert or Nexus), use it as a prototyping tool till you know what you want, then write the production version in an efficient and portable language like C, FORTRAN 77, PASCAL or even FORTH.

You don't have to wait for the promised fifth-generation dream machines either. As long as your computer is not bigger than a VAX nor smaller than a Sinclair QL it can do the job. An IBM PC or Apple MacIntosh, especially with a hard disc, would do quite nicely.

2.10 CONCLUSION

When it comes to knowledge-based systems, ignorance is just not a viable option. Nobody in the information business can afford a wait-and-see attitude, because the future has already begun.

REFERENCES

Feigenbaum, E. and McCorduck, P. (1983) *The Fifth Generation*, Michael Joseph, London.

Forsyth, R. (1981) BEAGLE: a Darwinian approach to pattern recognition. *Kybernetes*, **10**.

Lenat, D. (1982) The nature of heuristics. *Artificial Intelligence*, **19**, 189–249.

Michalski, R.S. and Chilausky, R.L. (1980) Learning by being told and learning from examples. *International Journal of Policy Analysis and Information Systems*, **4**.

Michie, D. (ed.) (1982) *Introductory Readings in Expert Systems*, Gordon and Breach, New York.

Naylor, C. (1983) *Build Your Own Expert System*, Sigma Technical Press/John Wiley, Chichester.

Quinlan, J.R. (1979) *Induction over Large Databases*, Report HPP-79–14, Stanford University, Palo Alto, California.

3

The Fifth Generation game

ANNIE G. BROOKING

3.1 BACKGROUND

Late in 1978, the Japanese Ministry of International Trade and Industry (MITI) gave the Electrical Laboratory (ETL) the task of defining a project to develop computer systems for the 1990s with the title 'Fifth Generation'. The project was supposed to avoid competing with IBM head-on. In addition to the commercial aspects, it also had to enhance Japan's international prestige.

After various committees had deliberated, it was decided to go ahead with the project in 1981. The project formally started in 1982.

A team was created under Hajame Karatsu to study the prospective functional requirements of the new machine. In order to do this they attempted to forecast the nature of the society of the next decade which the new machine would serve.

Having done this, and having compared the results with the ways that computers are currently used, the team concluded that various impediments existed to providing for perceived 'social needs', but that these would be alleviated by the new machine. These included:

(a) Expectation for improvement in the fields of low productivity.
(b) Internationalization of Japan.
(c) The shortage of energy and natural resources.
(d) High age and high education (Aged and educated society.)
(e) Information society for human beings.

These goals for a new society could be perceived as stressful to the human race because of the mismatch between the human being and current machines. Therefore, the function of the Fifth Generation machine would be to bridge that gap.

As Hajame Karatsu stated:

> . . . human beings are soft. So, many troubles can happen between the hard machine and the soft human being. From this consideration the Fifth Generation must be the machine that should work to fit the human being intimately, contrary to the present way when the human being has to approach the machine to match it and to follow the rule of it.

Dr Kazuhiro Fuchi (now head of ICOT, the Fifth Generation centre), further stated:

> Many voices are raised in dissatisfaction over present day computers. One of the complaints is that today's technology is far from the idea of being truly 'handy' for the user.

He further says that one of the factors for 'handiness' is the aspect of man-machine interface. Most people would agree that graphical and natural language communication would be preferable to typewritten QWERTY I/O. However, a factor to the detriment of 'handiness' is that any solution for a given problem has to be programmed.

If it is possible to integrate information relative to the object areas of the program, together with laws governing those areas, it will greatly benefit the problem solving capacities of the system. Knowledge of this kind corresponds to knowledge on the human side. This view reflected those long held in the United Kingdom and by researchers working in the area of artificial intelligence. In order that machines should be truly handy, it would be necessary to have a more natural interface between man and machine, in fact, more like the man to man interface. This poses many problems for the Japanese, including emulation of human sensory functions such as vision, touch, speech synthesis and speech understanding. All of these areas require a vast backup of support knowledge. Pure data processing functions would not support the sophistication of input required to supply these highly complex functions. To this end the Fifth Generation was designed to provide the support technologies – both hardware and software.

3.2 OVERVIEW OF THE PROJECT

The Fifth Generation project has broad scope because the proposal is to design an alternative architecture and supporting software. Seven research themes have been specified in the project (Table 3.1). These themes are each highly complex and will require thousands of man-years to cover adequately.

Table 3.1 Themes in research and development of the Fifth Generation computer system

Basic application system	1.1 Machine translation system. 1.2 Question answering system. 1.3 Applied speech understanding system. 1.4 Applied picture and image understanding system. 1.5 Applied problem solving system.
Basic software systems	2.1 Knowledge-base management system. 2.2 Problem solving and inference system. 2.3 Intelligent interface system.
New advanced architecture	3.1 Logic programming machine. 3.2 Functional machine. 3.3 Relational algebraic machine. 3.4 Abstract data type support machine. 3.5 Data flow machine. 3.6 Innovative Von Neumann machine.
Distributed function architecture	4.1 Distributed function architecture. 4.2 Network architecture. 4.3 Data base machine. 4.4 High speed numerical computation machine. 4.5 High level man-machine communication system.
Very large scale integration (VLSI)	5.1 VLSI architecture. 5.2 Intelligent VLSI CAD system.
Systematization technology	6.1 Intelligent programming system. 6.2 Knowledge-base design system. 6.3 Systematization technology for computer architecture 6.4 Data base and distributed data base system.
Development supporting technology	7.1 Development support system.

The Fifth Generation computer system will be oriented towards processing knowledge. It will have a high logic capability. Its greatest feature will be that the interface will approach the human level. The software modeling system is intended to be highly effective for use of the hardware and will serve mainly to perform meta-inference functions for problem solving such as understanding problems and synthesizing programs. Input to such systems is intended to include everyday language, pictures, images, etc.

There will not be one Fifth Generation machine, however, but several, each module made up of a number of modules, either hardware or software, each designed for a specific function. To that end, the user should ultimately be able to configure a speech machine for a specific function, a robot with high visual processing capabilities, etc.

However, the success of all of these modules will ultimately rely on high quality knowledge information processing and its management. To this end, it can be said that the success of the Fifth Generation project lies in the successful application of techniques to each of the problem areas.

The hardware intended to support the core of these activities will not be of the classical Von Neumann architecture. Research has already been done on languages which better support problem solving techniques. Currently PROLOG is the only language well known to support this problem solving strategy. The Japanese have decided to build upon the experiences of the advocates of logic programming and design a new language (to be called HIMIKO) which better reflects the concepts in logic. Initially the processing will be performed on a serial architecture especially designed for the purpose, the PSI machine (Personal Sequential Inference machine). During later stages of the project, a parallel machine will be developed.

The proposed speed for such a machine is measured in LIPS (Logical Inferences Per Second). Target Speeds quoted to date are in GIGALIPS.

> 1 GIGALIP = 1 000 000 000 logical inferences per second.
> 1 LIP = between 100 and 100 000 MIPS (Machine Instructions Per Second; approximately 30 000 times the processing capacity of a present-day DEC KL-10 processor.)

Table 3.2 shows a conceptual picture of the Fifth Generation machine as seen from the top down. As previously stated not all elements will be included in all of the proposed machines, but some idea of the potential complexity of a machine can be understood from the table.

A research and development schedule has been planned which specifies three stages – initial, interim, and final – for each of the seven research themes. The initial stage is three years' duration and amongst its goals are:

- A high performance personal PROLOG machine.
- A relational data base machine.
- Basic research.

Thus the first results should become available in April 1985.

Table 3.2 From the top down

	Three layers
User language – (speech, natural language picture)	
Analysis comprehension and speech synthesis	
Knowledge (language and picture domain)	
Intermediate specification response	
Intelligent programming system	
Problem understanding and response generation	
Knowledge (problem domain)	
Knowledge base system	
Program synthesis and optimization	
Knowledge machine model – (knowledge representation)	
Logic programming language	
Problem solving and inference machine	
Knowledge-base machine	
Interface for Fourth Generation machine	
Symbol manipulation machine	
Numerical computation machine	
Data base machine	

3.3 RESULTS TO DATE

By virtue of the nature of the implementation of the Fifth Generation project, it is extemely difficult to measure success accurately at each stage.

There is one official 'voice' for the project, namely ICOT. However, the majority of the research is not being done at ICOT. (At the time of writing ICOT is believed to have 30–40 researchers.) Most of the research effort comes from those companies who are working on some specific part of the project, agreed together with MITI. Such companies include giants like FUJITSU, MITSUBISHI and NEC. However, unlike other national and international IT projects they are not collaborative, and are, in some cases, competitive. This means that many results of research are company confidential. So the Fifth Generation project has levels – one public and several private.

One result which is visible is the PSI. Three machines have been built by MITSUBISHI. The first machine was delivered to ICOT in December 1983 for the first layer of software to be implemented in time for the second Fifth Generation Conference to be held in Tokyo, in November 1984.

Various research is underway in speech recognition and speech synthesis looks promising. The Japanese have an additional incentive to develop such systems because their written language is too complex to be easily implemented on a machine. Novel approaches to word processing, including high resolution FAX input, will no doubt have strong influence on the Japanese market place.

Surprisingly, there appears to be little activity on the development of expert systems. Whilst nearly all computer manufacturers in the world have some VLSI expert systems project underway, other applications are not evident in Japan. Clearly unlike Europe and America, the Japanese do not consider knowledge engineering and techniques for Fifth Generation software engineering to be as important as the development of the host hardware.

3.4 THE BRITISH RESPONSE

Japan invited several countries including the UK to send a team of scientists to Japan to discuss participation in their national program. As a result of this invitation a committee was formed, headed by John Alvey of British Telecom. The team of twelve consisted of computer scientists and technologists from British Industry, and Government departments. The only 'academic' invited was Roger Needham, who is director of the Computer Laboratory at Cambridge University. Notable omissions from the committee were Donald Michie, probably Britain's most famous AI expert and Alex d'Agapeyeff, Chairman of the first British Computer Society expert systems group. In fact, it now seems that none of the committee members had any extensive experience of artificial intelligence.

Nevertheless, the Alvey team attended the first Fifth Generation Conference, where the Japanese announced their program. The scale and cohesiveness of the program were seen as a major competitive threat. Also, it was assumed that the Americans would respond, further threatening the British information technology industry.

Upon their return to the UK, the team made a study of possible areas where collaborative research could be established within the UK. This study was published in September 1982, by Her Majesty's Stationery Office, and became known as the Alvey Report.

The report identified four key areas in which the committee believed major technical advances were necessary, if more wide ranging application of IT in the future were to be achieved. These four areas are:

- Software engineering.
- Very large scale integration (VLSI).
- Intelligent knowledge based systems (IKBS).
- Man-machine interface (MMI).

The program is for advanced information processing, which is intended to be highly collaborative between industry and academia. Like the Fifth Generation project, the program is a national one intended to inject the necessary impetus into the British IT industry, so that it will be able to compete with Japan and America in the future. The report was presented to the Government who subsequently voted it 350 million pounds (sterling), for a program designed to run for five years. A directorate was appointed, the Alvey directorate, headed by Brian Oakley CBE, formerly Secretary of the SERC. Four managers were also appointed, one to manage each of the four areas of research.

Four studies were commissioned from the four areas. These studies were intended to pinpoint possible areas for research projects. These studies were widely publicized, and industry and academia were invited to collaborate and comment. The four reports were:

(1) IKBS architecture study.
(2) Software engineering strategy.
(3) VLSI strategy.
(4) MMI strategy.

Within these studies clear guidelines were given, as to the nature and scope of future Alvey projects. More particularly the IKBS architecture study which was the first to be published, outlined the proposed strategy for IKBS activity within the UK.

3.4.1 The research and development program

This comprises five main styles of activity over the next 5–10 years, each with different timescales and objectives:

- **'Show Me' projects** providing immediate industrial demonstrations of existing IKBS technology.
- **Short term development projects** aimed at producing marketable products within 2–3 years, based on low risk developments from current technology.
- **Demonstrator projects** involving industry-led collaborative research and development aimed at building complete prototypes of possible future systems requiring substantial research and development progress.
- **Research themes** involving medium to long term directed research by collaborating teams on a limited number of carefully chosen topics likely to be crucial to success in building an advanced IKBS.
- **General research** accelerated progress in the directed part of the research and development program will only be possible against a

background of a well balanced portfolio of high quality, speculative research in all the important aspects of IKBS and related topics such as software technology and man-machine interaction.

Approximately one year after the report was published, the first contracts were awarded for feasibility studies for projects which fell into the demonstrator category. These projects were intended to be led by industry. They were invariably large, in some cases the consortium included more than eight organizations with 30–40 people working together. However, they were not to involve themselves in basic research, only identify needs where and when they arose. At the time of writing, the first contracts for those successful feasibility studies had just been awarded. As yet contracts for smaller projects or basic research had not yet been awarded, although the Alvey Directorate have received many proposals.

One factor in the Alvey strategy, which is interesting, is the high ratio of Government funding. This is seen as necessary for collaboration, especially if small companies are to be attracted into the program. Also, academia is 100% funded, again an essential ingredient in these times of cut-backs within the education sector.

As I have already stated, the Alvey programme has four main areas for research and development. I shall outline the objectives under each heading below.

(a) Software engineering

The British have always seen themselves as good software engineers, and it is true to say that we export a lot of software and design 'know how' to other countries.

However, despite the advent of structured techniques over ten years ago, the Alvey committee perceived that too much trust is still put into the use of *ad hoc* design techniques. In order for the UK to become a world leader in software engineering technology new techniques will have to be developed.

Research activities for software engineering are mostly concerned with the production of various generations of integrated programming support environment (IPSE). It is interesting however to note that the Alvey Report recommends the establishment of a software production centre and a national quality control centre.

(b) Man-machine interface

The area of man-machine interface has been identified as one which is in dire need of structured research. Thus the MMI program is extremely diverse including:

- Design of dialogs.
- Input/output modes and their effectiveness.
- Identification of communicative skills of humans such that systems can be better designed as consultants or tutors.
- Human/system cognitive compatibility – identify the cognitive mismatch between the user and the system.
- Analysis of problem solving behavior in complex tasks.
- Investigation of the extent to which systems will need to emulate human problem solving behavior.
- Alternative I/O devices such as high resolution scanners and complementary hard copy devices.
- Speech and image processing to include feature extraction, speech recognition and speech synthesis.

(c) IKBS

Research in IKBS was identified by the committee as not only difficult, but also long term. Themes identified requiring immediate attention include:

- Knowledge representation.
- Inferential problem solving.
- Development of functional languages.
- Development of functional machines.
- Development of smart data bases.
- Knowledge acquisition techniques.
- Natural language communication.
- Development of prototype IKBS.

The IKBS program is seen to be highly dependant upon other areas encompassed within the Alvery program such as MMI and new hardware which will no doubt be developed as a result of advances in VLSI design.

However, much theoretical work can still be done without new fast parallel hardware. In particular, knowledge acquisition is one of the bottlenecks in the design of expert systems needing attention.

(d) VLSI

VLSI design is important to the advanced information processing program because it will enable an order of magnitude increase in the number of interactions between circuits as compared to connecting LSI devices together on a printed circuitboard. The goal here is to ensure that the UK has secure access to internationally competitive VLSI.

Existing design tools are seen as being far from adequate to exploit the full potential of VLSI. Therefore, a substantial program for computer aided design is proposed. The objective has been stated as a set of tools which translates a system description into three outputs:

(1) Geometrical definition for reticule manufacture.
(2) Test programs.
(3) Process definition.

An indigenous capability to produce silicon chips is also necessary, and this must be world class silicon technology.
Several processes will be needed.

- Micron bi-polar.
- Micron MOS – digital/analogue MOS.
- 0.5 micron research.

For these processes, a number of process techniques need to be developed concurrently.

- Electron beam microfabrication.
- X-ray lithography – whole slice DSW.
- Direct-step-on-wafer (DSW) production aligners for high yield fine-line processing.
- 'Dry' etching using a combination of plasma and ion bombardment to replace wet chemistry.
- Ion implantation.
- Elitaxial growth – whether on silicon, sapphire or other insulating substances.
- Layer processing – metals and dielectrics on the silicon surface, for contacts, interconnections, device delineation and passivation.
- Annealing/depart drive in.

The research program targets over the next five years lead towards the maintenance flow of one micron demonstrator chip designs which will respond to the needs of MMI and IKBS programs.

The Alvey program was the first national response to the Fifth Generation Report. The scheme itself is only just underway and it will probably be at least another two years before results can be evaluated.

Meanwhile, the UK was still fighting to keep up in the IT race, not under its own flag, but under the combined European response managed by the EEC ESPRIT.

3.5 THE EUROPEAN RESPONSE

The European response came from Brussels, the headquarters of the EEC. The Commission employs teams of consultants to examine and monitor various trends in diverse areas affecting the Community. In the early 1980s the framework for the 1984–87 program had been structured around six major goals of community policies;

- Improving agricultural competitiveness.
- Improving industrial competitiveness.
- Improving the management of energy resources.
- Strengthening aid to developing countries.
- Improving living and working conditions.
- Making better use of the scientific and technical resources of the community.

At the European Council meeting in Brussels on 28th – 29th June 1982, information technology was singled out as an urgent subject for increased action. Further, at the Summit meeting in Versailles in June 1982 the leaders of industrialized nations agreed on the need for collaboration in the new technologies such as information technology.

The Commission had already identified the weakness of the European situation in a communication submitted to the Council on 25th May 1982, on the need for a European strategic program for research and development in information technologies.

The Commission then called together the major information technology companies to discuss the problem. These companies, which became known as the 'big twelve', were:

AEG	
Nixdorf	*W. Germany*
Siemens	
Olivetti	*Italy*
Stet	
Bull	
CGE	*France*
Thompson CSS	
GEC	
ICL	*Britain*
Plessey	
Phillips	*Netherlands*

Each sent representatives to form a panel whose task it was to work with the Commission in formulating the intiative which became known as ESPRIT (European Strategic Program for Research in Information

Technology). In some ways it could be said that ESPRIT was not a direct response to the Fifth Generation plan. European concern was not just with the Fifth Generation challenge, but something which could potentially occur tomorrow.

Over the past few years Europe had become increasingly dependent upon Japan for its chip productivity, and the USA for its software. The success of the UNIX operating system is testimony to this fact. Recently the Americans have become more cautious about exporting software, mainly because of tales of their technology finishing up in communist bloc countries. Specifically there have been instances when it has taken up to one year to acquire an export licence for a piece of non-commercial software. At the time of writing we have just been informed that UNIX, a doctored version, will once again be available outside the USA.

So, the big twelve were concerned as to the impact of the cessation of the software flow from America to Europe. Worse still, what would happen to Europe's IT industry should the Japanese simultaneously decide to stop exporting chips to Europe?

On the political level it can also be argued that he who wins the IT race will, in doing so, control the flow of information. Further, that he who controls information, controls the world!

All heady stuff but, as I have said, we have already seen some of these symptoms this year. Faced with such a dilemma, the Council of the EEC made the decision to formulate an IT task force, the function of which would be to manage the emerging program. A plan was formulated. It was decided that there would be six areas of research;

(1) Advanced microelectronics.
(2) Software technology.
(3) Advanced information processing.
(4) Office automation.
(5) Computer integrated manufacture.
(6) Information exchange system.

Each of these areas had a panel appointed to formulate a workplan. Panel members came from representatives of each of the big twelve, and from experts in the field. The panels wrote an initial workplan for the first part of the program. This part, known as the pilot phase, was intended for the duration of one year leading to the main phase which would continue for a further four years.

The pilot phase began in July 1983. Approximately 35 contracts were awarded to consortia who submitted successful research proposals in the preceding February. These contracts were fairly evenly spread over the five areas which had been further refined into fifteen research themes.

1.   **Advanced microelectronics**
    1.1 Advanced interconnect for VLSI.
    1.2 High level computer aided design.
2.   **Software technology**
    2.1 Portable common tool environment.
    2.2 Formal specification and systematic program development.
    2.3 Software production and maintenance management systems.
3.   **Advanced information processing**
    3.1 Advanced algorithms and architectures for signal processing.
    3.2 Knowledge information management system.
    3.3 Interactive query system.
4.   **Office automation**
    4.1 Functional analysis of office requirements.
    4.2 Multi-media user interface at the office workstation.
    4.3 Local wideband communication system.
    4.4 Office filing and retrieval of unstructured information.
5.   **Computer integrated manufacturing**
    5.1 Design rules for computer integrated manufacturing systems.
    5.2 Integrated microelectronics sub-systems.
    5.3 Process and production control based on real time imaging
        systems.
6.   **Information exchange system**

The EEC provided not only management for ESPRIT, but also funding. Projects mostly received 50%. This particular fact made it quite difficult for academia to participate in a capacity other than subcontract (for which they receive 100% funding from the partner). Nonetheless, many academic partners are participating in ESPRIT, but there are also contracts in which all the partners are industrial. At least two industrial partners are necessary for ESPRIT participation. Further at least two of the partners need to be doing research in separate EEC member states.

Once the pilot phase was underway, the commission set about detailing the workplan for years 1–5 (the pilot phase termed as year 0). The workplans as designed by the panels for the five areas were then published throughout Europe and the Commission invited contributions, comments and amendments. To facilitate these amendments workshops were run; participants were invited from those who made the most useful contribution in response to the call. These revised workplans were then laid down as the direction, widely agreed upon, for the next five years.

Whilst this makes ESPRIT extremely difficult to manage because of the vast quantity of information the task force has to cope with (more than

1000 contributions were received to the AIP workplan alone), it does show that ESPRIT is intended, and appears to be, a very democratic program, run by Europe, for Europe.

The call for proposals for the ESPRIT main phase began in March 1983, the deadline being May 7th. It is intended that the main phase should begin in the early autumn of 1984. Needless to say all the pilot phase projects hope to proceed to the main phase; whether that is the case remains to be seen.

3.6 THE AMERICAN RESPONSE

The first and most important thing to say about the American response is that there isn't one; at least not a nationally co-ordinated project.

However, America is highly active in all areas of research in the Fifth Generation project. In particular, several businesses have sprung up around MIT and Stanford whose goals include expert systems development and the application of artificial intelligence techniques to industrial problems.

A recent survey showed the following organizations to be actively involved in knowledge based systems research.

Universities	CMU
	MIT
	Stanford
	and perhaps a dozen others.
Non profit	JPL
	Rand
	SRI
Government	NOSC, San Diego Cal.
	NRL AI Lab. Washington DC
Industrial	Aids
	AMOCO
	BBN
	Bell Labs
	DEC
	Fairchild
	Hewlett Packard
	Hughes
	IBM
	Intelligenetics
	Jaycor
	Machine Intelligence Corp.
	Martin Marietta

Schlumberger
Systems Control Inc.
Teknowledge
TRW
Texas Instruments
Xerox PARC

To date the government has been the principal source of funds of work in expert systems. Recently DARPA has launched an initiative in AI research which is highly focused on the application of AI techniques to military problems. Such projects include intelligent pilot assistant, intelligent submersibles and the like.

At a recent SPL Insight meeting, Professor Edward Feigenbaum suggested that Americans treated national initiatives from Washington with suspicion, and that such an initiative on the American continent may prove unsuccessful for that reason. Whether or not an American national project emerges will remain to be seen.

However, one could argue that they do not need one. American academics have been working with industry for some time. One shining example of success in this field is the DEC–CMU partnership which led to the building of R1 (now called XCON), DEC's expert system for configuring VAX and PDP machines. This system was just the first in the family DEC are currently using inhouse.

Also, the Americans seem to be able to cope with the split of basic and applied research quite well. This has led to the recent growth of companies around universities such as Stanford where university prototype research is taken through to a marketable product by the companies, leaving the universities free to continue with basic research.

Activity in Silicon Valley is hectic. Several companies are working on alternative architectures and chip design. Perhaps the best known leader in this field, Gene Amdahl, plans to have his wafer chip on the market within the next two years.

Xerox and Symbolics both have had AI workstations on the market for some time, and both have extensive software for rapid prototyping available. Meanwhile, the Japanese are still developing the operating system for their Personal Sequential Inference Machine, (PSI). This product will not be available for viewing until the end of 1984.

Finally, there is the question, 'what is the giant IBM up to?' which remains difficult to answer. There is no doubt that IBM does have an interest in Fifth Generation research, but exactly what, is largely rumour. However, one rumour is that IBM has its own ICOT equivalent, and has done so for quite some time.

3.7 CONCLUSIONS

The most obvious fact the Fifth Generation game has brought to light is, there aren't enough people to play the game. Manpower shortage in this area is enormous, and the demands upon the leading players are great.

At present the requirements include:

(a) Education of the next generation of researchers.
(b) Course design for the future.
(c) Setting up of research projects.
(d) Advising various funding agencies.
(e) Writing books and research papers.
(f) Speaking at conferences, seminars etc.
(g) Advising industry.
(h) . . . and of course, research.

At a time when mass unemployment is rife, it seems crazy that a small section of our society should be so hopelessly overworked.

Given that this is the situation in all the countries involved in Fifth Generation research one could argue that the player with the most experience and the best strategy should win.

The Europeans have ESPRIT. There is no doubt that the aims of ESPRIT are laudable. On the other hand, international collaborative research is extremely difficult and time consuming to manage. If collaboration were the main objective of ESPRIT, then one could say that the project was working very well indeed. An example of success here is the joint research centre which ICL, Siemens and Bull have established, independently of any external funding, in Munich. Maybe if it wasn't for the ESPRIT initiative this would not have occurred.

ESPRIT seems to be a very fair program; the Commission is dedicated to its success. Certainly there is no doubt that Europe is doing things, and in a concerted way – at last.

Britain is busy. We have the Alvey initiative and ESPRIT. Our experts in the field are contributing to both programs and are probably the busiest in Europe as a result. Unfortunately our reputation abroad is now abysmal. Recently Professor Edward Feigenbaum referred to Brian Oakley, head of the Alvey Directorate as a 'hospital administrator'.

Certainly, we have been slow in the past to take our ideas past research and into the market place. The question now is whether or not it is now too late for us to catch up. I think not. Alvey is forcing industry and academia to work much more closely together. One pitfall we should be careful to avoid is that all research is not Alvey directed; we must still retain separate funds for basic research. One interesting recent development is the announcement by Brian Oakley that we will collaborate with the Japanese. Previously, there seems to have been some confusion as to whether or not we ought to have been talking to, let alone working with, the Japanese. Perhaps the myth that we cannot build hardware and the Japanese cannot build software does have some substance after all!

The Americans have always been busy in the field. When AI research was effectively stopped in the UK by the Lighthill Report in 1972, the Americans forged ahead, and some of our best researchers, Mike Brady, Pat Hayes and David Warren, went to the States in order to get things done. The fact that major American funding comes from the military will mean that they will not be short of necessary hardware, and other equipment that we are starved of in Europe.

Lastly, there is the Japanese Fifth Generation project. There is no doubt that Dr. Fuchi's observation that computers are not 'handy' is both correct and timely. With the popularization of microcomputers in the office, school and home, we are creating a society adept at using a badly designed tool. The time has come for someone to perform a functional analysis of human requirements for a computing tool. Knowledge engineering is the first step in this process.

Whether or not the Japanese will achieve the goals they have set themselves, resulting in a set of machines which will alter the common perception of computing, remains to be seen. If they are successful, no doubt they will ultimately steal the lion's share of IT business from the western world. On the other hand, it seems that the western world was not capable of formulating such a plan, even when it prepared nearly all the basic research.

If Japan intended to increase national 'prestige' with this project, then it could be argued that this goal has already been achieved. Europe, Great Britain and America have their own projects for high technology in an attempt to stave off Japan's bid for world IT domination.

Ultimately, whether the Fifth Generation machine will be developed as the result of a race, or world-wide collaboration, is the more interesting question. In conclusion I would like to thank the Japanese for initiating the Game for without it no doubt the rest of us would still be waiting for its counterpart before actively doing anything at all.

REFERENCES

The Alvey Directorate (1984) *Alvey MMI Strategy*, Department of Industry, London.
The Alvey Directorate (1982) *The Alvey Report*, Department of Industry, London.

The Alvey Directorate (1983) Alvey VLSI and CAD strategy. *ALVEY News*, Department of Industry, London.

Commission of the European Communities (1982) *On Laying the Foundations for a European Strategic Program of Research and Development in Information Technology: The Pilot Phase*. COM (82) 486 final /2, Commission of the European Communities, Brussels.

d'Agapeyeff, A. (1982) The fifth generation. In *The Fifth Generation – Dawn of the Second Computer Age*, SPL International, Abingdon, Oxfordshire.

Fuch, F. (1983) Final aiming for knowledge information processing systems. In *Adopting the First European Strategic Programme for Research and Development in Information Technologies*, (ESPRIT)COM (83) 258, Commission of the European Communities, Brussels.

Gevarter, W.B. (1982) *An Overview of Expert Systems*. NBSIR 1982 – 2505, US Department of Commerce, National Bureau of Standards, Washington, D.C.

JIPDEC (1981) *Preliminary Report on Study and Research on Fifth Generation Computers 1979–1980*. Japan Information Processing Development Centre, Keidan-Ren-Kaikan, Tokyo.

Muller, B. (ed.) (1983) *SPL Insight Program*. The Fifth Generation World Conference 1983, SPL International, Abingdon, Oxfordshire.

Point Paper (1983) *DARPA Strategic Computing Program*, US Department of Defence, Washington, D.C.

SERC–DOI (1982) *IKBS Architecture Study*, HMSO, London.

Talbot, D. and Witty, R.W. (1983) *Alvey Program – Software Engineering Strategy*. Department of Industry, London.

Yokoi, T. (1983) *A Perspective of the Japanese Fifth Generation Computer Systems Project*. ICOT TM – 0026, Minato-Ku, Tokyo.

4

How shall we judge an expert system?

ANTONY STEVENS

I have chosen to interpret this question in two ways. The first assumes that expert systems will perform according to expectation and this leads me to speculate about the possible social consequences that arise from this. The second interpretation leads me to discuss the technical problems associated with the design of an experiment which compares the merits of different experts, whether they be systems or humans. Finally I close with some thoughts about expert systems when viewed from very far away.

If we assume that expert systems fulfill their promise then our judging can be about what they are going to do to us.

It is tempting when writing about technology to forget the political context in which it exists. So much of the imagination of the writer may be absorbed by explaining the technology that he may forget that its effect may not be uniformly good or bad. The writer of popular science settles for describing the effect on 'man' rather than 'working man' or 'governing man'. One does not have to be a socialist to acknowledge that industrial society is deeply divided with different groups in strong antagonism and power in the hands of a few.

4.1 THE SOCIAL IMPACT OF EXPERT SYSTEMS

It is commonly asserted that knowledge is power. Where industrial society is concerned we would have to feel, if we believed the maxim, that the agents of government derive their power from their knowledge. But since they can have the same knowledge whether in or out of power we shall perhaps have to settle for the statement that knowledge goes hand in hand with power.

Inside the government there must be a quantifiable idea of how society should be managed. If a figure is provided for the number of workers that must lose their jobs it must in some sense have been reached through the application of a chain of reasoning. Of course, we do not know whether this chain of reasoning has taken place, or whether it is one that we would agree with. But we can be sure that, when a politician is confronted and asked to produce an argument for a policy, the reply must contain more than just moral and political force to support it.

Suppose then that an administration has put a considerable amount of thought into its planning. The public is entitled to ask the administration to come clean about the reasoning. If this is not done then we are permitted to believe that the administrators have a cynical approach to the task that they have set themselves.

Let us assume there is a free flow of information and that the reasoning is codified. If it is not codifiable, then perhaps we may feel that it is not logical and therefore does not merit attention. If it is codifiable then what is to prevent us from constructing an expert system to embody this reasoning? Clearly there are the perennial technical problems associated with expert systems – opaque explanations, combinatorial explosion (Sir James Lighthill's major criticism of artificial intelligence which, I am sure, scholars will enjoy rediscovering in a year or two*) and the difficulties with casting human reasoning into the form that an expert systems shell expects.

A speculative enquiry, however, into the impact of expert systems must rely on the assumption that these problems will seem smaller as technical development takes place. We assume that the technology will be there to fulfill the wish. The wish is to sell the government's version of how society should be run as a type of arcade game where you keep the finger down on the redundancy button until the level of the other variables is satisfactory. The 'treasury model', or something like it, then becomes a plug-in game for your home computer.

If knowledge goes hand in hand with power and the administration has knowledge and if expert systems do what is claimed for them then their knowledge will be on a chip in due course. This may be resisted by those in power. But we can expect that there will always be some among the higher echelons of an administration who will allow their reasoning to be placed on a chip. When the knowledge is available to both sides in a social conflict then the power relations between the two sides must also change.

* 'Combinatorial explosion' describes the way in which the possible states in a multi-step task increase exponentially with the number of choices at each choice point. (See Lighthill, 1973.)

The situation at present is that the administration of a country knows best and the public had better listen to it. If what we read about expert systems is true then the situation in a fairly short while will be that not only will the administration know best but so will every home computer which has the administrations knowledge on a chip. What are we going to do with the administration?

We cannot guess what the chip will tell us. It may tell us something unpleasant. We still have bad news but this time we do not need the government to tell us. It is much more likely that the chip will lead us into a labyrinth of technical argument. The state of society will be like an intricate spreadsheet calculation and everyone using it will be conscious of the tentativeness of the assumptions on which it is based. Instead of feeling that we all know what is going on we shall realize that no one ever had a firm basis for taking decisions.

It is a common prejudice that those in power are stupid and self-seeking. We may see the possibility of this prejudice turning into a certainty when we put what they know on a chip and find that they know nothing. An interesting psychological situation. A mandarin earning much better money than a labourer is shown to have nothing to offer in return.

For these reasons therefore the political consequences of expert systems merit study. It is possible that our perception of social questions will be much modified when we can get a properly documented account of the management of society on a chip.

If therefore there are expert systems which give political and economic opinions then how shall we judge them? If we say that an expert system will gain more marks if it brings about radical change are we saying that we shall applaud an expert system if it encourages the growth of political anarchy? Is something necessarily good because it promotes a redistribution of power?

Now to those who also have knowledge but much less power than the mandarin. These are the advisers; the lawyers, doctors and accountants. It is normally assumed that an entrepreneur who produces an expert system for one of the advising professions has the members of that profession in mind when he thinks of selling it. If we have the very best tax-advisor on a chip how much money will we make if we sell it to every tax accountant? The complexity of a tax-advisors work is not in the human interface but in the juggling of the facts once they have been elicited. Having built the tax-advisor chip shall we not then build the human-interface co-processor and bypass the accountant altogether?

Clearly many of us feel that an effective product along these lines is very far away. However, much of the white-collar activity of an industrial society has already been automated and no doubt tax-experts will also be gobbled up eventually. Is a good payroll program very much less than the embodiment of how a payroll expert would behave when asked to produce a set of payslips? Goodbye tax-accountant.

The balance of knowledge will change. Will the power relationship as well? Well, we need the accountant for those things which the law says should be done by an accountant. If a chip turns up which does it more accurately will not the law change as well?

When workers in a primary industry feel threatened they can go on strike, march and threaten the rest of society. Will the accountants have such muscle? Are there enough accountants for the government in power to want to please them in case they vote for the opposition? And further, if we have tax and other accounting advice on a chip will we notice if they stop work?

The same kind of reasoning could be applied to all the professions which currently feature brain power and experience as the main commodity that they have to sell. Clearly the impact will not be uniform. We shall still need surgeons, though the scarcity value of a specialist in internal medicine may be much diminished.

If expert systems are what they are claimed to be and even if they are no more than rigorous and formal statements of areas of professional expertise, they are going to change radically the knowledge relationships in our society. If we believe that power goes with knowledge then the power relations will change as well.

I must emphasize, in case it is not yet clear, that by presenting this picture of what is to come I am not exulting in the possibility of a social revolution. I am, rather, extremely curious to know just what exactly will be considered valuable when the romance between society and human intelligence comes to an end because intelligence will be so cheap. Does any one these days admire someone who can dig a hole or paint a car quickly? We shall soon feel the same dullness about brainwork.

These then are some thoughts about the possible social consequences of the new developments in expert systems. Now a few brief remarks about the possible effect of expert systems on cultural life. I use the term 'cultural life' loosely to mean what we talk about and enjoy doing when we are not working. So much of the conversation of the middle classes is taken up with the exchange of erudition that one wonders whether the disappearance of erudition because of the widespread availability of knowledge will leave everyone at a loss for something new to say. It is always nice to have something interesting to say so how will you feel when there is a chip that is better at dinner conservation than you are?

The idea of information reverberating everywhere making it difficult for any of us to be original reminds us of the Global Village of an earlier generation. Much of the psychology of Western Man is bound up with what he thinks goes on inside his brain. It should be very interesting to see what happens when that brain is thought to have a competitor.

Our cultural attitude to computers has changed considerably in the last twenty years. Consider the difference between HAL (Kubrick, 1968) and the spaceship computer in *The Hitchhiker's Guide to the Galaxy* (Adams, 1979). HAL was the computer that controlled the spacecraft in *2001: A Space Odyssey*. Everything about HAL was clean and logical. We as the audience bought the idea that something so clean and logical would necessarily destroy humans. HAL only had one program and it was bound to have bugs in it. In Hitchhiker we are already in the age of the program-generator. No program is perfect but we can have several versions of it (these are the different personalities that the onboard computer has) and we can see if we can live with the faults of each. It won't kill us; at most we shall see it as a piece of inadequate engineering.

Perhaps the appeal of Marvin the robot is a sign of what is to come. He has a brain as big as a planet and he is chronically depressed. These two features in the same personality may become a more frequent cultural stereotype, a kind of robot 'Nowhere Man'.

The reader may be used to reading more technical works and will be irritated with the facility with which I use words like 'cultural', 'political' and 'economic' and may also ask where I get the evidence for what I am saying. And yet the computing community has uncritically accepted terms like 'expert' and 'knowledge engineer' for several years without the close scrutiny that their use should undergo before they are accepted. If my sociological comments have any merit it is surely that they try to relate the possible developments in expert systems with a more realistic view of what is going on in Western Society.

4.2 EVALUATING AN EXPERT SYSTEM

Now to the second meaning of the word *judge*. That is the meaning that is more allied to product evaluation. Does the program do the job?

When we are in the business of assessing something we wish to compare its performance against a competitor or against a standard. Although some of the problems associated with this comparison will be outlined below let us first consider the situation where two parties already have similar or nearly similar expert systems for a particular task. Suppose that in a shop we can choose either a Honda tax-advisor or one from British Leyland. Which shall we choose? Presumably we shall choose the one that can be delivered that afternoon, that fits nicely into the machine we have at home, and which is easy to use.

Are any of these factors that may influence our choice dependent on research on expert systems? Clearly if we cannot cobble together an expert system then we have nothing to sell, but is the expert system part of the product all that difficult? Chips are getting faster, and software support more widely available. Does the success of the product depend so critically on the response time? We may find that we have spent an awful lot of money on expert systems research to catch up with the Japanese effort (which some believe has been given an undue import-ance) only to find that we shall not be able to sell the stuff anyway because of our national disaffection with marketing.

Perhaps we should forget expert systems and concentrate on trying to produce cheap and reliable cars. Certainly the market for cars can be quantified but no one seems to be able or willing to estimate of the future market for expert systems. Clearly there will be expert systems, but will they be profitable?

Now suppose you buy an expert system because it will enable you to identify the location of uranium better. What is to prevent the expert systems supplier from selling the same system to your competitor or, if he has agreed not to, what is to prevent your competitor from commissioning his own expert system?

We then have two moderately similar expert systems chasing the same uranium. Has anybody gained? It depends on your attitude to where wealth comes from. If there is enough uranium in the world such that two expert systems chasing uranium will result in twice as much uranium being found then expert systems have indeed participated in the discovery of wealth. If, instead, we are in a situation where everyone is after the same thing do we want to use it up quicker?

This is obviously a very simplified view of the economic effects of intelligent products but it may be a useful thought to bear in mind when attempting to design viable products – look for the product that addresses the problem that is always there. Perhaps this is why expert systems have had some success in medicine. There will always be people and they will always have illnesses.

Expert systems can be divided into two groups according to whether they do or do not employ reasoning based on probability. If probability is not employed the question of assessing the performance of a system should be relatively simple – we can either agree or disagree with the chain of reasoning since the results from this sort of expert system are supposed to have the force of logic.

A whole series of difficulties arises if an expert system uses pseudo-probability. This is because we cannot guarantee that the conclusions are necessarily true. A theoretical framework is missing that can assure the user that the conclusion reached is the best possible. This problem awaits the attention of a new mathematical genius.

The science of statistics contains many technical results which support the view that one method of estimation is better than a wide range of competing methods. These results are based on mathematical arguments which make assumptions about the context in which the estimation is taking place. It could be that the notion of best estimation is an illusion or refinement which is rarely put to the test because differing but moderately good practices will always agree and when they do not a situation exists where further exploration is required. Nevertheless statisticians seem to need and try to develop something which is undoubtedly the best possible.

With this high-minded tradition already embedded in our thinking we find that when we consider the technical assessment of expert systems that we become very uneasy. That is because we know right from the start that the behaviour that we are studying is somewhat imperfect and that we cannot define perfection easily. In the climate in which statistical work is conducted the possibility always exists that assumptions may be rigorously tested and confidence increased by repeated experiments. It is as if you can chart your way towards certainty, even if the certainty is merely that you know nothing. The expert system or human presents an altogether different proposition.

We are supposed to accept from the start that the performance will not be perfect. What is more, we do not know how imperfect. If an expert system is to achieve more than any competent statistician has been doing for years then it must show competency over a wide range of questions. This means that our notion of what its performance is has to be split up into its ability to perform different tasks, some simple and others not so simple.

How shall we combine these different performances in one overall measure? We shall not be able to avoid the requirement for an assessment of some kind as the pressure builds up to allow what an expert system tells us to have a formal status in society.

Where are these thoughts leading us? The expert systems community claims that computer programs can be written which can combine evidence to produce reliable advice in a way that any statistician would be most uneasy about. (Some of these techniques, including fuzzy logic, are discussed in Part Two of this book.) Why, we may ask, has not the statistical profession taken this path before? There are enough statisticians who travel freely between statistics and computing to suggest that it was not lack of understanding that prevented them from developing the techniques of fuzzy logic. It is surely more likely that they did not pursue this line of enquiry because they felt it would lead them to a situation where they would be comparing imperfections. They could not see what they would be measuring and therefore did not get involved.

Various approaches to the assessment of expert systems have been proposed. These, simply described, count how successfully an expert system achieves the right conclusion. If we have to decide whether a coin is biased we can toss it and compare the number of heads obtained with a theoretical expectation and assign a probability to the data obtained.

A similar line of reasoning would allow us to decide whether enough information was available to determine whether a coin that gave more heads than another coin was really biased.

No such theoretical framework exists for comparing two expert systems. If a modification to a system means that the number of times it is correct increases from say 60% to 65% how can we know whether this increase is significant? We cannot even enumerate all the possible outcomes from such a program (if we interpret the chain of reasoning as being part of the outcome) so how can we exclude the possibility that an improvement is the result of chance?

If expert systems based on probability are doing something new then they must be a source of knowledge that is inaccessible to the practitioner of statistics. If this is the case, we have competing approaches to the truth. If however the expert systems attitude is merely heretical then perhaps it is motivated less by a desire for truth than for the traditional reasons which give rise to heresies. These are that they come from new social groupings which require an identity which must be protected from other social groupings. One of the ways of achieving this protection is to develop an ideology which may be used in combat with the presiding ones.

The antagonism that I have described between statisticians and knowledge engineers is not necessarily a conflict in which any individual must be seen to be on one side or the other. It is more simply an antagonism that exists between two sets of ideas about what constitutes good practice in the provision of advice. Obviously the two sets of ideas could reside in the same individual. He could believe on Monday that the pursuit of knowledge is best carried out in the circumspect and secure way of the statistician and then on Tuesday wish and believe that it is possible to make the obscure become clear by simply supplying a collection of mental jottings to a computer program that is advertised as being capable of unscrambling them and producing knowledge. I believe that the two attitudes cannot coexist indefinitely and it will be interesting to see which predominates in the future.

The signs are increasing that those who work with expert systems feel that what they produce will have to undergo the same kind of testing that is now given to other products such as new drugs and engineering designs. Let us hope that the scientific reading public will not be insulted for very much longer by statements like 'Computer discovers ore deposit worth countless millions'. This statement is banal because it ignores the costs of extracting the material and whether it is really needed. It reminds one of the exaggeration of customs officials who, when they discover a suitcase on a ship full of old and dry grass, claim that they have impounded thousands of pounds worth of drugs. It is only worth that amount when it reaches the streets. In a suitcase on a ship it is worth very much less.

Suppose that the design of experiments for the assessment of expert systems derives its initial inspiration from what is known about how to conduct clinical trials. At its simplest, a clinical trial compares two pills. The pills are allocated to the patients at random and the survival experience of the two groups is compared. An opinion is then formed about which pill is better. The remarks that follow are made in a medical context but they could be transposed to other fields where experts are recognized.

In our context one pill could be the advice from an expert system and the other pill the advice from a human expert. A number of problems however exist if we want to pursue this analogy. When we compare two pills we can do a lot to assure ourselves that the pills are homogeneous. It is possible that two patients receiving the same pill are in fact receiving different treatment because of some unknown consequence of the manufacturing process that makes pills from the same box have different properties. We however perceive this variation as very much less than the variation that would be obtained when the treatment came from the advice of a doctor. How could we obtain the equivalent of a box of identical doctors? If we choose to standardize by comparing the performance of a system against one doctor alone then that doctor has a great responsibility to bear. If we choose a panel of doctors then on what basis are they going to be selected? If we know that we must choose the treatment that patients receive at random then perhaps the same principle should be applied to the choice of doctors.

If competence is claimed for the expert system in a specialized area of medicine we are faced with the choice of judging the performance of the system in relation to the non-specialist doctor or in relation to the best in the field.

It may be argued that since the target audience is the doctor who has not specialized then it is he who should participate in the comparison. We are then faced with the thought that the non-specialist will be sold something that is known to be worth less than the advice of the specialist. It is therefore most likely that the system will fall into disuse because no one is going to settle for second best. If it is as good as the specialist then we must ask whether the specialist is going to let it be developed and further, whether, if it can be so easily codified, the specialist knew anything worth knowing in the first place.

We are forced by this kind of thinking to believe that it is only worth assessing an expert system that can compete with the best because no one is going to find much of interest in an expert system that is known to be second best.

Is it realistic to think that a clinical trial can be set up which allows one patient to be treated by an expert system and another by a panel of specialists? When two pills are being compared a doctor cannot complain about a treatment, at least not at the start of the investigation, because the reason the experiment was started in the first place was that he did not know what the properties of that treatment were. But who will have the courage to give a patient a treatment suggested by an expert system when it goes against received opinion?

So our field of enquiry is restricted even further. We need only reasonably compare expert systems that compete with experts because we can anticipate that the second best will always fall into desuetude. And further we can only compare expert systems with what the experts think of them because they cannot realistically be trusted with the lives of humans. It may be argued that an expert system methodology can acquire its prestige in a non-dangerous area and that this therefore may give it some credibility in those situations where much more is at risk. If an expert systems shell is extremely useful for the design of systems that route traffic through a city could it not have some intrinsic merit which would allow us to trust it in another context? This is very indirect thinking.

The position is now fairly ludicrous. On the one hand we have the opinions of experts and on the other we have the conclusions of a computer system which we shall judge by using the opinions of experts.

There is a trick that can be used which may give us the feeling of greater objectivity. If we mix the opinions from the computer system with the opinions of the experts and ask the experts to judge each on its merits and not tell them the origin of each then we may feel that a better comparison is being obtained. The disappointment lies in the fact that we are not actually learning anything in this situation about the treatment of patients but only about what is going on in the minds of the specialists. We have by this method constrained the perceived perform-ance of the expert system to be no better than that of the specialists. And yet if expert systems based on probability are to have novel features that result in new knowledge then they must sometimes surprise the specialist.

Suppose that all these problems are somehow overcome, the experiment is designed, the validation is performed and agreement reached that a particular system performs to a certain level of competence. This competence is in relation to a human standard. If I then buy the system and start using it in my daily work I shall with little effort begin to assimilate much of the knowledge it contains. The relative standing between me and the system will be altered. Of course this could also go the other way. When I come back from a long holiday the system will have gained in relation to me because I will have forgotten some of what it knows.

I wish I had a sensible criterion to offer the reader but I fear that, when we wish to assess the performance of an expert system, we are talking about something very ephemeral. Great store is set in the advertising industry in the television ratings of different programs. Their use in judging when to place commercials is very haphazard, but there is precious little else to go on. By promoting this new type of programming methodology the expert systems community has created a medium that has many of the properties of show-business. We have created something whose performance can only be measured very crudely and whose usefulness may depend mainly on the enthusiasm of those participating in it. Is MYCIN a viable program? Let me ask the reader to answer that question for himself rather than accept what he is told.

4.3 CONCLUDING REMARKS

There are two more aspects of the expert systems phenomenon that need to be discussed. The first aspect is that the need to develop expert systems appears in the main to represent an attempt by the computing community to sell something to the other academic disciplines.

In the prehistory of computer applications (that is 20 years ago) it was possible to obtain mileage by putting together projects which had the title 'The application of computer based analysis to subject X' where subject X could be really obscure topics like Population Genetics, Prehistoric Cave Art or Guppy Social Behaviour.

There was a generous feeling in the world academic community that cross-fertilization was exciting and that the fertilizing power of data processing was immense.

With the passage of time these attempts lost their attraction. Very often the new technology required that the investigator in subject X employ statistical notions of random sampling and experimental design in a systematic way. How do you take a random sample of stone-age hunter-gatherers when you do not even know how many there were or, even, where they were?

I think it is fair to say that the computing community had in the end contributed very little to knowledge. It had made it possible for the methods of the statisticians to have been tried out sometimes with great success. But the computing profession had only provided the engine for some one else to drive.

So the pressure has always been there for people in computing to show that there is an original contribution that they can make to Western scientific culture. This has now brought a completely new emphasis to their efforts. The promoters of expert systems derive their livelihood from computing and they wish to secure that livelihood by taking over other subject areas. It is as if they are no longer inspired by what they do and wish to obtain inspiration from the liveliness that they think exists in the work of others.

My final remark may be the sort of remark that an anthropologist might make about the expert systems movement as an aspect of human society. I wonder whether we shall ever have an explanation for the attractiveness of disembodied intelligence. Why are we thrilled when a machine thinks like us? If we look at the mental life of people from long ago we can see that much of what we would now call their decision support came from what were perceived as outside agencies, embedded in a supernatural framework. In the book *The Origin of Consciousness in the Breakdown of the Bicameral Mind* the psychologist Julian Jaynes (1976) charts in great detail how humans stopped receiving advice from external voices and other oracles and began to make up their own minds about what to do. I see a great similarity between the ancient role of Delphi and the hopes that people have for the part that expert systems will play in our lives.

It is too soon to tell whether what is happening is healthy. If it isn't then expert systems will join the ground-nut scheme and the Brabazon airplane on the rubbish tip of history and we shall have an interesting time trying to work out how it was that so many otherwise gifted people chose to believe that something new had appeared on the face of the earth.

ACKNOWLEDGEMENTS

I am very happy to acknowledge that I have derived great benefit from discussing some of the ideas contained in this chapter with the following people (who clearly do not bear any responsibility for what I have written).

1. Mlle. Noelle Burgi, Department of Political Science, Sorbonne.

2. Mr Henry Elliott, Department of Mathematics and Computing, Slough College.
3. Mr Brian Johnson, ISTEL Ltd.
4. Mr Tim Johnson, OVUM Ltd.
5. Mr Alan Parkin, Computer Techniques International Ltd.
6. Mr Richard Rowland, Allen and Overy partnership.

REFERENCES

Adams, D. (1979) *The Hitchhiker's Guide to the Galaxy*, Pan, London.
Jaynes, J. (1976) *The Origin of Consciousness in the Breakdown of the Bicameral Mind*, Houghton Mifflin, New York.
Kubrick, S. (1968) *2001: A Space Odyssey* (from *The Sentinel* by Arthur C. Clarke) MGM.
Lighthill, J. (1973) *Report to the Science Research Council on Funding for Artificial Intelligence Research*, HMSO, London.

INFERENCE

5

Fuzzy reasoning systems

RICHARD FORSYTH

One problem faced by all experts, whether human or inhuman, is that nothing in life is certain except death, and even that may arrive unexpectedly. Real-life problem-solving demands an acceptance of uncertainty, in order to minimize the difficulties it poses. Various schemes have been tried, some quite successfully, which allow the use of fragmentary and uncertain information to reach an estimate of the truth.

Indeed one of the great benefits of expert systems research has been the development of methods for being precise about imprecision. In this chapter we examine some ways of reasoning under uncertainty – where the problem data or the rules of inference (or both) are not 100% reliable.

5.1 A HACKER'S GUIDE TO FUZZY LOGIC

Fuzzy logic (also called 'possibilistic logic') was invented by Lotfi Zadeh (1965) who extended classical Boolean logic to real numbers. In Boolean algebra, 1 represents truth and 0 is falsity. So it is in fuzzy logic; but, in addition, all the fractions between zero and one are employed to indicate partial truth. Thus

$$p(tall(X)) = 0.75$$

states that the proposition that 'X is tall' is in some sense three quarters true. It is, by the same token, one quarter false. To combine non-integer truth-values, fuzzy logic defines the equivalent of the AND, OR and NOT operators.

```
p1 AND p2 = MIN(p1,p2)  (* smaller *)
p1 OR p2 = MAX(p1,p2)   (* greater *)
NOT p1 = 1 − p1         (* inverse *)
```

Thus pieces of evidence can be combined in a rigorous and consistent manner; and fuzzy logic is used successfully for example in the decision-support system REVEAL.

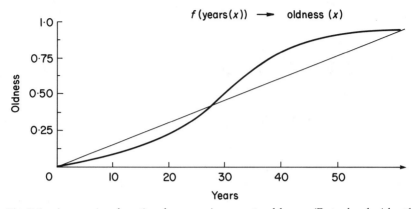

Fig. 5.1   A mapping function from age in years to oldness. (But who decides the shape of the curve or line?)

A weak point in the application of fuzzy logic is the mapping or membership function. Suppose I am 35, how true is the statement that I am old? Is it 0.5, since that is about half a lifetime? Or would 0.4 or 0.6 be more realistic?

Someone has to decide the shape of a graph such as Fig. 5.1. But who is to say whether the curve or the straight line is better? There are no strong rational grounds for preferring one mapping function to another; and in a real problem there will be scores or hundreds of such functions, each to some degree arbitrary. For this reason, practical systems that employ fuzzy logic such as REVEAL (see Chapter 9 of this volume) allow the user to modify various mapping functions easily, and thus to find out experimentally whether the precise shape of the curve is critical or not. There is much more to fuzzy logic than that, but we only have room for an introduction.

One matter we have skated over, however, which deserves further consideration before moving on, is the problem of weighing disparate pieces of evidence. Suppose, for example, we have a collection of 'fuzzy' rules on political preferences, including the following.

> *Rule 1*
> IF   X drives a Volvo car
> AND   X reads the Guardian newspaper
> THEN X will vote for the Social Democratic Party (SDP).
> *Rule 2*
> IF   X dislikes Mrs Margaret Thatcher
> AND   X supports UK membership of the EEC
> THEN X will vote for the SDP.

Let us further suppose that we have seen X driving a Volvo with our own eyes (certainty 1.0) and are fairly sure (0.8) that X usually reads the Guardian. Then the premises of Rule 1 have a joint truth value of 0.8, since we use MIN for AND.

Of course the rule itself may not be wholly reliable, but to keep things simple for the moment we assume the same degree of truth for the conclusion as the premises, giving a level of 0.8 for the statement, 'X will vote SDP'.

Now supposing we find out that X dislikes Mrs Thatcher only moderately (0.5) and does not support continued British membership of the European Community (truth level 0.25) then the degree of truth in, 'X will vote SDP' is only 0.25 (the lesser value) according to Rule 2.

How are we to reconcile these conflicting truth values of 0.8 and 0.25 for the same proposition? Do we take the minimum, the maximum, the average or some other function of the two numbers?

The problem would still exist even if the two pieces of evidence were not in conflict, since different rules pointing in the same direction would tend to confirm each other and reinforce belief in the conclusion, indicating a higher degree of truth than the average or even the maximum.

Likewise, several indicators pointing in one direction are not completely cancelled by a single item of negative evidence.

This takes us out of the realm of fuzzy logic proper into the theory of evidence, which is beyond the scope of this review. The point I wish to emphasize here is that the use of fuzzy logic does not in itself solve the problems associated with weighing up disparate sources of (possibly contradictory) evidence.

5.2 THE USE OF CERTAINTY FACTORS

One of MYCIN's many contributions was a solution (not *the* solution) to this problem (Shortliffe, 1976).

Shortliffe devised a scheme based on what he called certainty factors (CFs) for measuring the confidence that could be placed in any given conclusion as a result of the evidence so far. A certainty factor is the difference between two component measures:

$$CF[h : e] = MB[h : e] - MD[h : e].$$

CF[h : e] is the certainty of the hypothesis h given evidence e. MB[h : e] is a measure of belief in h given e, while MD[h : e] is a measure of disbelief in h given e.

CFs can range from -1 (completely false) to $+1$ (completely true) with fractional values in between, zero representing ignorance. MBs and

MDs on the other hand can range from 0 to 1 only. Thus the CF reflects a simple balancing of evidence for and against.

Note that this formula does not permit any distinction between conflict of evidence (MB and MD both high) as opposed to lack of evidence (MB and MD both low), which could sometimes be very important.

Notice also, in passing, that neither CF nor MB nor MD is a measure of probability. MBs and MDs obey some of the axioms of probability but are not derived from a population sample of any kind and therefore cannot be given a statistical interpretation. They merely allow the system to grade hypotheses according to their strength of support.

5.3 WEIGHING THE EVIDENCE

So far we have made no advance on fuzzy logic; and in fact, MIN, MAX and $1-M$ are employed for AND, OR and NOT respectively in MYCIN just as in fuzzy logic.

What Shortliffe also provided, however, was an updating formula whereby new information could be combined in a straightforward fashion with previous results. This applies to the measures of belief and disbelief associated with each proposition. The formula for MBs is as follows

$$MB[h:e1,e2] = MB[h:e1] + MB[h:e2] \times (1 - MB[h:e1])$$

where the comma between e1 and e2 is to be read as 'followed by'. MDs are updated in the same way.

This states that the effect of a second piece of evidence (e2) on the hypothesis h given earlier evidence e1 is to move the fraction of the distance remaining towards certainty indicated by the strength of the second piece of evidence. The formula has two important properties:

(1) It is symmetric in that the order of e1 and e2 does not matter.
(2) It moves MB (or MD) asymptotically towards certainty as supporting evidence piles up.

Let us return to our fictitious political rules, this time with a transatlantic version.

> *Rule 1*
> IF   X drives a Volkswagen
> AND   X reads the Washington Post
> THEN X will vote Democrat.
> *Rule 2*
> IF   X dislikes Ronald Reagan

OR   X wants the US to pull out of El Salvador
THEN X will vote Democrat.

We assume that the individual MBs are as follows:

1a. X drive VW	0.8 }	
1b. X reads Wash. Post	0.75 }	AND <=> MIN
2a. X dislikes Reagan	0.4 }	
2b. X wants to quit El Sal.	0.6 }	OR <=> MAX

Then the hypothesis that X votes Democrat is supported at the level 0.75 by Rule 1 and 0.6 by Rule 2. Applying the formula we have

$$\begin{aligned}
\text{MB[Democrat : Rule 1, Rule 2]} &= \text{MB[Democrat : Rule 1]} + \\
\text{MB[Democrat : Rule 2]} &\times (1 - \text{MB[Democrat : Rule 1]}) \\
&= 0.75 + 0.6 \times 0.25 \\
&= 0.9.
\end{aligned}$$

Thus the combined measure of belief 0.9 is stronger than either separately. This accords with our intuition that several concordant indicators reinforce one another. Moreover the order of Rules 1 and 2 could be interchanged without affecting the outcome.

Shortliffe's scheme also provides for the possibility that inference rules may be uncertain as well as data. This is a highly significant step forward.

Each rule has an 'attenuation', a number from 0 to 1 which indicates its reliability. Thus, returning to our notional voters once more, we might have said something like

Rule 3 (credibility 0.64)
IF   X drives a Chevrolet
AND X reads Readers' Digest
THEN X will vote Republican.
Rule 4 (credibility 0.8)
IF   X likes retired actors
OR   X wants the US to invade Nicaragua
THEN X will vote Republican.

Here Rule 3 is less trustworthy than Rule 4. If the degrees of support for the premises were

3a. X drives Chevvy	0.88 }	
3b. X reads Readers' Digest	0.5 }	AND <=> MIN
4a. X likes retired actors	0.5 }	
4b. X wants US into Nicaragua	0.7 }	OR <=> MAX

the unmodified strength of the conclusions would be 0.5 and 0.7, but these MBs would have to be multiplied by the attenuation factors of 0.64 and 0.8 – giving attenuated levels of 0.32 from Rule 3 and 0.56 from Rule 4. Applying the updating formula we get

$$MB[Republican : R3,R4] = 0.32 + 0.56 \times 0.68$$
$$= 0.7008.$$

Shortliffe does attempt a theoretical justification for these methods, but in my view the rationale is somewhat shaky. The important point is that this set of techniques has served well in a significant program, MYCIN, and its successors. In other words the empirical results are encouraging enough to warrant further investigation and use.

5.4 THE QUINTESSENCE OF BAYESIANISM

One calculus of uncertainty which does have a comparatively firm theoretical foundation is probability theory.

Many systems, including the PROSPECTOR mineral exploration system (Duda *et al.*, 1978), have used Bayes's Theorem as the thread for tying together information from disparate sources. Bayes's Rule provides for computation of relative likelihoods between competing hypotheses on the strength of the evidence. It depends on the formula

$$LR(H : E) = P(E : H) / P(E : H')$$

where the likelihood ratio LR is defined as the probability of the event or evidence E given a particular hypothesis H divided by the probability of the evidence given the falsity of that hypothesis (H'). Thus if we know the probability of the evidence given the hypothesis, and its negation, we can work out the likelihood of the hypothesis in the light of the evidence. For instance, if we know the probability of spots given chicken-pox and the probability of spots among non-chicken-pox patients we can compute the probability of chicken-pox given spots. It is usually easier to work this way round.

The likelihood ratio can be used to adjust the odds in favour of the hypothesis in question if it becomes known that the event E has occurred.

Chris Naylor (see Chapter 6 of this volume) expresses Bayes's Rule in terms of probabilities. For the sake of variety, and because it is often computationally more convenient to work with odds, I give it in terms of odds here. Odds in favour (O) and probabilities (P) can be interconverted quite simply:

$$O = P/(1-P) ; P = O/(1+O).$$

Bookmakers' odds, e.g. in horse racing, are typically quoted as odds against; but the conversion of odds against (A) to odds on (O) is also simple:

$$O = 1/A.$$

Thus 7 to 4 against can be expressed as 1.75 to 1 against, which is 0.5714 (to 1) in favour (or 4 to 7 in favour).

The entire Bayesian updating scheme can be encapsulated in the expression

$$O'(H) = O(H) \times LR(H : E)$$

where O(H) is the *prior* odds in favour of H and O'(H) is the resulting *posterior* odds given event E as determined by the likelihood ratio.

Information from a variety of different knowledge sources can then be combined just by multiplication. Given the prior odds of the competing hypotheses and the events (observations) which are known to have happened, the posterior odds – and thence the probabilities – are easily calculated. The likelihood ratios can be obtained from a simple 2-dimensional frequency table showing how often each event occurs under each hypothesis.

Underneath is a simple example. To give our mythical voters a rest, we have tabulated some imaginary data which might (just might) be of use in forecasting life expectancy. Anyway, it illustrates the principles involved.

	Lifetime in years:		
Cigarette smoking habits	*>75*	*75 or less*	*Totals*
Smoker	20	33	53
Non-smoker	24	23	47
Totals:	44	56	100

Here we have a sample of 100 deaths of which 44 were over 75 years of age on death (> 75 column) and the rest, 56 people, were 75 years old or less. They have been divided into those who smoked and those who did not smoke. (Caution: this is not real data.)

The prior odds in this sample of 100 cases in favour of living more than 75 years are

$$O(Longlife) = 44/56 = 11/14 = 0.7857$$

and the likelihood ratios are

$$LR(Longlife : Smoker) = (20/44)/(33/56) = (20 \times 56)/(44 \times 33)$$
$$= 320/363 = 0.8815$$

$$\text{LR(Longlife : Nonsmoker)} = (24 \times 56)/(44 \times 23) = 336/253$$
$$= 1.3280.$$

Suppose further for the sake of illustration that we also look at sex as another variable with a bearing on longevity.

Sex	>75	75 or less	Totals
Male	24	36	60
Female	20	20	40
Totals:	44	56	100

Here the likelihood ratio for men is

$$\text{LR(Longlife : Male)} = (24/44) / (36/56) = 0.8484.$$

For women it is

$$\text{LR(Longlife : Female)} = (20/44) / (20/56) = 1.2727.$$

Then given the prior odds of 11/14 in favour of a long life (over 75 years) we can compute the posterior odds that a male smoker will have a long life as defined in this way by

$$O'(\text{Longlife}) = \text{LR(Longlife : Smoker)} \times \text{LR(Longlife : Male)}$$
$$\times O(\text{Longlife})$$

or

$$O'(\text{Longlife}) = 0.8815 \times 0.8484 \times 11/14$$

which is approximately 0.5876 according to my home computer. This corresponds to a probability of 0.3701, as compared to an initial probability of 0.44. So we have taken account of two rather negative indicators.

The same principle can be adapted to deal with more than two hypotheses (columns) without much difficulty.

Likelihood ratios must always be positive. Zero and infinity are conceivable, but we strive to avoid them (slugging the data to do so if necessary). If $LR > 1$ it indicates evidence favourable to the hypothesis, if $LR < 1$ the evidence is contra-indicative and if $LR = 1$ then it is neutral.

The LR multiplier tells us how much more likely the hypothesis in question becomes if we know the evidence than it would be otherwise.

If the evidence itself is doubtful it is a simple matter to compute a scaled ratio LR' such that

$$LR' = LR \times PE + (1-PE)$$

where PE is the probability that the evidence is valid. For instance, a likelihood ratio of 1.2 (supportive) would become an adjusted ratio of

$$1.2 \times 0.8 + 0.2 = 0.96 + 0.2 = 1.16$$

(less supportive) if the evidence were known with probability $p = 0.8$; while a ratio of 0.5 (strongly against) would become

$$0.5 \times 0.5 + 0.5 = 0.75$$

(less strongly against) if the evidence were known with $p = 0.5$ only.

To sum up, likelihood ratios have two great advantages: (1) they allow combination of several independent sources of evidence; (2) they can be adjusted easily if the evidence is itself uncertain.

There is a catch, however. The alert reader will have seized on the word 'independent' in point (1) above. And statisticians will have thrown up their hands in horror at the calculations involving male smokers in the preceding section. After all, it may well be that there are more male smokers than female ones. To treat Male/Female and Smoker/Nonsmoker as two independent sources of information is not justified without further investigation. Yet to carry out that further investigation would not only take time, it would create a bigger table with far more cells, each containing a meaninglessly small sample.

There is almost bound to be some degree of association in any real set of indicators. The practical problem is to minimize it. In other words, we would be most unwise to add Bearded/Beardless to our list of indicators since we know that there are hardly any bearded women. Nor would Persistent-Cough/No-Cough be a good additional variable, because many more smokers are likely to have persistent coughs. We would be in danger of measuring the same effect twice.

These are fairly obvious, but other correlations may be less clear, and so the software should be designed to filter them out or recalibrate the ratios when they are found. As an example, the HULK package (Helps Uncover Latent Knowledge) which uses Bayes's rule in a fairly simple-minded way, has an entropy measure that warns the user against adding a new rule which, in effect, duplicates a previous rule. This avoids any gross misuse of Bayes's rule. Most other Bayesian reasoning programs insert checks of a similar kind.

5.5 THE INCREDIBLE HULK

The HULK system (Forsyth, 1984) relies heavily on the use of likelihood ratios. It consists of two main modules which are run in sequence.

LOOK – Logical Organizer Of Knowledge
LEAP – Likelihood Estimator And Predictor

LOOK is a rule-testing program. It allows the user to try out decision rules. A new rule is typed in as a Boolean expression using the names of the problem variables. LOOK then uses the suggested rule to categorize each sample in the datafile and reports back with its success rate, the likelihood ratios derived and (most significant) an assessment of its efficacy in combination with all the other rules generated so far. Only if the new rule improves this score will it recommend its retention. The user then makes the final choice of whether to keep the rule or discard it.

Thus LOOK can be thought of as a software sieve for filtering out bad conjectures by running them against trial data. It does not invent its own rules but it does allow for the build-up of a collection of several rules working together. It facilitates the method of conjecture and refutation which is at the heart of science. The user does the guesswork (which people are good at) leaving the testing to the machine (which it is better at).

If two rules draw on the same underlying factor then the second one, although apparently predictive in its own right, will not contribute to any information gain and the system will not recommend its inclusion in the rule set.

LEAP allows the hard-won expertise in the form of rules generated using LOOK to be applied to forecast the probability of a number of samples belonging to any given category. The cases in the test data set for LEAP need not have their actual class membership known (unlike LOOK's training data). Samples are ranked by descending order of probability in the output.

5.6 CONCLUSIONS

The methods of inexact reasoning presented here – fuzzy logic, certainty factors and Bayesian logic – all have their uses. They have proved their worth in serious applications.

But they have their critics too. Some philosophers object to the exclusion of the 'law of the excluded middle' from fuzzy set theory, as that has been a cornerstone of logic since the days of Aristotle. Many mathematicians regard Shortliffe's reliance on certainty factors with misgivings, as an *ad hoc* 'fix' introduced with a cavalier disregard for the underlying problems.

And Bayes's theorem has been a focus for over 200 years of controversy among statisticians. In particular, the estimation of prior probabilities can be highly problematical. If you want the prior probability of, say, gastric cancer, do you take the proportion of patients reporting to their doctor with stomach pains, the proportion of the US population with the disease, an estimate of the proportion of the world population suffering from the disease, or something else? Often the true value simply is not known, so someone makes a guess. Fortunately the more evidence that accumulates, the less important the accuracy of the prior odds; but that is hardly a cogent argument for using the first estimate that comes to hand, as most systems do.

Being precise about uncertainty is an endeavour fraught with hazards for the unwary. That is what gives the subject of probability its special fascination. It also makes it an arena for heated debate. Even the meaning of innocuous probabilistic statements like 'the chance that it will rain tomorrow is 0.55' or 'the probability of my drawing an ace from a well shuffled deck of cards is 1/13' cannot be regarded as settled. The theorists still debate over the frequency interpretation of unrepeatable events and the relationship between degree of rational belief and probability, among other topics. (See Efstathiou, 1984; Weiss and Kulikowski, 1983; Mamdani and Gaines, 1981.)

Leaving aside the theoretical objections, there are practical difficulties too. Fuzzy logic, for example, has been promoted as one way to capture the meaning of inherently vague linguistic concepts like 'tall' and 'old'. But of course an old athlete (aged 36) is very much younger than a young pensioner (at 55), just as a small elephant is bigger than a large mouse. Context is all-important.

Then there is the question of assigning numeric values to subjective judgements. Many systems follow PROSPECTOR in allowing the user to reply with a rating on a scale −5 (definitely not) to +5 (absolutely certain). But let us suppose a system for tree identification asks

> On a scale −5 to +5 how sure are you that the leaves have a strong pungent aroma?

and receives the number nought in reply. Clearly the user does not know the answer, but this noncommittal zero could have a wide variety of meanings.

(1) As a professional botanist of many years standing I have smelt the leaves and in my considered judgement they are intermediate between a strong pungent aroma and no smell at all.
(2) Some people are colour blind, but as for me, I'm afraid my olfactory sense is defective.
(3) Look, all I have to go on is a photograph.
(4) It's winter, for heaven's sake: there are no leaves.
(5) What! Go out in that hailstorm and sniff the damn thing? You must be joking.
(6) 'Pungent'? What is that supposed to smell like?
(7) The local tom cat uses this tree as a boundary marker. It's pungent all right, but it may not be the tree's fault.

Uncertainty has many facets. Their implications are not all equivalent. Trees are relatively familiar objects; consider sympathetically the plight of the poor user who is asked by PROSPECTOR whether 'Hornblende has been pervasively altered to Biotite'!

Having raised these issues, we must not duck the need to deal with uncertainty somehow. Heuristic knowledge is never cut and dried. If we insist on dealing only with indisputable 'facts' we will miss out all the interesting problems.

The competent knowledge engineer must be prepared to build some kind of weighting procedure into an expert system, perhaps based on one of the schemes outlined in this chapter. He or she must also be aware that any such procedure will have its limitations. That is an argument for providing safeguards and consistency checks, not an excuse for waiting till absolute certainty (i.e. death) arrives.

REFERENCES

Duda, R., Hart, P., Barrett, p. *et al.* (1978) *Development of the PROSPECTOR System for Mineral Exploration*, SRI Report Projects 5822 and 6415, Stanford Research Institute, Palo Alto, Ca.

Efstathiou, J. (1984) Non-classical logics and the handling of uncertainty. *British Computer Society Specialist Group on Expert Systems Newsletter*, **10**.

Forsyth, R. (1984) *HULK User Guide*, Brainstorm Computer Publications, London.

Mamdani, A. and Gaines, B.R. (1981) *Fuzzy Reasoning and its Applications*, Academic Press, New York.

Shortliffe, E. (1976) *Computer Based Medical Consultations: MYCIN*, American Elsevier, New York.

Weiss, S. and Kulikowski, C. (1983) *A Practical Guide to Designing Expert Systems*, Methuen, New York.

Zadeh, L. (1965) Fuzzy sets. *Information and Control*, **8**, 338–353.

6

How to build an inferencing engine

CHRIS NAYLOR

There is something about the title of this chapter which seems to contain an implicit clang. The title, in case you hadn't noticed, is 'How to build an inferencing engine' and the clang seems to lie in the apparent disparity between the esoteric smoothness of the phrase 'Inferencing engine' and the rather prosaic dullness of the phrase 'How to build . . .'.

An inferencing engine would be fine. Talking about such things, we could very well feel that we are at the cutting edge of modern computer thinking. But 'How to build . . .'; that's a different matter altogether. Because we all know that, when we get back to wherever we call home, we're going to have the same old keyboard and screen in front of us and, on the machine, will be loaded the same old computer languages with which we have always worked.

The tools we have aren't *bad* tools by any means. But they are *familiar* tools about which there is nothing esoteric at all. And it is with these tools that we are going to have to build our inferencing engine. And suddenly, the esoteric nature of the engine itself begins to lessen. Because with those tools we can write programs, and nothing more – at which point our super smooth inferencing engine becomes a program, and nothing more.

The end product of this chapter – if there is an end product – is an approach which might be used next time you feel like spending a few weeks sweating in front of a keyboard and screen. It is not even a close cousin of the magic wand approach to solving problems. I wish it was but, outside of the funny papers, such approaches just don't exist.

However, having poured out a modicum of cold water, let's go back to the esoteric-sounding bit – the 'inferencing engine' itself. What is it? A simple enough question, but not such a simple answer is available. For just about everything we do can be subsumed under the general heading of 'inferencing'. Clearly, if we had a program which would do our inferencing for us, then we could call such a program an inferencing engine. That would then sound super-smooth and we could use the end-product to impress friends and enemies alike (if only by a description of the same, rather than by its actual workings).

But again: what is inferencing?

Let me give you an example of an inference. I am a large employer and I employ Fred Bloggs and pay him £1 per hour for each hour that he works. Last week he worked 20 hours for me. Therefore, I infer, I shall this Friday pay him £20. That is an inference.

It is also, of course, the essence of a payroll program. And, frankly, anyone who starts to sell their payroll programs as inferencing engines may be, semantically, correct but I would have certain reservations about buying the product from them.

But return to that payroll example again because there are a couple of interesting (if obvious) points to be made about it. The first is that the inference we made (concerning Fred Bloggs' requirement for £20) was *exact*. The second is that the inference was also made very *easily*. And, to date, this has tended to be a prime feature of a very great deal of work done in the field of computers. The tasks which they have been set to solve have, in general, been tasks which have exact solutions and, almost by virtue of this, the solution of those tasks has been easy. It is, in a way, the very exactness of the solutions which has enabled pro-grammers to see a way straight through the problem and solve it without too much difficulty.

Now, of course, there will be some groans when I say that all current computer programs produce exact solutions easily. I, too, have at least a limited groan when I think of some of the things with which I have had difficulty in the computer field.

Consider, for instance, numerical analysis. Does that have an exact solution? Is that easy? No, in general it is neither of those things. But, at least, you can buy a book on numerical analysis, look up an appropriate method, and use that. And, having done so, the book will usually give a pretty thorough analysis of the likely range and type of errors that might be inherent in the system. It may not be exact in the analytical sense, but it is exact in the sense that, using a given method, we would know exactly what order of error was involved.

But now turn to a different sort of problem, the problem of medical diagnosis. Is that exact or easy? It *might* be. Maybe doctors find it to be both exact and easy – after all, they've spent their lives doing it. But *how* do they do it? If you were to ask them you would almost certainly get some very woolly answers indeed. It all seems to be a curious mixture of guesses, hunches, direct observations, reported comments, practical experience . . . You name it and they use it. The whole thing is about as coherent as any witches' brew you care to imagine. And yet, of course, *we* understand perfectly well what it is that they are doing. We may not understand medicine, and we may not be able to program their activities on to a computer, but we certainly *understand* the type of thing that a doctor does when faced with a patient. And that is simply because, like the doctor, we are human too. And we work in just the same way in our own various fields of expertise.

Now that the word 'expertise' has crept in, it may be possible to see how the subject of inferencing engines links through to expert systems.

The kind of inference with which we are concerned is not the simple, exact and easy inference. It is the very opposite. The *inexact* and *difficult* inferences which, typically, human experts use in all walks of life. It is these which we are trying to build and our problem is that, unlike the payroll problem, we don't really know even what the basic equations are, never mind how to program them to a solution.

Upon reflecting now on what I have just said it seems to me that I could almost stop there with the claim that the subject is so riddled with problems that there is no hope left for those who would wish to proceed. But, in fact, things aren't quite as bad as that and, if they were, those of you who have parted with good money to buy this book would feel, possibly, that the next reasonable thing for you to do would be to lynch me.

So what I propose to do is to describe an inferencing engine (that esoteric phrase once more!) which I have worked on, which seems to give good-ish results on certain types of problems, and which is, really, fairly easy to build.

I think it possible that, in the course of what follows, you may find some of the things I have to say familiar and I hope that you will bear with this because for anyone unfamiliar with some of the ideas to leave them out would possibly be to leave them in the dark. This is particularly true, I think, of the occasions when I shall have to mention certain aspects of statistics.

6.1 THE INFERENCING ENGINE AND THE KNOWLEDGE BASE

In a very great deal of expert systems work there has been a conscious effort to divide the problem into two parts – the inferencing engine and the knowledge base. The idea is that the inferencing engine is the general purpose thinking machine and the knowledge base is that about which the engine shall think.

The former, if you like, is the equivalent of a 'raw' human brain with the inbuilt capacity to do anything. Whereas the latter is the sum of all human experience in some particular field. Add the two together and you have the equivalent of a human expert. Or so, at any rate, the theory goes.

In many ways, of course, it's a good idea. After all, suppose that you had just such an inferencing engine and that you had, also, a knowledge base applicable to the field of medical diagnosis. Why waste the engine at such time as you wanted an expert on, say, weather forecasting? Why not simply unplug the medical bit and design and plug in the meteorological bit? Well, the reason 'why not' is simply that – as yet – your inferencing engine might not be up to handling knowledge from two such disparate fields. But that doesn't prevent anyone from trying. A much more practical point from my own standpoint is this: even if you were only working on a single problem (such as medical diagnosis) breaking the problem into the two parts – knowledge base and inferencing engine – does make the problem much more tractable. It allows you to spend one day worrying about why the inferencing engine won't work and the next day worrying about what's wrong with the knowledge base. This is, I find, much better than having to spend two days worrying about the both of them as would happen with more conventional techniques. And, if maybe that sounded a bit like a joke, it isn't really so funny.

Obviously, you'll realize that, put like that, it's little more than saying that one has a program and one has data. Life is then made much easier if, for the time being, you forget about the data and, using test data maybe, spend the day getting the program itself to work.

But the fact is that, when working with rather diffuse problems, there is often a great deal of uncertainty about what, exactly, is the program and which is the data. The overlap between the two can be considerable and the trick is to draw the dividing line so that absolutely as much as possible of the problem is defined as data (the knowledge base) rather than as the program (the inferencing engine). A side advantage of doing this is that it enables you to see just to what extent you really can write a general-purpose inferencing engine. After all, if every single bit of 'data' were excluded from the program it really could be general purpose and, with a different knowledge base, it really could be used again for something else.

I think now that in order to help make the discussion a little more concrete I ought to say something about one particular knowledge base. Now, obviously, the knowledge base isn't the inferencing engine which you were promised – but it's what that engine has to drive and the format.it comes in will have to be the same format as a knowledge base in some other field if the inferencing engine is to work in another field.

The examples I give, incidentally, will almost all be in the field of medical diagnosis although I think most people will accept that there are many other fields which could be formulated in the same way to be driven by the same engine.

Anyway, there are two basic data formats within this particular knowledge base.

(1) The first format holds the knowledge on a particular illness:

Illness name, p, no. of applicable symptoms (j, py, pn)

The first item is the name of the illness. The second item is the prior probability of that illness being present in any member of the population taken at random. In Bayesian language, it is the prior probability of that illness. The third item is the number of symptoms which are applicable to that illness – either as indications of the condition or as contra-indications. After this there are a series of triples – three-element fields – corresponding to each of the applicable symptoms. The first item in the triple is a reference number giving the symptom which is now being considered. The second item in the triple is the probability that this symptom will be observed given that the patient has the illness in question. The third element of the triple is the probability that the symptom will be observed given that the patient does *not* have this illness.

(2) The second type of data is that concerning the symptoms:

Symptom number, symptom name, question to be asked
concerning this symptom

There are three fields. The first is the symptom number – and you will recall that this is the reference used in the illness data – the first item in those triples. The second is the name of the symptom. The third field is a question which may be asked of the user of the system in an attempt to determine whether he or she is exhibiting this particular symptom or not.

Anyway, so far so good. That's the knowledge base as it is used. there's nothing sacred about it, but it seems roughly adequate for our purposes. Maybe it would shed a little more light if you were to think of Influenza. That's the first field – illness name – completed. Now, what's the probability of any random person having influenza? Let's say it's one in a thousand. That's the second field, p, completed: $p = 0.001$. Now, how many symptoms indicate or contra-indicate influenza? Lots of course, but, say, fever and runny nose – 2 symptoms. If the patient has influenza then he certainly has a fever and he probably has a runny nose. If he doesn't have influenza then he may still have a fever, but it's much less likely, and the same goes for noses of the runny variety.

So we finish up with something like this:

INFLUENZA, 0.001, 2, 1, 1, 0.01, 2, 0.9, 0.1

which fairly neatly summarizes what any doctor would tell you about influenza. Or it would do if, for instance, that particular doctor had a rather limited knowledge of his subject.

Corresponding to this we have the following items concerning the symptoms:

1, FEVER, DO YOU HAVE A HIGH TEMPERATURE?
2, RUNNY NOSE, DO YOU HAVE A RUNNY NOSE?

And that is the knowledge base (summarized in Fig. 6.1). Obviously it can be fairly quickly and easily modified to refine the knowledge therein and so, at this stage, that particular problem is dealt with.

The real problem now remains – how are we going to drive this thing? What does the inferencing engine look like?

And, at this stage, I am going to divide the problem into two parts. The first part will be concerned with the inference itself; and, the second part with the engine within which the inferences fit. If it sounds a little odd to draw this distinction then bear with me because by 'inference' what I am really referring to is more-or-less a single calculation. By

---

(1) Illness name, p, number of applicable symptoms (j, py, pn)

(2) Symptom number, symptom name, question to be asked

e.g.

(1) INFLUENZA, 0.001, 2, 1, 1, 0.01, 2, 0.9, 0.1
with two associated symptoms:

1, FEVER, DO YOU HAVE A HIGH TEMPERATURE?
2, RUNNY NOSE, DO YOU HAVE A RUNNY NOSE?

So the prior probability of anyone having influenza is 0.001

There are two symptoms associated with influenza.

The first symptom is fever. The probability of fever given influenza is 1

The probability of fever given NOT influenza is 0.01.

The second symptom is runny nose. The probability of runny nose given influenza is 0.9

The probability of runny nose given NOT influenza is 0.1

Fig. 6.1   The format of the knowledge base

'engine' I really mean the system by which we shall determine – or the system shall determine – exactly what order it is to carry out its inferences.

6.2 BAYES'S THEOREM

The whole essence of the approach I have used towards inferencing is Bayes's approach. And, for those of you who didn't already know this, the Reverend Bayes was an 18th Century English vicar who spent his life studying statistics. Now, just as a safeguard for myself, I will say that Bayes's approach to inferencing is not the only approach possible. There are others, such as the methods of classical statistics and the more recent methods of pattern matching. I am not going to dwell on these alternative approaches simply because I feel that to do so would widen the topic of this chapter beyond belief. I, personally, have found a Bayesian approach extremely useful and I think that to concentrate on the one method and see it through is likely to give you the maximum benefit from this contribution.

Essentially, Bayes's theories rest on the belief that for everything, no matter how unlikely it is, there is a prior probability that it could be true. It may be a very low probability. It may, in fact, be zero. But that does not prevent us from calculating as if there were a probability there. Now, given a prior probability about some hypothesis (does the patient have influenza, say, or is the world flat?) there must be some evidence we can call on to adjust our views (beliefs, if you like) on the matter. If there were not then the process would stop right there with the prior probability remaining forever unchanged. But, given relevant evidence, we can modify this prior probability to produce a posterior probability of the same hypothesis given some new evidence.

For those who like to think in terms of equations, it goes like this (see Fig. 6.2). $P(H)$ is the prior probability of some hypothesis. $P(H : E)$ is the posterior probability of the same hypothesis given some item of relevant evidence E. Now, by definition,

$$P(H : E) = \frac{P(H\&E)}{P(E)} \quad \text{and} \quad P(E : H) = \frac{P(E\&H)}{P(H)}$$

So, with a bit of re-arranging, we get:

$$P(H : E) = \frac{P(E : H)\, P(H)}{P(E)}$$

and the question that then remains is: have we achieved anything useful? Well, yes. We started off with $P(H)$ and we wanted $P(H : E)$.

P(H) = the prior probability of H given no evidence.
P(H : E) = the posterior probability of H given evidence E.

Now

$$P(H : E) = \frac{P(H\&E)}{P(E)} \quad \text{and} \quad P(E : H) = \frac{P(E\&H)}{P(H)}$$

So

$$P(H : E) = \frac{P(E : H) \, P(H)}{P(E)}$$

and

$$P(E) = P(E : H) \, P(H) + P(E : \text{not } H) \, P(\text{not } H)$$

Relating this to the format of the knowledge base:

$$P(H : E) = \frac{py \times p}{py \times p + pn \times (1-p)}$$

Fig.6.2   Bayes's Theorem

Now, think about our patient with influenza (or not with influenza – that is the problem, to find out). We know roughly what the prior probability of influenza for patients in general is – that is P(H). But we want to know the probability for influenza in this patient in particular.

We find that he has a fever (the evidence is there) and we now want to know P(H : E) – the probability of the patient's having influenza given that he has a fever. Well, we could make a guess on it, but somehow that isn't really a very easy question to answer. It would be very much easier to answer the opposite question: If the patient has influenza what is the probability that he has a fever? The answer is that a fever is certain – the probability is 1 – and that seems a much better way to proceed. And that is how Bayes theory allows us to proceed.

We are still left with one other item to clear up – the bottom line in the equation – P(E) the probability of the evidence as a stand-alone item. In this case, what is the probability of *anyone* having a fever? Because, obviously, if everybody always had a fever all the time then the fact that this patient has a fever would tell us nothing. Our patient has a fever, but are fevers, in general, rare events?

And the way we can proceed on this is to calculate P(E) as

$$P(E) = P(E : H) P(H) + P(E : \text{not } H) P(\text{not } H).$$

In other words, the probability of a fever occurring in anyone is the probability of a fever occurring in an influenza patient times the probability of anyone having influenza plus the probability of fever occurring in a non-influenza patient times the probability of this person being a non-influenza case.

And now, maybe, you see how this all fits in with the previous definition of our knowledge base. For $P(E : H)$ is the py associated with influenza and $P(E : \text{not } H)$ is the pn we had associated with influenza. So we get the formula:

$$P(H : E) = \frac{py \times p}{py \times p + pn \times (1-p)}$$

This is where the Bayesian neatness now comes into play. For the original value of $P(H)$ that we used was the 'p' (prior probability) that we held in our knowledge base. But, having calculated a new $P(H : E)$ (i.e. having asked about the patient's fever, say) we can now forget the original $P(H)$ and, instead, use this new $P(H : E)$ as a new $P(H)$. So the whole process can be repeated time and time again as new evidence comes in from the keyboard, each time the probability of the illness being shifted up a bit or down a bit using exactly the same Bayesian equation each time with, simply, a different prior probability being used derived from the last posterior probability.

Eventually, having gathered in all of the evidence concerning all of the hypotheses we, or the system, can come to a final conclusion having successfully inferred the correct hypothesis to be true (if nothing goes wrong, that is).

Now that may have sounded good, but there are one or two criticisms of the method which could be made and so I will make a few here and now. The first is the calculation of $P(E)$. The calculation presented here is accurate, but fairly simple. That is, it is accurate if we know $P(E : \text{not } H)$ but we might not know this very accurately. Think, by way of illustration, of the probability of someone having a fever given that he does not have influenza. Typically, we would know $P(E : H)$, the probability of a fever given the patient has influenza, very accurately, but not always $P(E : \text{not } H)$.

One way around this is to use the fuller formula (see Fig. 6.3):

$$P(E) = \sum_{i=1}^{n} P(E : H_i) P(H_i)$$

of which our previous formula was a subset.

A general formula for the probability of some item of evidence is

$$P(E) = \sum_{i=1}^{n} P(E : H_i)P(H_i)$$

So, as the $P(H_i)$ are continually updated at runtime, $P(E)$ could, in theory, be continually updated also.

Fig. 6.3

In many ways it is tempting to do this, because what it says is that the probability of E, the evidence, is the probability of E given every single condition with which E might occur multiplied by the probability of that condition. It is very complete. Of course, if our knowledge base held details of each and every single condition with which fever might occur and the current probabilities of those conditions then we would have an exact estimate of P(E) being constantly updated as $P(H_i)$ changes and being always accurate. It would be very nice to work like this. The problem really lies in the fact that our system is liable in some ways to be less than perfect. For instance, Lassa fever causes a fever but if we do not have Lassa fever in the knowledge base then our calculations of P(E) will be that much in error as a result. Similarly for each and every item in which our knowledge base is deficient.

From a practical point of view a rough estimate using P(E : H) and P(E : not H) is probably good enough and, if it makes you feel uneasy, then you can always console yourself with the thought that, by using the simpler method, we reduce the computational overhead and get answers today, rather than, say, next week.

The second criticism to be made of the method is that it assumes independence of the variables being used. Theoretically, this is quite a serious point. Suppose in our knowledge base we had two symptoms. The first was 'fever' as previously mentioned. The second was 'high temperature'. Now, of course, there would be no point in having both items because they mean the same thing. They are exactly correlated. But, if they did both creep in, what then? We would have included the same evidence twice and therefore, either incremented, or decremented, the probability of influenza more than we should have done and the final posterior probabilities would be wrong.

Now, on a small scale, this sort of trouble is almost bound to occur simply because most symptoms (in medical diagnosis: 'items of evidence' in some other field) will tend to have some correlation one with the other somewhere. And there is no theoretically nice way out of this problem. I say 'theoretically nice' because the problem worries statisticians much more than it worries anyone else. The reason for this is as follows.

If, at the end of the process, we wanted the exact probabilities to be attached to each of the hypotheses under consideration then there are plenty of criticisms which could be made of this method. But if, at the end, we were happy just to have an idea of the relative magnitude of the various probabilities then the problems tend to disappear. As long as the information in the knowledge base is equally erroneous for every item and a similar number of items of evidence are available for each hypothesis then the relative order of the errors which occur tends to be much the same throughout. The last few decimal places may be somewhat shaky, but the overall picture which the system infers appears to be, generally, quite reasonable. Perhaps the point will be made a little more strongly if I just digress into a consideration of the matter of odds. (See Fig. 6.4.)

$$O(H) = \frac{P(H)}{1 - P(H)}$$

$$O(H : E) = \frac{P(E : H)}{P(E : \text{not } H)} O(H)$$

$$= \frac{py}{pn} \times O(H)$$

So

$$\ln|O(H : E)| = \ln\left|\frac{py}{pn}\right| + \ln|O(H)|$$

Fig. 6.4 Odds versus Probabilities

Now, odds and probabilities are related in a way by the formula:

$$O(H) = \frac{P(H)}{1 - P(H)}$$

So, for a hypothesis with probability 0.5 the odds on that hypothesis are 1 to 1.

Now, some workers prefer to do their Bayesian sums using odds rather than probabilities simply because it is computationally easier.

Using odds our earlier formula becomes:

$$O(H : E) = \frac{py}{pn} O(H)$$

In other words, the odds change as a straight linear function of P(E : H) and P(E : not H) – and, of course, if we took logs and held in our knowledge base log (py/pn) then the calculations would be a matter of simple addition.

I, personally, have objections to the use of odds in this way. The main one being that the end points of the range are at plus and minus infinity rather than the 0 and 1 of probabilities. Infinity being outside the range of most machines, it seems to me that some very valuable information is lost about these end points, for events which occur with probabilities 0 and 1 are very interesting events and can greatly help to solve a problem quickly.

As a further digression it will be apparent that the odds relationship, being a straight line one, means that the probability relationships are not. P(H : E) tends to move asymptotically towards its end points of 0 and 1. (See Fig. 6.5.) It may, given strong evidence, actually get to its

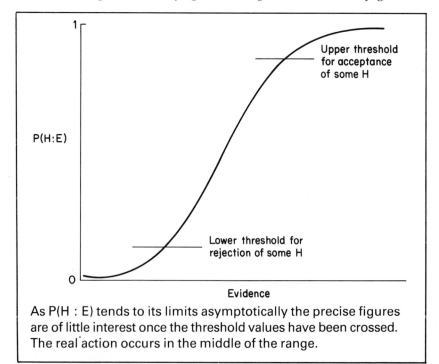

As P(H : E) tends to its limits asymptotically the precise figures are of little interest once the threshold values have been crossed. The real action occurs in the middle of the range.

Fig. 6.5   Thresholds

end points. But, in the meantime, when it is simply approaching them, it means that the probability change induced by any item of evidence tends to get progressively less, and this helps to ameliorate the effects of possibly correlated items in the knowledge base. Maybe the same question is being asked twice but it will hardly show in the final result if we stick with probabilities and there is a reasonable body of other evidence available to the system as well. The essence of this point is that I, and I think other people, tend to perceive probabilistic events in fairly close accord with probability measures rather than as odds, and that makes the use of probabilities preferable.

Well, that was a quick skim through Bayes and outlines the inferencing process, but, before we pass on, we should look at the criterion the system uses for making a decision. What we could have the system do, if we wanted, would be to simply print out at the end of each session a listing of all the hypotheses and the probabilities associated now with each one of them. And that would be rather unimaginative.

Typically, what most workers do is to set two thresholds – an upper and a lower. If the probability exceeds the upper threshold that hypothesis is accepted as a likely conclusion to make. If it falls below the lower threshold it is rejected as unlikely. So the system is able to display some fairly intelligent inferencing behaviour. In practice this method of rigidly setting threshold criteria is open to criticism and to show what I mean consider one hypothesis about which certain items of evidence are all instantly available.

Assuming all of these items to be independent, we could, instead of proceeding stepwise as we have done before, just consider the one big calculation to find P(H : all the relevant supportive evidence).

The basic calculation is the same as before but this time we use, instead of P(E : H), P(all supportive evidence : H) which is simply the product of all of the supportive P(E : H) for that hypothesis.

By doing this we obtain the maximum possible posterior probability which that hypothesis could achieve if every single item of evidence went in its favour given what is in the knowledge base at the moment.

Likewise, we can calculate a minimum possible probability for that hypothesis supposing that all the evidence currently in the knowledge base worked against it.

Clearly, these values are unlikely to be the same for all hypotheses. In fact, we might find that for some hypotheses the maximum possible probability attainable might only be, say, 0.5. So, if we set a rigid upper probability threshold of 0.9 and a lower of 0.6 this particular hypothesis would always be rejected as unlikely.

However, suppose the hypothesis was: the patient has lung cancer. Now, you simply cannot accurately diagnose lung cancer via a computer keyboard. You need, at the very least, the addition of X-ray evidence. So what you want to do is to get the system to report on a particular hypothesis if the system thinks that, to the extent of its own internal knowledge, the patient might have lung cancer. That is to say, you want the system to tell you if it is as certain *as it can be* about the hypothesis given its own internal constraints of having, for instance, no X-ray machine and no eyesight of its own.

The better approach to adopt on threshold criteria is to simply set an upper limit, M1, as maybe 0.9 of the maximum attainable for that hypothesis given the current knowledge base. Similarly, a lower threshold, M2, can be calculated as, maybe, half of this maximum or some multiplier of the minimum value possible. This way both the upper and lower threshold criterion values are specific to each particular hypothesis. (See Fig. 6.6.)

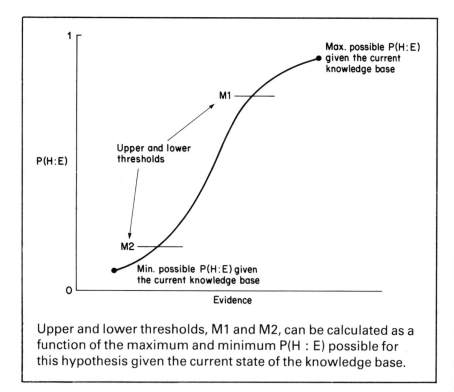

Upper and lower thresholds, M1 and M2, can be calculated as a function of the maximum and minimum P(H : E) possible for this hypothesis given the current state of the knowledge base.

Fig. 6.6

6.3 UNCERTAINTY IN USERS' RESPONSES

Just in case anyone thought that we were getting to the end of the inference itself there is a bit more to come. This concerns uncertainty in the users' responses.

Ideally, when the system requests a certain piece of information, the user can give a straight answer. But it may be that the user is not sure of what answer to give. The example I personally like occurs in the case of that excellent system PROSPECTOR which at some point in its process of mineral exploration asks the user the question: 'Has hornblende been pervasively altered to biotite?' I sympathize with anyone who isn't quite sure about the answer to that one.

The problem can occur in other fields. 'Do you have a bad cough?' can be a pretty subjective question to answer and so it becomes necessary to allow the user to reply on, say, an 11 point scale with +5 being Yes and −5 being No, 0 being Don't Know and everything else being somewhere in between.

The calculations then proceed much as before except that $P(H : E)$ is replaced by $P(H : R)$ calculated as:

$$P(H : R) = P(H : E)P(E : R) + P(H : \text{not } E)P(\text{not } E : R)$$

where R is the user's response. In other words, to allow for uncertainty the system has to allow for a bit of $P(H : E)$ and a bit of $P(H : \text{not } E)$ and the amount of each it uses depends on the extent to which the user's response supports the presence or absence of this particular item of evidence. See Fig. 6.7.

Clearly, if the response is nought then $P(H : R) = P(H)$, nothing changes, and for other responses a system of linear interpolation between $P(H : E)$ and $P(H : \text{not } E)$ allows for uncertainty.

And that, more or less, covers the inferencing system used.

6.4 THE ENGINE

This brings us now to the engine part – the means the system is to use to drive around amongst the various inferences it might make. The obvious question to ask is: does it matter? After all, the system could just start at the front of its list of questions and work through them until it got to the end and then stop.

You *could* do it that way and, if you did, you could call it forward chaining. A data driven strategy, this simply asks a question, or takes what the user gives it, and then makes what inferences it can from that data, after which it asks another question, and so on until all of the hypotheses have been resolved one way or the other.

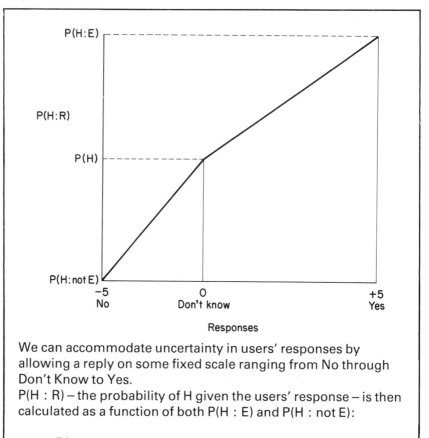

We can accommodate uncertainty in users' responses by allowing a reply on some fixed scale ranging from No through Don't Know to Yes.

P(H : R) – the probability of H given the users' response – is then calculated as a function of both P(H : E) and P(H : not E):

$$P(H : R) = P(H : E) \, P(E : R) + P(H : \text{not } E) \, P(\text{not } E : R)$$

subject to the constraint that P(H : R = 0) = P(H) i.e. a Don't Know reply leaves P(H) unchanged.

Fig. 6.7   Uncertainty in users' responses

Essentially, there are two problems with this approach. The first is that it can be very wasteful in time. Some items of evidence are obviously going to be much more generally important than others so that to leave them until last simply because, by historical accident, they happened to be at the end of the list would be wasteful.

Consider two questions: (1) Do you feel generally ill? (2) Do you have clubbed fingers? Now the first question is obviously a good question to ask very early on in a medical diagnosis session because a *No* answer would instantly rule out a very large slab of illnesses whereas a *Yes* answer would raise the probabilities of many others. The second question, however, can often be used as an indication of certain lung complaints, but, even at that, it is by no means a very certain indication and its absence would rule out very few, if any, items at all.

The second problem with forward chaining is that, to the user, it can seem a bit purposeless. Just a series of questions being fired out at random until the system either stops or gives up.

Of course, if the first problem were solved (that of asking 'good' questions first) then probably the second problem would tend to be solved also because the user might well perceive that the system was at least trying to help.

The second method often used is that of backward chaining. What the system does here is to select a hypothesis from its knowledge base. Having done so, it then looks backwards, as it were, in order to try to see what items of evidence it needs in order to resolve that hypothesis one way or the other and so it asks the user for these items.

Such a system obviously looks a lot more purposeful in its behaviour because it can always say just what it has 'on its mind' by way of a current theory, the current theory being the hypothesis it is currently trying to resolve. But, in its basic form, it has serious disadvantages. Primarily these stem from the problem of deciding in which order it shall consider the various hypotheses open to it and then in which order it shall try to obtain the relevant evidence for these hypotheses.

Suppose the first illness in the knowledge base is acne rosacea. Backward chaining as ever, the system decides to purposefully resolve that hypothesis first. Looking at the 'evidence' for acne rosacea it finds that the condition is often associated with excessive tea drinking. Or, at least, of the various items of evidence associated with the condition excessive tea drinking is the first item in its knowledge base.

So the user switches on his favourite doctor and the first question he or she is asked is: Do you drink a lot of tea? The system is purposeful but to the user it might appear just a trifle obsessive. It reminds me of a medical officer from whom I once suffered who was convinced that the world was divided into two parts – those who had glandular fever and those who did not.

6.5 THE RULE VALUE APPROACH

The approach to this general problem – which is really the problem of which question to ask next – that I have developed is a Rule Value approach, which it has been suggested could also be called 'Sideways Chaining'. It uses neither forward nor backward chaining, both of which tend to concentrate on the hypotheses, but, rather, it concentrates on the evidence. Essentially, for each item of evidence it assigns a value – the value of this rule in the process of inferencing – and asks that question with the highest value first.

Intuitively, the method seems reasonable, because the system simply asks questions which seem kind of important to it, continually modifying its ideas of what questions are important as the answers come in. This, it seems likely, is something like the way human experts behave.

The problem is, of course, how to define an important question. And the answer, in its simplest form, goes like this: We can calculate the value of each item of evidence as the total sum of the maximum probability shifts which it can induce in the whole of the hypotheses currently in the knowledge base. So calculate:

$$RV = \sum_{i=1}^{n} |P(H_i : E) - P(H_i : \text{not } E)|$$

(See Fig. 6.8.) In this way we develop an RV for each item of evidence in the knowledge base. The system can then search for the maximum RV and request information on that item.

$$RV = \sum_{i=1}^{n} \left| P(H_i : E) - P(H_i : \text{not } E) \right|$$

So the rule values are calculated for each item of evidence as the sum of the maximum probability shifts that they can induce in all of the n hypotheses to which this evidence is applicable. That question is always asked first which has the highest rule value.

Fig. 6.8   Rule values (or sideways chaining)

Now, obviously, these rule values are not static. As the posterior probabilities, the $P(H_i : E)$, become continually updated they will continually cause the rule values to be altered. For instance, if a particular set of hypotheses are 'killed' during questioning then there becomes little scope for their probabilities being changed so, consequently, the items of evidence which would have applied to them become less important, as they are re-calculated, and there is a reducing chance that those questions will now be asked. Conversely, as certain hypotheses become increasingly likely there is an increasing scope for their probabilities to be altered by any relevant remaining items of evidence. So these acquire higher rule values and are more likely to be asked next. It is as if the system had a measure of 'attention' in it paying heed to those hypotheses which it had the greatest scope for resolving at any given moment.

Another big advantage of this method is that it is relatively easy to implement – which is not a point to be ignored.

There are, of course, variations on the theme. For instance, we might take RV squared instead of plain RV because, by doing so, we will emphasize those items which produce large shifts in certain hypotheses at the expense of those items which only produce small shifts in a large number of hypotheses. Of course, large shifts are the ones most likely to quickly reject or accept a hypothesis and cut down on the need for further processing.

Yet another variant is to take the sum of squares of RV about its mean value. The purpose of doing this is, again, to try to slice up the problem more cleanly, emphasizing even more those items which can produce a big shift in some hypotheses at the expense of the many small shifts in a large number of hypotheses which might merely cause a large number of hypotheses to wobble up and down around their middle values without coming to any very definite conclusions quickly.

A further refinement to the method is to 'weight' the Rule Values in such a way that those items of evidence which were applicable to hypotheses which were relevant to the last-asked item of evidence receive an increased Rule Value.

The purpose of this is to try to avoid 'jitter' in the system. Suppose our system is running and there are two 'kinds' of hypothesis currently being considered, say Group A and Group B. The highest Rule Value is found and a question is asked and it so happens that this item of evidence is mainly applicable to Group A hypotheses. However, the next question to be asked, with the next highest Rule Value, is, by a small margin, mainly applicable to Group B hypotheses. Then the next question is Group A, and then Group B and so on.

It all occurs by chance and the differences in Rule Values which cause this jitter might be very small. But, to the user, it could appear that the system was jumping around the subject in a very odd fashion. What is needed is to slug the system with a bit of inertia to try to make it stay on the point for a while and to give it some greater sense of 'attention'.

The extent to which these refinements are worthwhile in practice, of course, depends on how much programming effort one wants to put into it and what sort of processor overhead you're willing to put up with. Basically, a simple Rule Value approach works well and is not too slow.

A very real difficulty lies in the problem of evaluating each approach, because in practice how would you assess a question-asking sequence as either good or bad? A horrendous sequence can be spotted very quickly by almost anyone. But a sequence which is good enough compared with one that, theoretically, might be better would be hard to evaluate.

This problem – of evaluating the running of such a system – is not at all trivial. If you have an expert inferencing system with 100 different items of evidence it could gather, all measured on an 11 point scale, then there are 1100 different ways it could be driven by the user.

For each of these 1100 ways there are 100! (factorial) different ways of ordering the question asking process. With numbers of that order, one's computer cannot even calculate how many different ways the thing might be made to run, let alone evaluate them all. And yet such a system fits quite comfortably inside an Apple II or a Sinclair Spectrum.

So, in essence, you dream up a method you like and see, roughly, what it does. And if it doesn't actually explode in your face then it's probably OK.

6.6 COMING TO A CONCLUSION

Essentially, the system is running, it is asking good questions and it is updating its hypotheses according to the answers it gets. It can carry on until it has no more questions to ask and then stop, but it can also come to a conclusion. It can say, 'This is what I think is the case, and maybe you should consider these other items too . . .'

The first item to consider is the Most Likely Outcome. At its simplest this might just be that outcome with the highest probability. But remember what I said about the minimum and maximum probabilities for each hypothesis depending on the information currently in the knowledge base.

Essentially, for each hypothesis we have five quantities each of which is a probability and each of which offers considerable scope for confusion. However, they are these (see Fig. 6.9):

P(H)   which is the current estimated probability of that hypothesis being true.

P(Max) which is the current maximum probability that this particular hypothesis could attain if all the remaining evidence went in its favour.

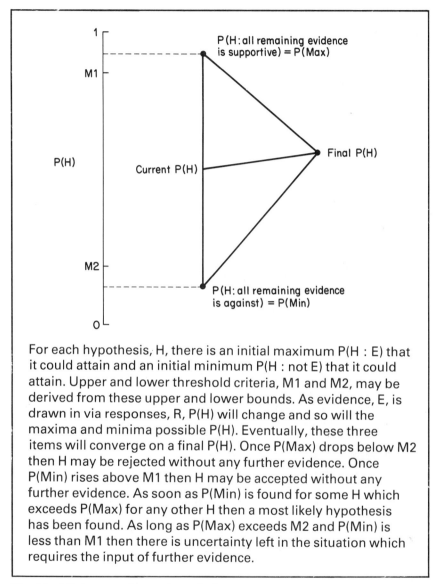

For each hypothesis, H, there is an initial maximum P(H : E) that
it could attain and an initial minimum P(H : not E) that it could
attain. Upper and lower threshold criteria, M1 and M2, may be
derived from these upper and lower bounds. As evidence, E, is
drawn in via responses, R, P(H) will change and so will the
maxima and minima possible P(H). Eventually, these three
items will converge on a final P(H). Once P(Max) drops below M2
then H may be rejected without any further evidence. Once
P(Min) rises above M1 then H may be accepted without any
further evidence. As soon as P(Min) is found for some H which
exceeds P(Max) for any other H then a most likely hypothesis
has been found. As long as P(Max) exceeds M2 and P(Min) is
less than M1 then there is uncertainty left in the situation which
requires the input of further evidence.

Fig. 6.9   Minima, maxima and conclusions

P(Min)   which is the current minimum probability which a particular hypothesis could attain if all of the remaining evidence worked against it.

M1   which is the upper threshold criterion for accepting a particular hypothesis calculated as a proportion of P(Max) before any evidence had been accumulated at all.

M2   which is the lower threshold criterion for rejecting a particular hypothesis calculated as a proportion either of P(Max) or P(Min) before any evidence had been collected at all.

Now, the most likely outcome has been found if there is some hypothesis for which P(Min) is greater than P(Max) for any other hypothesis. In other words, even if all of the evidence has not yet been gathered in, it may still be possible to say which outcome is the most likely if no other outcome can conceivably overturn this particular hypothesis. This may well help to cut the session a little shorter than it might otherwise have been.

The next category of conclusion is that of Likely Conclusions. These are hypotheses which have P(Min) greater than M1 i.e. their minimum attainable probability is greater than the upper threshold.

The next category is Uncertain Conclusions. These are items for which P(Min) is less than M1 but for which P(Max) is greater than M2. In other words, they have not exceeded the upper threshold (although with more evidence they might) but they are still likely to exceed the lower threshold so they should still be considered. These items are prime candidates for the system to extend its questioning session in an attempt to resolve uncertainty.

At the bottom of the list we get No Inferences Possible – except, of course, for the obvious inference that none of the hypotheses are true. In this case the greatest P(Max) is less than M2, the lower threshold. In general, some uncertainty still exists in the system whenever P(Max) is not equal to P(Min) and equal to P(H). But whether it is worth resolving this uncertainty depends on the extent to which the various hypotheses may be made to cross the two thresholds M1 and M2 and this can be seen by examining P(Min) and P(Max) against M1 and M2.

I will now come to *my* conclusion simply by giving a general overview of the process I have described so far:

(1) For each hypothesis establish a prior probability. This is done by scanning the knowledge base and extracting the variable p for each hypothesis (see Fig. 6.1). This is held as P(H) to be later updated.

(2) For each item of evidence establish a Rule Value. This is done by scanning the knowledge base to extract the variables (j,py,pn) where j is the 'evidence number' and py,pn are, respectively,

P(E : H) and P(E : not H) for this item of evidence, j. Then calculate RV for each item of evidence as in Fig. 6.8.
(3) Of all the RVs find the greatest RV to identify that item of evidence which can induce the greatest probability shift in all the hypotheses under consideration.
(4) Interrogate the user on that item of evidence using the question stored in the knowledge base. The user's response may be on a scale from -5 to $+5$ and is the variable R.
(5) Given R, recalculate all hypotheses which referenced that item of evidence in their knowledge base to find P(H : R) (see Fig. 6.7).
(6) Recalculate the Rule Values for all items of evidence to allow for the change in probabilities that have taken place given the last response.
(7) Calculate the minimum and maximum values which each hypothesis may yet attain (see Fig. 6.9).
(8) Find the greatest of the possible minima of these hypotheses.
(9) Check to see if any hypothesis has a maximum possible value which exceeds this maximum of the minima. If there is such a maximum exceeding the greatest minimum then go back to (3) and ask another question. If there is not then there is a most likely outcome and this is it.
(10) Send the system into a summary routine during which it announces, possibly with a fanfare of trumpets, the exact details of all of the inferences it has made.

Finally, never ever tell the end user what was involved in writing this inferencing engine. He'll never believe you if you do tell him because, like most people, he thinks that inferencing is easy. And, of course, he's right (as long as you don't have to use a computer, that is).

APPENDIX: An example knowledge base

Suppose that you wanted an expert system that could act as your own personal car mechanic. This example is of a knowledge base, a very small knowledge base, designed to offer expertise in the field of car mechanics using the methods described so far:

> FLAT BATTERY,
>   0.1, 5, 1, 0, 0.99, 2, 0.7, 0.05, 4, 0.2, 0.5, 5, 0, 0.99, 6, 1, 0.01
> NO PETROL, 0.05, 2, 2, 1, 0.01, 6, 0.9, 0.02
> DAMP IN IGNITION,
>   0.01, 3, 3, 0.9, 0.1, 4, 0.25, 0.5, 6, 0.9, 0.02
> DIRTY SPARK PLUGS, 0.01, 2, 4, 0.01, 0.5, 6, 0.9, 0.02

1, LIGHTS WORKING, ARE THE LIGHTS WORKING?
2, PETROL GAUGE LOW, IS THE PETROL GAUGE READING LOW?
3, VEHICLE EXPOSED TO DAMP, HAS THE VEHICLE BEEN PARKED IN DAMP CONDITIONS?
4, VEHICLE RECENTLY SERVICED, HAS THE VEHICLE BEEN RECENTLY SERVICED?
5, STARTER MOTOR TURNING, IS THE STARTER MOTOR TURNING?
6, CAR WON'T START, WILL THE CAR NOT START?

Just skimming briefly through all this, the first group of items are the hypotheses – for instance, the hypothesis that there is a flat battery. The second groups of items are the items of evidence; for instance, the evidence that the lights are working.

As I am not a brilliant car mechanic the probabilities may be a little adrift from the exact truth but, despite that, consider the first hypothesis – that the car has a flat battery. The prior probability of this on any given car, knowing nothing further about the situation is, we'll say, 0.1, i.e. every tenth car is normally reckoned to have a flat battery.

There are, we reckon, 5 different items of evidence that could be used to establish whether or not the car did, in fact, have a flat battery. The first of these is item 1 (lights working). If the battery is flat then the probability of observing that the lights are working is 0. If, on the other hand, the battery is not flat then $P(E : \text{not } H)$, the probability of observing that the lights are working is, say, 0.99 (i.e. almost certainly they will be working, except in the event that a bulb or fuse has blown).

The second item of evidence is 2. Petrol gauge low. Since the petrol gauge is electrically operated, this could also be relevant. It isn't quite so important, because it doesn't take much electricity to run a petrol gauge. So we reckon that the probability of observing a low petrol gauge reading if the battery is flat is 0.7 and the probability of observing a low petrol gauge reading if the battery is not flat is 0.05. (We could have a low reading for some other reason, such as a lack of petrol!) Note that this probability corresponds to the prior probability of the hypothesis 'no petrol' since that is the only other reason we can think of for the petrol gauge reading low. And so on through the list of applicable items of evidence. The car is less likely to have a flat battery if it has been recently serviced; it is totally unlikely to have a flat battery if the starter motor is turning; and the car definitely won't start if the battery is flat (probability 1) although it might not start even if the battery isn't flat (probability 0.01, say).

The next hypothesis, that there is no petrol, is influenced by the items of evidence: petrol gauge low, and car won't start. Similarly, the hypothesis 'damp in ignition', is influenced by the evidence: vehicle exposed to damp, car recently serviced, and, car won't start. Dirty spark plugs are influenced by the evidence: vehicle recently serviced, and, car won't start (the former contra-indicating dirty spark plugs, the latter giving a positive indication). These probabilities may be judged from experience or may be built up in a more exact and rigorous fashion, but the final proof is to run the thing to see what it does.

Consider Fig. 6.8 and the equation given there for working out Rule Values. If we look at the Rule Values using that equation on this example knowledge base we get the following values:

Evidence	Rule value
Lights working	0.9174
Petrol gauge low	1.4151
Vehicle exposed to damp	0.0822
Vehicle recently serviced	0.1376
Starter motor turning	0.9174
Car won't start	2.3807

Every time the system is run, the first question it will always ask is: Will the car not start? After that it adjusts its Rule Values according to how you reply. But a glance at the table of Rule Values shows that, after 'car won't start', this particular expert is most interested in the matter of whether or not the petrol gauge is reading low and whether or not the starter motor will turn, all of which seems eminently sensible.

Just out of interest, if you give a definite Yes reply to the question 'Will the car not start?', the system then recalculates its Rule Values to give:

Evidence	Rule value
Lights working	0.9991
Petrol gauge low	1.2135
Vehicle exposed to damp	0.7554
Vehicle recently serviced	0.8153
Starter motor turning	0.9991
Car won't start	0

So the next question it asks concerns the petrol gauge. But note how all of the remaining Rule Values have shot up in value on hearing the news that your car won't start. Suddenly, the expert car mechanic has started to take an interest in a large number of things that didn't really interest it before.

If, on the other hand, you had replied No to the question 'Will the car not start?' (i.e. it's working OK) then all of the Rule Values plummet. The expert car mechanic discounts all of the four hypotheses it was considering, concludes that there's nothing wrong with the car, and asks you no more questions.

KNOWLEDGE ENGINEERING

7

Knowledge engineering in PROLOG

MASOUD YAZDANI

7.1 INTRODUCTION: WHERE DO EXPERT SYSTEMS COME FROM?

During the last 25 years the discipline of artificial intelligence (or AI for short) has been growing somewhere between psychology and computer science on the map of sciences. This is due to the fact that researchers in this field are preoccupied with the task of making computers do things which, if done by human beings, would require intelligence (Minsky, 1968).

Early work in AI has had an exploratory nature. The initial concern of AI researchers has been with finding possible ways of doing intelligent things. Therefore, early AI work (however much claimed otherwise) has addressed a different field from that of psychology. Where psychology is concerned with the actual way people do things, AI has been attempting to map out the possible ways that those things can be done on a computer.

Although AI has not yet finished its initial task of exploration, it has become a source of theories for psychologists. This attention has affected AI, in return, towards a change of emphasis in favour of cognitive simulation, whereby efforts to produce possible intelligent artefacts are constrained by the need to make them operate in a similar fashion to a human being.

The second source of influence has been the attitude of the sponsoring organizations. In the USA the exploratory phase of AI research has been generously sponsored, and now AI is expected to produce results. In the UK where, thanks to the Lighthill Report (1972) sponsorship of AI research has been rather strict, a turning point has occurred. The Alvey Report (1982) suggests rather generous support for areas of AI work where medium-term results are considered possible. This second source of influence has affected AI, towards a change of emphasis in favour of building useful computing systems.

7.2 WHAT ARE KNOWLEDGE-BASED SYSTEMS?

The initial phase of AI research (Winston, 1977) has led to a general realization that world knowledge is behind peoples' intelligent behaviour. AI, in its attempt to produce intelligent behaviour on a computer, is limited by the amount of knowledge about peoples' general knowledge. Other disciplines, such as psychology, have not been able to provide AI with explicit exposition of the general knowledge that people show in their behaviour. Due to this problem, some attention is focused on the form of behaviour which most appropriately should be called intellectual behaviour. This is the sort of knowledge which a professional expert has. Such domains are already well defined and well documented in professional journals. Law, citizens' advice, geological and mechanical expertise are easily separable from the whole wealth of general human knowledge. These are exactly those under consideration as intelligent knowledge-based systems in the Alvey initiative:

> An intelligent knowledge-based system is a system which uses inference to apply knowledge to perform a task. Such systems can be envisaged handling knowledge in many areas of human thought and activity from medical diagnosis to complex engineering design, from oil technology to agriculture, from military strategy to citizens' advice.
>
> [Section 4.4.1. of the Alvey report.]

The attempt to deal only with a small bandwidth of human knowledge reduces the complexity of the task faced by an AI researcher, and enables him to offer some working system to users on a reasonable time scale, while major problems of intelligence remain long-term research objectives. Nevertheless, there are numerous problems which need to be tackled, however much the bandwidth is narrowed down:

(1) How is the knowledge acquired in the first place?
(2) How is it represented?
(3) How are the representations implemented on particular hardware?
(4) How is the knowledge accessed inside the system?
(5) How is the knowledge applied to a particular situation?
(6) How is the knowledge modified in the light of experience?
(7) How is it maintained (and, in most cases, irrelevant knowledge disposed of)?

The list is endless.

7.3 WHAT DOES AN EXPERT SYSTEM LOOK LIKE?

Let's look at one example of an expert system, before we consider the question of how to build one ourselves. The AI Handbook (Barr and Feigenbaum, 1982), describes MYCIN, the most widely known expert system, as follows:

> The MYCIN system (Shortliffe, 1976) was designed to provide consultative advice on diagnosis and therapy for infectious diseases. Such advice is often required in hospital care because the attending physician may not be an expert on infectious diseases that show themselves during hospitalization – for example, an infection that develops in a cardiology patient after heart surgery. Time considerations compound the problem. A specimen (blood or urine, etc.) from a patient can show some evidence of bacterial growth within 12 hours, but generally it takes 24 to 48 hours (or more) for positive identification. The physician must, therefore, often decide in the absence of complete information whether or not to start treatment and what drugs to use if treatment is required. Both of these may be difficult questions.

The following is a sample interaction between a physician and the system.

- What is the patient's name?
  John Doe
- Male or female?
  Male.
- Age?
  He is 55.
- Have you obtained positive cultures indicating general type?
  Yes.
- What type of infection is it?
  Primary Bacteremia.
- When did symptoms first appear?
  May 5, 1975.
- Let's call the most recent positive culture CULTURE-1. From what site was CULTURE-1 taken?
  From the blood.
- When?
  May 9, 1975.
- Let's call the first significant organism from this blood culture ORGANISM-1. Do you know the identity of ORGANISM-1?
  No.

- Is ORGANISM-1 a rod or a coccus or something else?
  Rod.
- What is the gram stain of ORGANISM-1?
  Gramnegative.
- Have there been positive cultures from sites which are not associated with infections about which you are seeking advice?
  No.
- Did ORGANISM-1 grow aerobically?
  Yes.
- Did ORGANISM-1 grow anaerobically?
  Yes.
- What is the suspected portal of entry of ORGANISM-1?
  The gastrointestinal tract.

.

.

.

When satisfied that it has a reasonably good feel for the situation, MYCIN starts a short line of questions in preparation for recommending a course of treatment:

- My recommendation will be based on the opinion that the identity of ORGANISM-1 may be 1 Pseudomonas-aeruginosa, 2 Klebsiella-pneumoniae, 3 E. Coli, 4 Bacteroides-fragilis, 5 Enterobacter, or 6 Proteus-non-mirabilis. On a scale of 0 to 4, where higher numbers indicate greater severity, how would you rate the patient's degree of sickness?
  3.
- Does the patient have a clinically significant allergic reaction to any antimicrobial agent?
  No.
- How much does the patient weigh?
  70 kilograms.
- My first recommendation is as follows: In order to cover for items 1, 2, 3, 5, and 6, give Gentamycin using a dose of 119 mg (1.7 mg/kg) q8h IV [or IM] for 10 days. Modify dose in renal failure. And in order to cover for item 4, give Clindamycin using a dose of 595 mg (8.5 mg/kg) q6h IV [or IM] for 14 days. If diarrhea or other gastrointestinal symptoms develop, check for pseudo-membranous colitis.
- Do you wish to see the second choice?

Figure 7.1 shows a superficial view of how the system operates.

AI programs in general, and expert systems in particular, are different from traditional computing packages in the way the programs are

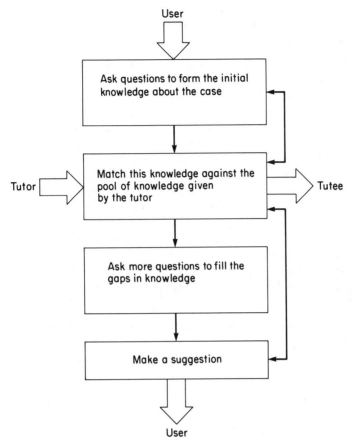

Fig. 7.1

organized. A program has traditionally been viewed as procedure and data. Expert systems however 'can all be fairly described as data base-driven' (Michie, 1980). There are, in fact, three distinct modules:

(1) Facts about features of a particular case.
(2) Rules about a domain of expertise.
(3) Rules for processing the rules in (2) or the 'inference engine'.

In most cases the distinction between the above three modules is conceptual and they would all exist within a single database.

7.4 EXPERT SYSTEMS ARCHITECTURE

If a computer program is to perform the task of an expert it needs a large amount of knowledge to carry out complex tasks in a manner comparable to that of humans. Such systems need to be organized in an orderly fashion to avoid complete confusion. In general the knowledge is divided into three kinds.

(1) **Factual (declarative) knowledge:** This knowledge represents a particular case and is usually gathered through a dialogue with the user to establish what facts are true at the present time. The way such information is represented is important, as the structure of the representation contains information. We need to choose the structure of the representation with reference to its content.

(2) **Procedural knowledge:** This knowledge is usually collected in advance from the domain specialist and forms the core of a knowledge base. This also forms the reasoning part of the system in order to infer conclusions. Such procedural rules can generate facts on demand. Therefore factual and procedural knowledge are interchangeable. Furthermore, these rules need to be open to manipulation by other rules at the run time.

(3) **Control knowledge:** The system needs to have a variety of control strategies available to it so that alternatives can be tried out at run time and be able to deal with failed attempts.

The Production Systems represent a particular method of organizing programs into groups (1), (2), and (3) above, where each part is kept separate and therefore the total system can be easily understood and used.

(1) → Data base (DB)
(2) → List of production rules (PR)
(3) → Method of choosing which production rule to apply to the current state of the data base.

Each production rule is of the form IF condition THEN action, or possibly, IF condition THEN action 1 ELSE action 2. Whether a production rule is applicable is determined by pattern matching.

The conditional part of production is matched against the current DB. If the matching process succeeds it also instantiates all pattern variables, that is variables occurring within the condition of a production rule, to specific matching values found in the DB. These values will then be used only by the action part of that same production. The action part can be any procedure and it is evaluated only if the match succeeds and the production is selected by the control mechanism. All such changes can be affected using two primitive functions – add and remove, e.g. (add item2 DB), (remove item1 DB). When the system starts, a simple rule is invoked which gathers some initial information about the case and adds that to the data base. From then onwards the system follows a basic 'select a production p – apply its associated actions'. The centralized data base is a focus for all activity and the programmer has to produce potentially complex control strategies to ensure that the so-very-possible anarchy in the system is controlled towards a successful conclusion. The most popular way of 'running' as well as 'controlling' a production system is through the devices known as 'demons'.

There are three possible types of demons: if-added, if-removed and if-needed. The demons are enabled by adding them to the DB. If-added demons would typically be used to make forward deductions, which have to be made automatically as soon as some fact becomes known. If-removed demons are invoked by the function remove. They are the opposite of the if-added demons and they work in very much the same way. If-removed demons would typically be used to mop up the explicit deductions made by if-added demons as soon as the item which caused those deductions was removed (for maintaining the consistency of the DB). If-needed demons are used to perform backward deduction.

The great bulk of the database is made up of rules which are invoked by pattern-matching with features of the case-environment and which can be added to, modified, or deleted by the user. A data base of this special type is ordinarily called a knowledge base.

There are three modes of user interface to an expert system, in contrast to the single mode (getting answers to problems) characteristic of more familiar types of computing:

(1) Getting answers to problems – user as client.
(2) Improving or increasing the system's knowledge – user as tutor.
(3) Harvesting the knowledge base for human use – user as a pupil.

Not all human experts can code their knowledge into explicit rules accessible to a computer system. Furthermore, some might not even know explicitly what rules they follow. A 'knowledge engineer' is a person who bridges this gap and codes the human expert's knowledge into a set of rules for an expert system.

7.5 THE BOTTLENECKS AND MINEFIELDS

The main bottleneck currently holding back the widespread use of expert systems, is the process by which the knowledge of the human expert is 'extracted' by the 'knowledge engineer'. Currently this process is *ad hoc* and is basically carried out by 'trial and error'. Nevertheless, a number of methodologies are emerging for this process, while the automatic induction of knowledge is on the horizon.

Despite the 'knowledge extraction bottleneck', a simple algorithm based around trial and error methods has led to a number of successful implementations where a 3-stage activity takes place.

(1) Structuring the domain by finding a good model of the problem-solving process performed by the human expert.
(2) Producing a prototype working model, knowing full well that you will not get it right first time, but that it will be easier to correct the specific errors and learn about the nature of the problems in this way.
(3) Following the eternal loop of 'testing', 'debugging', and 'refining' the prototype until the system is satisfactory, or until you have learned enough to design a new version.

The rather *ad hoc* methodology has found popularity with some designers (for a more detailed survey, see Wellbank, 1983) due to a number of reasons:

- Human experts find it easier to criticize a working system than say what is needed.
- Engineers find it easy to give exceptions to rules, e.g. if A do B, unless C (it shouldn't do that because . . .).
- The prototype keeps human experts interested.
- In general it is useful to get a system working as soon as possible.

In addition to this, the number of choices needing to be made regarding the tools to be used by designers (see Barber, 1984) puts a minefield in front of newcomers to the expert systems world. Current tools for developing expert systems in the order of their pre-packed sophistication are:

- Expert systems shells (such as EMYCIN, SAGE, REVEAL, Micro Expert etc.).
- Development environments (loops, POPLOG etc.).
- Symbolic languages (PROLOG, LISP).
- Algorithmic languages (C, FORTRAN, BASIC).

As there are not many off-the-shelf expert systems, anybody wanting to use one in their work needs to construct one for themselves.

(1) Expert system shells (ESS) are very useful when applicable but in many cases no use at all, except from an introductory training point of view. ESSs are usually constructed by taking an existing expert system, such as MYCIN, and generalizing it into a shell such as Empty-MYCIN. These constrain the solutions to a problem by composing a design methodology best suited to the class of problems to which the original expert system belonged.

(2) Development environments such as POPLOG (Sloman *et al.* 1983) provide less ready-made solutions but more possibilities. POPLOG, for example, provides not only symbolic languages PROLOG, POP-11 and LISP under one environment, but also provides a task-oriented screen editor as well as some partially-working modules in a number of libraries. These systems, however, are only available on large computers and are rather expensive.

(3) Symbolic languages such as LISP and PROLOG, which are becoming widely available for microcomputers, are the most cost effective entry level for a newcomer who only wants to learn about the issues and who is prepared to learn the language and spend some time programming. However, this route does not provide such a cost effective program generation as (2) above is; nor does it provide such efficient implementation as (4) below.

(4) Despite concentrated efforts by some people to portray otherwise, algorithmic languages such as C or BASIC can be used for constructing an expert system. These would act as an implementation language for a production system architecture. The designer, however, needs to be well aware of the internal workings of 'inference engines' and production systems, to avoid writing a program which does not exhibit any of the novel characteristics of expert systems. These languages could, however, lead to the most effective implementations on current hardware.

The final choice is to identify the domain of application and see whether the expert system or AI technology is yet advanced enough to tackle it. Currently, any diagnostic application which depends on the knowledge of a very narrow domain is a 'good' application, while anything depending on creative and commonsense reasoning in a wide-ranging domain is a 'bad' one. Some difficult domains are where:

- Experts do not generally agree.
- The strategies in reasoning are complicated.
- The knowledge includes spatial and/or temporal relationships.
- The problems take a long time to be solved by people.
- A lot of actions hinge on a lot of conditions.
- There are too many objects and too much reliance on commonsense concepts.

7.6 INDIRECT BENEFITS

There are a number of areas of application of expert systems which are not directly noted for short-term commercial applications, but which could prove to have great potential in the future. The first such application is where an expert system is devised which is an expert on the workings of another computer package. Such systems are also referred to as 'intelligent front ends'. Using such a system, the user of a complicated statistics package could interact with such an expert and be advised on how to use the system, or even act as an intelligent mediator between the computing package and a naive user.

There are a number of other ways in which an expert system can successfully be added to an existing package (e.g. a relational database), in order to infer new information by looking at the data for patterns of relationships.

Finally, the potential of using expert systems as novel ways of producing computer-based tutoring systems is very promising. One such novel way of teaching a subject such as physics or medicine, would be to produce an intelligent program which would behave like a skilled physicist or a medical consultant (O'Shea and Self, 1983). The trainee can then observe the knowledge and the line of reasoning of the program and learn in a way that they would have been unable to do before. Trainee doctors could simply be asked to look over MYCIN's shoulder as it sets about solving its problems. This is possible because MYCIN can explain in English what it is doing, MYCIN's decision-making processes are similar to those which students are supposed to develop and MYCIN's representation of medical information is in a human-like manner. The use of MYCIN in this educational role has, in fact, been its most successful application so far, while overshadowed by MYCIN's consulting potential.

A further, slightly different, use of expert systems is in containing the domain knowledge of a tutor in the form of an intelligent tutoring system (Sleeman and Brown, 1982). Computer-based tutoring packages up to now have tended to be basically drill-and-practice. While using expert systems methodology, we can design diagnostic systems which could also form a model of the user more similar to a human teacher. The following incorrect subtraction and addition

$$
\begin{array}{r@{\qquad}r}
170 & 33 \\
-\ 93 & +\ 179 \\
\hline
187 & 102 \\
\end{array}
$$

will not result in 'wrong, you lose a point' being printed on the screen. An ITS will diagnose correctly the misconception of the pupil in forgetting the borrow or the carry over. Using expert systems methodology, we have produced such sophisticated tutoring packages running even on microcomputers (see Attisha and Yazdani, 1983, 1984). The educational potential is exciting.

7.7 USING PROLOG AS A PRODUCTION SYSTEM

In order to demonstrate the ideas presented earlier in this chapter, we shall use PROLOG (Clocksin and Mellish, 1982), to construct a toy expert system. Interested readers should also consult Clark and McCabe (1982) for a successful exposition of PROLOG as an expert system construction tool in which they not only go further than our toy example, but also remain true to PROLOG's 'logical' view of the world. Here we use PROLOG as if it were a production system, in a similar manner to that of Spacek (1981).

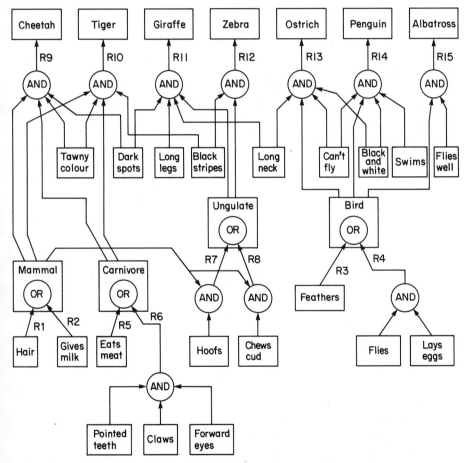

Fig. 7.2 A sample network for a simple rule-based system. Boxes represent assertions, circles represent ways of combining assertions and the labels R1, R2, etc. . . . identify rules. (From Duda and Gaschnig, 1981. Used with permission.)

(1) PROLOG provides us with a database in which we can accommodate our production rules in the form:

conclusion IF   precondition1
                AND precondition2

In the 'logical' interpretation of PROLOG this means:

To prove conclusion

prove precondition1 and
prove precondition2

The PROLOG syntax for all this is simple, with ':-' standing for IF, and ',' for AND.

(2) PROLOG also enables us to accommodate facts as rules such as the above, where there are no preconditions.

(3) The control mechanism provided by PROLOG is what is known as depth-first-search, or backward chaining, similar to that of if-needed demons described earlier. The order of the appearance of facts and rules in the database also guides this control process. PROLOG does not, however, require any numbering of rules or facts in the database. We have numbered the lines to make the exposition of ideas clearer.

A toy expert system on animals discrimination (as in Winston and Horn, 1980) written in PROLOG with the rules in the structure in Fig. 7.2 would be as follows:

```
1.1.0    it-is-a (cheetah):-
1.1.1         it-is (mammal),
    2         it-is (carnivore),
    3         has (tawny-colour),
    4         has (dark-spots).
1.2.0    it-is-a (tiger):-
1.2.1         it-is (mammal),
    2         it-is (carnivore),
    3         has (tawny-colour),
    4         has (black-stripes).
1.3.0    it-is-a (giraffe):-
1.3.1         it-is (ungulate),
    2         has (long-neck),
    3         has (long-legs),
    4         has (dark-spots).
1.4.0    it-is-a (zebra):-
1.4.1         is (ungulate),
    2         has (black-stripes).
1.5.0    it-is-a (ostrich):-
1.5.1         it-is (bird),
    2         does (not-fly),
```

3	has (long-neck),
4	has (long-legs),
5	has (black-and-white-colour).
1.6.0	it-is-a (penguin):-
1.6.1	it-is (bird),
2	does (not-fly),
3	does (swim),
4	has (black-and-white-colour).
1.7.0	it-is-a (albatross):-
1.7.1	it-is (bird),
2	does (fly-well).

We also need the following:

2.1.0	it-is (mammal):-
2.1.1	has (hair).
2.2.0	it-is (mammal):-
2.2.1	does (give-milk).
2.3.0	it-is (bird):-
2.3.1	has (feathers).
2.4.0	it-is (bird):-
2.4.1	does (fly),
2	does (lay-eggs).
2.5.0	it-is (carnivore):-
2.5.1	does (eat-meat).
2.6.0	it-is (carnivore):-
2.6.1	has (pointed-teeth),
2	has (claws),
3	has (forward-eyes).
2.7.0	it-is (ungulate):-
2.7.1	it-is (mammal),
2	has (hoofs).
2.8.0	it-is (ungulate):-
2.8.1	it-is (mammal),
2	does (chew-cud).

As we said in the description based around production systems, initially the database would be free of any facts about the current situation. Therefore we need a simple conversational section in our program to gather information from the user:

3.1.0	has (Y):-
3.1.1	write ('has it got'),
2	write (Y),nl,
3	read (Reply),

```
4              positive (Reply),
5              asserta (has(Y)).
```

```
4.1.0   does (Y):-
4.1.1          write ('does it'),
2              write (Y),nl,
3              read (Reply),
4              positive (Reply),
5              asserta (does(Y)).
```

```
5.1.0   positive (yes)
5.2.0   positive (y).
```

We finally need a definition of the overall task:

```
6.1.0   run:-
6.1.1          it-is-a (Y),
2              write ('i think it is a'),
3              write (Y),nl,nl.
6.2.0   run:-
6.2.1          write ('i dont know what your animal is'), nl.
```

All the user needs to do now is type **run** and the system will do the rest.

7.8 HOW DOES PROLOG WORK IT OUT?

Due to the control mechanism provided by PROLOG, the result would be a search through the database for the meaning of **run**. This is provided on line 6.1.0. In order to satisfy the request to 'run' by the user, PROLOG then has to prove what appears under 6.1.1 to 6.1.3. The system starts from the top attempting 6.1.1 first. This leads to another search in the database, taking us to 1.1.0 where Y is instantiated with 'cheetah' and control passed to 1.1.1 in order to prove 'it-is-mammal'. Another search in the database takes us to 2.1.0 instantiating Y in this case to 'mammal' which is our current item of search. Item 2.1.0 has one precondition; has (hair). The next search through the database leads us to 3.1.0. Precondition 3.1.1 is satisfied by an inbuilt operator resulting in the message 'has it got' being printed out at the user's terminal. Precondition 3.1.2 leads to 'mammal' plus a new line to follow. Precondition 3.1.3 is also satisfied by an inbuilt operator which reads the user's input and instantiates 'Reply' with it. Note that variables in PROLOG all start with an upper case letter (constants with lower case) and have a scope limited to one rule only.

Now the user has the first question on his terminal: 'has it got hair'. Let us be positive to start with and say 'yes'. This would lead to an instantiation of 'Reply' with 'yes'. Precondition 3.1.4 takes us back to another search of the database taking us to 5.1.0 which would be a successful match with no preconditions to follow. Precondition 3.1.5 uses another inbuilt operator which would 'assert' a new fact to the database before other similar facts. In this case has (hair) will be added just before 5.1.0. The system has collected its first fact about the animal in question.

We can now go back and see what other preconditions at a higher level are not yet checked. PROLOG's control mechanism has put all of the previous unattended preconditions on a stack and will follow a 'last in – first out' strategy, taking us to a satisfaction of 2.1.0, which, in turn, will lead us back to 1.1.1. We are now ready to try 1.1.2.

Precondition 1.1.2 takes us to 2.5.0 which follows the same steps above and which leads to the following being printed on the user's terminal: 'does it eat-meat'. Let us see what happens if we are negative and say 'no'. Well, 4.1.0 will lead to a search of the database looking for 'positive (no)'. This will reach the end without success, and therefore will be considered as a failure by PROLOG, resulting in 4.1.0 also failing, due to one of its preconditions failing. Precondition 2.5.0 therefore will also fail.

It should be noted, however, that when a precondition has failed and we are 'backtracking' to the preconditions which called it, we will try other possible alternatives, if they are available. Therefore, in this case, we would try 2.6.0, leading to a further question: 'has it pointed-teeth'.

Let us still be negative and say 'no'. This will lead to a failure of 1.1.2. PROLOG will try still another alternative for 1.2.1 before giving up on 1.2.0. A new version of 1.2.1 will lead to 2.2.0 which would lead to a question: 'does it give-milk'.

Let us say 'yes', leading to the success of 1.2.1. This means that we are ready to try to go forward. PROLOG's philosophy will be: 'Maybe things further away have changed now that we have another success'. Trying 1.2.2 will lead to the same question as we have already been asked: 'does it eat-meat'.

This is due to the fact that our program is not sophisticated enough to remember negative facts in the same way as it remembers positive ones. Appendix A provides an improved version which remedies this problem and others in the above program. However, let's try the alternative, to be consistent, and say 'no' again! This leads to 1.2.2 failing. As we have now tried all the alternatives of 1.2.1, we have 1.1.0 failing too. Well, all that we have done is fail to prove that the animal in question is a cheetah, having learned that it has hair!

You can guess that we shall be trying to prove that it is a tiger next and so on, in the order of the rules presented until we finally succeed, depending on the order of the user's positive and negative answers.

7.9 FURTHER EXTENSIONS

In this chapter we have presented a brief overview of the issues involved in building an expert system. We have used the example of the animal discrimination problem as a means of demonstrating the reasoning behaviour of such systems. The proposed PROLOG 'program' for the solution of the above problem, although simple enough for demonstration purposes, is far from being satisfactory. If you try this program, in fact, with a variety of different data you will discover that it will ask questions to which you have already provided answers. One reason behind this inadequacy is that it does not remember negative facts which it has been told.

Appendix A presents an improvement of the program which remedies some of the problems by using a more complex structure for the representation of facts as well as using an inbuilt non-logical predicate of PROLOG, namely! (called *cut*), which *prunes* the search tree leading to more efficient routes to the solution.

The program used here, however, incorporates only one of the general features of expert systems: that of 'inference generated requests for data'. This means that the system does not request information at random but asks only for what it requires for its reasoning process. In fact a further extension would enable the user to ask 'why' a request for information is made. The system could then present the current rule it is following as the reason behind the request.

Clark and McCabe (1982) present a tutorial on features such as 'explanation of behaviour' which can be added to such a system using PROLOG as a basic building block. Hardy (1983) has also extended PROLOG syntax successfully for a sophisticated example in which the rules are written in a more natural way:

> *Rule 100*
> IF   property = hairy
> THEN group = mammal cf 800.

In the above example cf stands for certainty factor, introducing some level of probabilistic reasoning into the system.

PROLOG syntax can in fact be easily extended through the definition of new operators so that rules presented in the form above are treated by the system as rules of the form presented in our animal discrimination example:

> :-op(975,xfy,:),
>   op(725,xfy,cf),

```
op(948,xfy,because),
op(800,xfy,and),
op(750,xfy,or),
op(959,fx,if),
op(949,xfy,then).
```

Using such a system we can note a rule which we are using so that later we can explain why we have asked a specific question. Invoking a rule then would be:

```
invoke (R):-
          R : if P then C cf N,
          (N < 200 ; note (C cf N because [R])).
```

Hence, if the certainty factor is less than 200 degrees, we ignore the rule, else (';' stands for the logical OR operation) we note the conclusion plus the rule number which leads to it. A predicate 'why' could then look into the database to see what the 'current' rule noted is and present it to the user as the reason behind the question.

```
why:-
     write ('Your answer will help me with rule'),
     current (RULE),
     show (RULE).
```

If we follow the path of adding more and more features to our system in this manner, we shall end up producing something very similar to the expert system shell to which we referred earlier but this time using an extension of PROLOG. We might, however, have been better off starting with an expert system shell. The issue of the choice of the right tools is beyond the scope of this introductory chapter, in addition to the fact that the choice would differ for each application. However, in most cases PROLOG will act as a good vehicle for 'knocking off' a cheap prototype before building an efficient system, using the appropriate tools.

The following is an incomplete list of features which needs to be added to an expert system either in an incremental fashion (such as the approach of this chapter) or right from the start:

(1) Inference generated request for data.
(2) Accountability (explanation of behaviour).
(3) Transparency (tutoring role).
(4) Automatic gathering of rules.
(5) Adult learning.
(6) Probabilistic reasoning (uncertainty in facts, rules and control).

APPENDIX A: An improved version of the animal discrimination program

```
it-is-a (cheetah):-
        it-is (mammal),
        it-is (carnivore),
        positive (has,tawny-colour),
        positive (has,dark-spots).
it-is-a (tiger):-
        it-is (mammal),
        it-is (carnivore),
        positive (has,tawny-colour),
        positive (has,black-stripes),
it-is-a (giraffe):-
        it-is (ungulate),
        positive (has,long-neck),
        positive (has,long-legs),
        positive (has,dark-spots).
it-is-a (zebra):-
        it-is (ungulate),
        positive (has,black-stripes).
it-is-a (ostrich):-
        it-is (bird),
        negative (does,fly),
        positive (has,long-neck),
        positive (has,long-legs),
        positive (has,black-and-white-colour).
it-is-a (penguin):-
        it-is (bird),
        negative (does,fly),
        positive (does,swim),
        positive (has,black-and-white-colour).
it-is-a (albatross):-
        it-is (bird),
        positive (does,fly-well).
    it-is (mammal):-
        positive (has,hair).
    it-is (mammal):-
        positive (does,give-milk).
    it-is (bird):-
        positive (has,feathers).
    it-is (bird):-
        positive (does,fly),
        positive (does,lay-eggs).
```

```
            it-is (carnivore):-
                 positive (does,eat-meat).
            it-is (carnivore):-
                 positive (has,pointed-teeth),
                 positive (has,claws),
                 positive (has,forward-eyes).
            it-is (ungulate):-
                 it-is (mammal),
                 positive (has,hoofs).
            it-is (ungulate):-
                 it-is (mammal),
                 positive (does,chew-cud).
        positive (X,Y):-
                 ask (X,Y,Reply),
                 yes-check (Reply).
        negative (X,Y):-
                 ask (X,Y,Reply),
                 no-check(Reply).
        yes-check (yes).
        no-check (no).
        ask (X,Y, Reply):-
                 write (X),
                 write ('it'),
                 write (Y),nl,
                 read (Reply),
                 remember (Reply,X,Y).
        remember (yes,X,Y):-
                 add (positive (X,Y)).
        remember (no,X,Y):-
                 add (negative (X,Y)).
        add (X):-
            run:- asserta (X:-!).
                 it-is-a (Y),
                 write ('i think it is a'),
                 write (Y),nl,nl.
```

APPENDIX B: EXERCISE FOR THE READER (courtesy of Lindsey Ford)

Write an expert system which has the following rules:

1 IF ball game, two teams with more than 2 players per team, number
   of players in team = 9 THEN 'is baseball'
2 IF ball game, two teams with more than 2 players per team, number
   of players in team = 13 THEN 'is rugby league'

   3 IF ball game, two teams with more than 2 players per team, number of players in team = 15, ball can legally be passed forward THEN 'is Gaelic football'

   4 IF ball game, two teams with more than 2 players per team, number of players in team = 15, NOT ball can legally be passed forward THEN 'is rugby union'

   5 IF ball game, two teams with more than 2 players per team, number of players in team = 11 NOT bat used THEN 'is hockey'

   6 IF ball game, two teams with more than 2 players per team, number of players in team = 11, bat used THEN 'is cricket'

   7 IF ball game, two teams with more than 2 players per team, number of players in team = 11, round ball, NOT ball solid THEN 'is association football'

   8 IF ball game, two teams with more than 2 players per team, number of players in team = 11, NOT round ball THEN 'is American football'

   9 IF ball game, two teams with more than 2 players per team, number of players in team = 5 THEN 'is basketball'

10 IF ball game, NOT two teams with more than 2 players per team, ball solid, NOT played indoors, round ball, NOT mallet used THEN 'is golf'

11 IF ball game, NOT two teams with more than 2 players per team, bat used THEN 'is table-tennis'

12 IF ball game, NOT two teams with more than 2 players per team, NOT played indoors, mallet used THEN 'is croquet'

13 IF ball game, NOT two teams with more than 2 players per team, NOT played indoors THEN 'is tennis'

14 IF ball game, NOT two teams with more than 2 players per team, played indoors, racquet used, NOT ball solid THEN 'is squash'

15 IF ball game, NOT two teams with more than 2 players per team, ball solid NOT round ball THEN 'is bowls'

16 IF ball game, NOT two teams with more than 2 players per team, ball solid played indoors, round ball THEN 'is snooker/billiards'

17 IF ball game, NOT two teams with more than 2 players per team, NOT ball solid, NOT bat used, NOT racquet used THEN 'is pelota'

18 IF NOT ball game, racquet used THEN 'is badminton'

19 IF NOT ball game, NOT played sitting down, played indoors, NOT racquet used THEN 'is darts'

20 IF NOT ball game, played sitting down, cards used, NOT board used THEN 'is bridge'

21 IF NOT ball game, played sitting down, NOT cards used, board used THEN 'is chess/draughts/snakes and ladders or something of that sort'

REFERENCES

Alvey, P. (1982) *A Programme for Advanced Information Technology, The Report of the Alvey Committee*, HMSO.

Attisha, M. and Yazdani, M. (1983) A microcomputer-based tutor for teaching arithmetic skills. *Instructional Science*, **12**, 333–342.

Attisha, M. and Yazdani, M. (1984) An expert system for diagnosing children's multiplication errors. *Instructional Science*, **13**.

Barber, E.O. (1984) Expert systems survey. *Working Paper W.122*, Department of Computer Science, University of Exeter.

Barr, A. and Feigenbaum, E. (1982) *Handbook of Artificial Intelligence*, Pitman Press, London.

Clark, K.L. and McCabe, F.G. (1982) PROLOG: a language for implementing expert systems. *Machine Intelligence*, **10**, 455–475.

Clocksin, W. and Mellish, C. (1982) *Programming in PROLOG*, Springer Verlag, Berlin.

Duda, R.O. and Gaschnig, J.G. (1981) Knowledge-based expert systems come of age. *Byte*, **6:9**, 238–278.

Hardy, S. (1983) *PROLOG for Knowledge Engineers*, Tecknowledge Internal Memo.

Lighthill, J. (1972) *Artificial Intelligence: Report to the Science Research Council*, Science Research Council.

Michie, D. (1980) Expert systems. *Computer Journal*, **23:4**, 369–377.

Minsky, M. (ed.) (1968) *Semantics Information Processing*, MIT Press.

O'Shea, T. and Self, J. (1983) *Learning and Teaching with Computers*, The Harvester Press, Brighton.

Shortliffe, E.H. (1976) *Computer-based Medical Consultations: MYCIN*, American Elsevier, New York.

Sleeman, D. and Brown, J.S. (eds.) (1982) *Intelligent Tutoring Systems*, Academic Press, London.

Sloman, A., Hardy, S. and Gibson, J. (1983) POPLOG: a multi-language program development environment. *Information Technology: Research and Development*, **2**, 109–122.

Spacek, L. (1981) *The Production Systems and PROLOG*, Department of Computer Science, University of Essex.

Wellbank, M. (1983) *A Review of Knowledge Acquisition Techniques for Expert Systems*, Issued by Martlesham Consultancy Services, British Telecom Research Laboratories, Ipswich, England.

Winston, P. (1977) *Artificial Intelligence*, Addison-Wesley, Reading, Mass.

Winston, P. and Horn, B. (1980) *LISP*, Addison-Wesley, Reading, Mass.

8

How we built Micro Expert

P. R. COX

Some time in 1981 a small group of us decided to design and write an expert system shell. I am going to attempt to recount some of our experiences while doing this. I will try to explain some of the decisions which we had to make while designing this system and our reasons for making the choices which we made.

I hope that this narrative approach will be helpful in bringing out some of the problems involved in designing an expert system shell and that it will also give potential users some insight into what can and what cannot be done with the shells currently available.

Of course, once we had written our expert system shell and had used it for a while, we very quickly became dissatisfied with it and thought that we could do better next time. It has taken us a long time to get our ideas straight as to exactly what the Mark II version should look like but we have finally got it written and into the final stages of testing. However this account is mainly about Micro Expert. We will need to get some experience using Expert II before we can sensibly evaluate our new set of choices, but I would expect that Expert II will be merely another step along the road.

The first set of choices which we had to make were concerned with the size of the system. Should we be aiming at a large system designed to run on a large mainframe or, going to the other extreme, should we be aiming at something which would run on a microprocessor? We chose to write a microprocessor-based system. The choice was made for a number of reasons, the first of which was availability of resources. We had several microprocessors available but we had not got and could not afford a mainframe. The second reason was the type of application which we anticipated. In many advice-giving applications there is a great advantage in using a machine which can be put in the boot of a car. Not all expert systems are necessarily interactive but the great majority of them are and it is often important to be able to take the system out on site. The third reason is to do with our background as programmers, our self image as a group if you like. We see ourselves as practical engineers rather than as theoretical scientists. We feel that our strengths lie in our ability to write well engineered programs which run with the minimum of resources rather than in our capacity to produce something completely original in conception.

If you look at the expert systems currently working or in the process of development you will be struck by the variety both of application area and of general approach taken by the writers of the various systems. Our next decision therefore was to choose the type of system which we wish to write. We decided to attempt to write a system of the type known as an advice language. A system of this type is primed with rules explaining to it how to perform a particular function. These rules are supplied to it by a knowledge engineer. In use, it is consulted by a user who has an appropriate problem and the system will attempt to give the user advice. The session proceeds in a manner which is analogous to the way your doctor behaves when you go to his surgery. It asks the 'patient' questions about his symptoms and attempts to diagnose his problem from the answers.

I do not think that there were many other options open to us at this stage as we had already decided that we were designing a system which was not aimed at any one application area. An advice language is probably the type of expert system which covers the broadest spectrum of applications.

The next factor which we had to consider was the computer language in which we intended to write the system. The first part of this choice is between one of the AI languages such as LISP or PROLOG and a conventional algorithmic language. While efficient implementations of both LISP and PROLOG exist on the larger mainframes, implementations for small machines tend to be rather heavy in their use of resources; both memory and machine time. The strength of the AI languages lies both in their flexibility which is extremely useful for experimental programming, and in their power which cuts down the amount of work involved in producing a large complex program. We were however intending to produce a system designed to run as efficiently as possible on a small microprocessor so we rather regrettably decided to use an algorithmic language. We decided to use the UCSD PASCAL system – PASCAL because we needed a language which would support recursion and a reasonable system of heap management, the UCSD PASCAL because it is available on a wide range of hardware and we were interested for commercial reasons in obtaining as much program portability as possible.

One of the ways of looking at an advice language is as an instance of a special purpose computer language. An advice language is a language in which you write expert systems in much the same way as SIMULA is a language in which you write programs concerned with simulation. Many of the choices which must be made when designing an advice language are the same as those which are pertinent to the design of any other computer language. Most AI languages are incremental. This implies that you can run bits of program as soon as you have written them just as you can in BASIC for instance. Following this tradition most of the early expert systems were also incremental. You could add rules to your model at any time. We decided, however, to go our own way and produce a system which had a separate rules compiler, so that to change your model you had first to edit a rules source file and then you had to recompile your model, just as you would if you were using FORTRAN or ALGOL. We did this for two reasons. First we think this enables us to run a bigger model on a machine with a given memory size. Secondly we can see occasions where it would not be advisable to issue a model to a user and to allow him to alter it if he felt fit. This can easily be stopped in a compiled model by not giving him the rules source or the compiler. Thirdly, we were concerned with the difficulty that the user of the language was going to have debugging his rules. We wished to produce a language which was as strongly typed as possible. Incremental languages are of necessity weakly typed languages.

You do not set out to design a system of this type in a vacuum. Any designer of a system is influenced by previous systems which have been built by other people in the same applications area. We read everything which we could find about previous expert systems and eventually decided to model our system on the PROSPECTOR system (Duda *et al.*, 1978). In particular we adopted its method of inference using Bayes's rule and its authors' way of looking at collections of rules as trees and their habit of expressing this diagramatically.

There are two features of PROSPECTOR which we did not implement. Firstly, PROSPECTOR, at the beginning of a session, asks the user for a list of the minerals which he has encountered. It processes this list against a table giving synonyms of common minerals and uses the standard names thus produced to answer some of the model's questions and thus get the session off to a good start. We thought at the time that this feature was too application dependent to be generalizable for use in a context-free shell and so decided not to adopt it. However I am now not so sure that this was a good decision. It is a very common situation that the user of a model has something which he wishes to say at the beginning of the session. He must have some sort of problem or he would not be using the model in the first place. It would be useful in future systems if some form of general purpose volunteering facility could be provided. This will not be easy to implement however.

The second feature of PROSPECTOR which we did not implement was its semantic net facility. This facility allows the model writer to specify that, for instance Granite, Periodite and Basalt are all igneous rocks. If the model knows, during a session, that Basalt is present, it knows without asking that igneous rocks are present. Alternatively, if the model has been told that igneous rocks are absent, it knows without asking that Granite, Periodite and Basalt are not present. You can get the effect you want without specifically having this feature in an advice language, so we decided not to implement it in our first system. However, it is a feature which can simplify things for the model builder and is a prime candidate for inclusion in future shells.

At this stage we had made our basic decisions which were to write an advice language type of expert system, to implement it in UCSD PASCAL to run on a microprocessor, to have a separate rules language compiler and run time system and to follow the style of system used in PROSPECTOR. Before we consider how these decisions worked out in use, I would like to explain in some detail how the system as implemented looks to the user.

Micro Expert consists of two programs, a rules language compiler called EXPCOMP and a run time system called RUNEXPT. To create a model the user first writes his rules in the Micro Expert rules language. I will say more about the rules language later, for the time being it is enough to say that it is a very simple language: each box in any of the figures in this chapter corresponds to one statement in the language.

The rules are entered into the microprocessor and written to disk using the standard UCSD system editor thus forming a source file in the conventional way. The source file is then compiled using the EXPCOMP compiler. The compiler produces two output files rather than the conventional single object file. The first output file, the object file, contains the structure of the model. This is in the form of tables which can be loaded into main memory and used by the run time system, rather than the executable code produced by most compilers. The second output file produced by the compiler, the message file, contains all the ASCII text strings from the source. Expert systems tend to contain large amounts of text and it is advisable not to hold this in main memory as this would severely restrict the size of model which could be handled on a microprocessor.

The compiler also produces a listing which can be directed to either the console or the printer. The listing contains first a copy of the source with line numbers followed by any error messages. It then gives a list of all the variables in the program and a separate list of goal variables. This is followed by a concordance.

The compiler checks for variable typing, it makes sure that we do not add numbers to probabilities for instance. It checks that all statements can be reached from at least one goal statement and that the leaf nodes of all trees are questions. It also checks for circular arguments in the model. Any model which will compile without errors will run and cannot hang up so a large class of errors which occur in conventional programming cannot get past the compiler. This is not to say however that the model is guaranteed correct. The logic of what the user has written could still be wrong.

I do not intend to go into any detail on the internal operation of the compiler. It is a very conventional compiler for what is a small and syntactically very simple language. For those of you who are interested in this subject I will merely state that the syntax is fully left context bounded and that the compiler parses using the method known as recursive descent. Many books on PASCAL contain an example of a compiler of this sort.

When the user has got a cleanly compiled model the next stage is to use it. To do this he executes the program RUNEXPT. This program commences by asking the user for the name of the model which he wishes to use. When he supplies the name, it reads the object file for this model and then starts the question and answer session. The method of operation of this session is best explained by demonstrating what a rule base looks like so we will proceed to look at an example of a rule base.

A small rule base is shown in diagrammatic form in Fig. 8.1. This example contains only one goal represented by the uppermost box in the figure. This goal is 'You should take your umbrella'. In other words the purpose of this model is to help the user decide whether or not he should take his umbrella and the model will ask him questions to enable it to decide what to advise him. There are arrows in the figure descending from this goal box to two boxes on the next level. These boxes are 'It is raining' and 'It will rain today'. This signifies that the decision to take your umbrella depends in some way on whether it is raining and whether it will rain today. Note that at this stage we have not specified what this relationship is, merely that there is one.

If you look at the box marked 'It will rain today' you will see that there are arrows descending from it pointing to three more boxes. These boxes contain the words 'The cows are standing up in the fields', 'The seaweed is damp' and 'The barometer is falling' so the truth of the statement 'It will rain today' depends in some way on the truth of these other three statements.

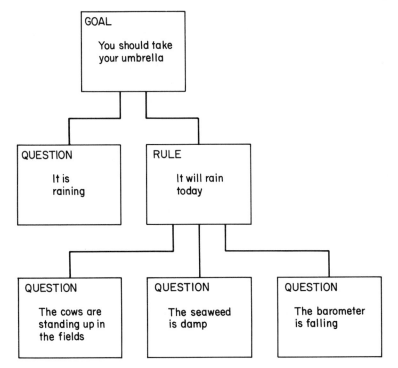

Fig. 8.1

The other four statements in the model do not have any arrows descending from them. There is no way for the model to deduce the truth or falsity of these statements except by asking the user. These four statements are therefore questions and are marked as such in Fig. 8.1. The statement 'It will rain today' is neither a goal nor a question. We therefore refer to it as a rule and as you can see it is marked as a rule on the figure.

To recapitulate, the boxes on these diagrams represent hypotheses in your model, these boxes are classified as goals, rules or questions. The boxes at the top of a tree must be goals, but boxes in the middle of a tree can be goals if you want. A goal has two attributes. Firstly, it is something which you can ask the system to prove and, secondly, it is a statement which will be reported on by the system in the final report. The leaf nodes of the trees must be questions. All other boxes are referred to as rules.

We have already said that the truth or falsity of each box in the diagram (except for the question boxes) is derived in some way from the truth or falsity of the boxes to which it points. We have not said anything yet about how it is derived. The first point to be noted is that there must be more than one way of performing this derivation, so that associated with each box there is an operator. If the system used Boolean logic the operators would be the usual Boolean operators; AND, OR and NOT. However the system is designed to handle uncertainty. That is to say that the contributory factors to a hypothesis will not usually be known to be true or false with certainty, they will merely have probabilities associated with them.

Figure 8.2 shows the same model as Fig. 8.1 but expanded to show the operators and question types which I am now going to discuss in more detail.

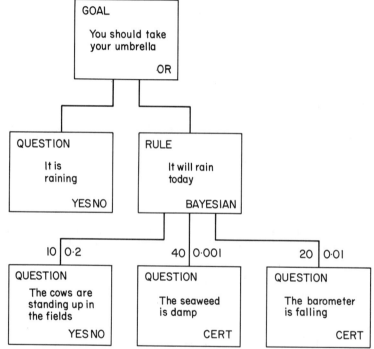

Fig. 8.2

The NOT operator is the simplest to implement. If A is not B then the probability of A is 1 − the probability of B.

IF   A = NOT B
THEN Pa = 1 − Pb

There are a number of ways of implementing a fuzzy AND and a fuzzy OR operator. However everyone is agreed that no matter how we do this the operators must behave like the equivalent Boolean operators at the limit, that is to say when the probabilities of the contributory factors are constricted to zero and one. We have chosen to follow the definitions used in PROSPECTOR for the Micro Expert implementation. AND is defined as minimum. That is to say, in the expression 'A is B AND C AND D' with the probabilities of A,B,C and D defined as Pa, Pb, Pc, Pd respectively, then Pa is the minimum of Pb, Pc, Pd.

Similarly the operator OR is defined as a maximum. In the expression 'A is B OR C OR D' with the probabilities of A, B, C and D defined as Pa, Pb, Pc and Pd, then Pa is the maximum of Pb, Pc, Pd.

At this point it must be said that there is more than one way of implementing the AND and the OR functions, for instance the AND function could be defined as probabilities of the contributory factors multiplied together. There is no general agreement on which formulae to use. However, as already mentioned, the operations must behave as if they were Boolean operators in the extremes. Furthermore it would seem logical that the pair of factors used should obey de Moivre's theorem. This states that:

A AND B = NOT ((NOT A) OR (NOT B))

The Max and Min operations do not obey this theorem however. As you can see the mathematics of these systems need further development.

In addition to these three fuzzy logic operators, AND, OR and NOT we need a fourth. We need to be able to say something like 'A depends on B and C, but B is more important than C'. For this type of operation we use an operation which we call Bayesian. Mathematically, the Bayesian operator is based on Bayes's rule. A rule with a Bayesian operator looks like this:

> *Rule measles* (Bayesian) 'The patient has measles'
>   Fever LS 10 LN 0.01
>   Spots LS 20 LN 0.001
>   Prior 0.25

The rule states that measles can be deduced from the presence of spots and the presence of fever. The last line of the example which reads 'Prior 0.25' signifies that 25 per cent of the cases seen by this model are expected to have measles, or to put this another way, if for some reason we are unable to check whether the patient has spots or fever the probability of measles would be 25 per cent. This number is known as the *a priori* probability of measles. The first stage of the calculation of the probability of measles is to turn this *a priori* probability into an *a priori* odds. A probability of 0.25 gives an odds of 1/3 that is one chance for and three chances against.

Associated with each contributory factor here are two numbers which are known as LS and LN. LS stands for logical sufficiency, LN stands for logical necessity. In the example fever is assigned an LS factor of 10 and an LN factor of 0.01. If we know that fever is present we multiply the *a priori* odds for measles by the LS factor. In this case this will give us a current, or *post priori* odds of (1/3) × 10 or 10/3.

If we know that spots are present as well, we also multiply by the LS factor for spots which is 20, giving a *post priori* odds of 1/3 × 10 × 20 with both spots and fever.

Similarly if we know that a symptom is not present we multiply by the appropriate LN factor.

If we do not know whether a symptom is present or not we multiply by one (or leave the odds alone).

The rule in the example can be translated into English as follows. 'If we have no evidence, the probability of measles is 0.25. The definite presence of fever makes measles 10 times as likely. The definite absence of fever makes measles 100 times less likely (i.e. 1 / 0.01). The definite presence of spots makes measles 20 times as likely and the definite absence of spots makes measles 1000 times less likely.

The possible outcomes are shown in Table 8.1.

Table 8.1

Fever	Spots	Odds	Probability
Yes	Yes	1/3 × 10 × 20= 66.6	0.98
Yes	Don't know	1/3 × 10= 3.33	0.77
Yes	No	1/3 × 10 × 0.001= .0033	0.003
Don't know	Yes	1/3 × 20= 6.67	0.86
Don't know	Don't know	1/3= 0.33	0.25
Don't know	No	1/3 × 0.001= 0.0003	0.0003
No	Yes	1/3 × 0.01 × 20= 0.066	0.06
No	Don't know	1/3 × 0.01= 0.0033	0.003
No	No	1/3 × 0.01 × 0.001= 0.000003	0.000003

The contributory factors to a Bayesian rule are not necessarily questions. They could be rules themselves. The question arises as to how we interpret the probabilities of these rules in terms of 'yes', 'no' and 'don't know'. 'Yes' is obviously equivalent to a probability of 1, 'no' is a probability of zero, 'don't know' is interpreted as a probability equal to the *a priori* probability. The problem remains, however, as to what we do if the probability is any other value.

Let us suppose for example that the probability of a contributory factor is greater than the *a priori*, that is to say somewhere between 'don't know' and 'yes'. Here are two possible courses of action open to us. Firstly, calculate the resultant probabilities for both the 'don't know' case and the 'yes' case and interpolate to get some intermediate result. Or, secondly, use a factor for the multiplication which lies between one and the LS factor. In practice we have chosen to take the second approach and to use linear interpolation on the LS or the LN factor whichever is appropriate. However there is really no theoretical justification for using one approach over another. It is not even clear from those published papers on PROSPECTOR which I have read, which approach it uses. The method which we have chosen will produce an engine which is more positive in its results than the other method.

If you refer to Fig. 8.2 again you will see that the leaf nodes of the trees are designated as questions. The model has no way of deducing the probabilities of these statements so it must ask the user. The user is being asked in effect to give his estimate of the probability of a statement being true. To expect the user to give an estimate of probability directly would make the model much too difficult to use. It is however reasonable in most cases to expect the user to be able to reply 'yes' 'no' or 'don't know' to a question. The reply is translated by the system into a probability where 'yes' equals 1, 'no' equals 0, and 'don't know' equals the *a priori* probability which is provided by the model builder. A second type of question is used in the system where the user replies using a scale running from 5 to −5. In this scale 5 is equivalent to 'yes' (or a probability of 1), −5 is equivalent to 'no' (or a probability of zero), and 0 is equivalent to 'don't know' (or the *a priori* probability). Intermediate values signify degrees of belief in the truth or falsity of the question. For instance, a reply of 4 could be interpreted as 'very probably', −2 as 'probably not' etc. These intermediate valued replies are translated by the system into probabilities by linear interpolation.

There are some problems associated with the interpretation of the meaning of this type of question when the answers are anything except 'yes' or 'no'. For instance, let us suppose that the system asks 'Are your spark plugs dirty?' and that the user replies 'don't know'. A number of meanings can be placed on the reply. For instance 'I am an experienced mechanic and in my opinion the degree of dirt on the spark plugs is borderline' or 'I have never looked at a spark plug before and I don't know how dirty is dirty' or again 'I can't find the plug wrench' or even 'What is a spark plug?'

There are a number of approaches to resolving this problem. The first one is that a 'don't know' answer means that the system cannot obtain any information about the degree of dirtiness of the spark plug. Therefore it will do nothing and the reason that it can obtain no information is not important. The second approach is that we could distinguish between the various interpretations of the answer by asking more questions. We must use discretion when doing this however as it could make the model very tedious to use.

Expert systems work and give results in spite of these unresolved problems. They appear to get their strength from the redundancy of the rules and to function in spite of the fact that the mathematics used is rather rudimentary, that many of the questions which they ask are ambiguous and that in most models some of the rules are dubious. However, when we can resolve some of these problems I would expect them to work even better.

The system as we have described it so far works purely in terms of probabilities. There are many places in most models where it is more natural to ask questions which are directly answered with a number.

For instance, 'Is the patient old?' is an ambiguous question in many circumstances. It assumes that the user knows what would be considered old for the purposes of this model. 'Enter the patient's age in years' is much less ambiguous. The system therefore has a type of question called numeric which can be answered with a number.

If we are going to include numeric questions in the system we will need to be able to do a certain amount of arithmetic with the numbers which we get. The system has rules of type Plus, Minus, Multiply and Divide. We can have rules which say things like:

> *Rule age-difference* 'The difference of their ages'
> Subtract mans-age womans-age

It would be tedious to do a lot of complicated calculations using a system as rudimentary as this but this is not usually necessary. There is another way to handle such cases as you will see when I come to discuss external functions. The system distinguishes between probabilities and numbers. It considers them to be different types of object and the compiler will not allow you to do arithmetic with probabilities.

To enable us to integrate numeric questions with the system, which is basically designed to reason in terms of probabilities, we need some way of converting numbers into probabilities in a controlled manner. There are two types of rule which do this. They are known as Range and Modulus. Mathematically this type of operator is called a fuzzy set membership function.

Let us assume that our model contains a question which asks 'Give the age of the patient in years' and that we want an assertion that says 'The patient is old' and that for our current purposes we define old as follows: anyone under 60 is definitely not old, anyone over seventy is old, anyone between 60 and 70 we are not sure. We would write two rules as follows.

Rule old-patient 'The patient is old'
  Range patients-age 60 70
Question patients-age 'The age of the patient in years'
  Numeric 0 120

The numbers 0 and 120 in this example are merely range checks on the validity of the answer to the question. For instance, if the user replied to the question with a value of 150 the system would refuse to accept it and would repeat the question.

Old-patient is calculated by the following procedure: if patients-age is less than 60 then the probability of old-patient is zero, if patients age is 70 or greater then the probability of old-patient is 1, if the value of patients-age lies between 60 and 70 then the probability of old-patient is found by linear interpolation. For instance, if patients-age is 65 then old-patient takes a value of 0.5.

Modulus is a similar function but its two parameters are a target value and a tolerance. For example let us say that the temperature of a chemical reaction should be 80 degrees centigrade and that we can accept a tolerance of plus or minus 5 degrees. We could write a rule which said:

Rule correct-temperature 'The temperature is correct'
  Modulus Temperature-reading 80 5

This would be calculated as:

  If reading is 80 then correct-temperature is 1.
  If reading is less than 75 or greater than 85 then correct-temperature is zero.
  For any intermediate values of reading correct-temperature found by linear interpolation.

Figure 8.3 shows these examples in graphical form. You will see that the graph of the modulus function is a pyramid. It could be argued that it would be more correct to use a nice bell shaped curve. We thought however that for a small system, the extra computational load of doing this outweighed any advantage to be gained.

It is possible to build up more complicated fuzzy set membership functions using range and modulus as basic building blocks and I will give a simple example of this which is often used. Let us suppose that we wish to decide whether we should consider a person to be a teenager. We will say that for our purposes thirteen year olds through 19 year olds are definitely teenagers, ten year olds and younger are definitely not, twenty two year olds and older are definitely not, and we

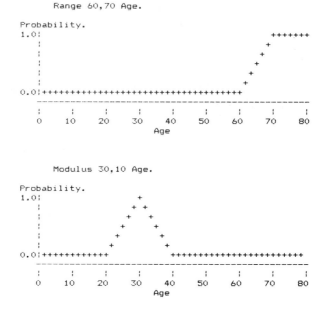

Fig. 8.3

are not sure about 11, 12, 20 or 21 year olds. We can write the following rules.

> *Rule teenager* 'A teenager'
>   And old-enough not-too-old
> *Rule old-enough* 'Old enough to be a teenager'
>   Range age 10 13
> *Rule not-too-old* 'Not too old to be a teenager'
>   Not too-old
> *Rule too-old* 'Too old to be a teenager'
>   Range age 19 22
> *Question age* 'What is the customers age in years'
>   Numeric 0 120

We have now described all the functions which we need to logically define our model. There is one further class of information which we must be able to write into our rule base to enable us to produce a viable system. We must be able to control in some way the order in which questions are asked and we must be able to specify that some of the questions are irrelevant under certain circumstances.

Let us consider the order of questioning first. There are circumstances where it would be very inconvenient to the user if the system was allowed to ask the questions in the order which was most convenient to it. For instance, let us suppose that our model contains these two questions, 'Are your spark plugs dirty?' and 'Do your spark plugs have a white deposit?' If these two questions were asked with a number of other questions between them, there would be a definite possibility that the user would be required to remove the spark plugs twice. This could make him distinctly unhappy. We need therefore to be able to force the system to ask these two questions together. There are also many instances where we need to control the order of questioning merely to make the computer structure its conversation in a more human-like way. The human users can find it rather disconcerting if the system jumps about from subject to subject in what appears a random manner and it is often necessary to be able to control this.

The second requirement is that we should be able to specify that certain questions are only relevant under certain circumstances. As an example let us suppose that the model contains these three questions; (1) 'What sex is the patient?' (2) 'What age is the patient?' and (3) 'How many times has the patient been pregnant?' It is obvious that if the sex of the patient is male then the number of pregnancies must be nil. A system which asked for the patient's sex, received an answer of 'male' and then proceeded to ask how many times the patient has been pregnant would not appear very intelligent to the user. There are other reasons for wanting to be able to control the questioning in this manner besides that of logical consistency.

Firstly, there is the question of implementing heuristics. For instance, your domain expert might say 'I find that under such and such circumstances it is better to investigate A before investigating B'. Secondly, there is the matter of making the model behave in a polite way. It is all too easy inadvertently to produce models which conduct a conversation with the user in a manner which can be interpreted as rude or uncouth. As an example, suppose our model produces the following dialogue:

> System: 'Are you married?'
> User: 'No'
> System: 'How many times have you been pregnant?'

This would be construed as an example of an uncouth system.

If you look at Fig. 8.4 you will see that it is the same as Fig. 8.2 but with the addition of one extra box. This box contains the words 'Do you have an umbrella?' It is joined to the goal box 'Should you take your umbrella?' with a dotted line. Next to the line are a pair of numbers 1 and 5. This signifies that 'Do you have an umbrella?' should be answered and that the answer should lie in the range 1 to 5 expressed as a certainty before we attempt to investigate whether or not you should take your umbrella.

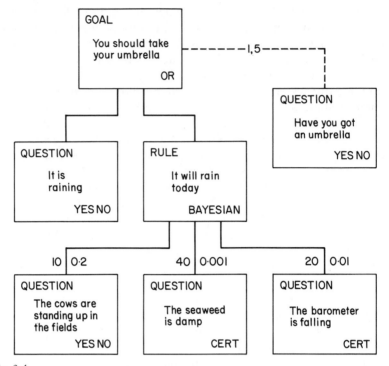

Fig. 8.4

This is written in the rules language using the keyword blocked and is commonly known as a blocking factor. The goal rule of the model depicted in Fig. 8.4 is written:

> *Goal take-umbrella* 'You should take your umbrella'
>   Blocked have-umbrella 1 5
>   Or raining will-rain

This simple mechanism will allow us to do all the types of control of question sequencing described above. If you merely wish to constrain the order of investigation of parts of the model you can write:

> Blocked age −5 5

for instance.

There is one other factor which needs to be taken into consideration when using blocking. Blocking solely affects the order in which the questions are asked in a model and whether they are asked at all. It has no effect on the probabilities which are calculated. In the last example the model will first ask 'Do you have an umbrella?' If the answer is 'No' the model will ask no further questions. This is the effect which we intended. However, it will give an answer of 'Don't know' to the goal statement 'You should take your umbrella'. This is because the value of this goal statement is defined as 'Raining' or 'Will-rain' and we have not investigated either of these hypotheses so they both have values of 'Don't know'. If, as seems more likely, you want the result to be 'No' in these circumstances you must specifically say so. This example will handle the situation adequately:

> *Goal take-umbrella* 'You should take your umbrella'
> Blocked have-umbrella 1 5
> And have-umbrella need-umbrella
> *Rule need-umbrella* 'You will need your umbrella'
> Or raining will-rain

You can see that the question 'Have-umbrella' is included in the goal 'Take-umbrella' both as a blocking factor and as part of the logical derivation so that if 'Have-umbrella' is answered in the negative it will both inhibit any further investigation of the hypothesis 'Take-umbrella' and force the result of this goal to be 'No'.

It is important to realize that the use of a blocking statement blocks a path through the model rather than the questions attached to this path. Let us look at the following example:

> *Goal A* ' . . . . . '
> Blocked B 1 5
> And C D
> *Goal E* ' . . . . . '
> Or C F

In this example the system will start out by investigating goal A. Goal A is blocked on B so it will investigate B first. Let us suppose that a result of −3 is obtained for B. The system will not investigate C or D. It will then go on to investigate the second goal, goal E. While it is investigating E it will investigate C even though C is blocked by B in goal A. As you will see it is only the path to C through goal A which is blocked, not C itself. D on the other hand has no alternative path, it can only be reached through A. D therefore will never be investigated.

We have now described all the main features of the advice language. However we have found in practice that, from time to time, a model designer will have some unique requirement which cannot be handled within the context of the system as defined. We have therefore included a facility which allows the user to write what are known as external functions or external questions. These are procedures written by the model designer, usually in PASCAL and linked with the system's run time program.

I will first describe an external question. Rather than displaying a message on the VDU and getting its value from a reply typed in by the user, it calls a PASCAL procedure which supplies a probability or a number which it places in the question's current value field. External questions can be used in a number of ways, they can be used to interrogate a piece of process equipment, or they can be used to interface an expert system to a database.

An external function is a rule which uses a user-supplied procedure to calculate its current value from the values of its contributory factors. For instance, in some circumstances a user may think that the system's convention of calculating a fuzzy AND as the minimum of the probabilities of its contributory factors is not what he requires. He may prefer to use a convention where AND is the product of the contributory factors. This could easily be implemented as an external function.

External functions can be numeric as well as probabilistic. We could if we needed, implement trigonometric functions in this manner. It is possible also to implement specialized fuzzy set membership functions; that bell shaped curve mentioned above for instance.

To take another example, let us suppose that our model contains a question which reads as follows:

What metal are the heat exchanger tubes?
Type 1 for Copper.
     2 for Nickel.
     3 for Mondmetal.
     4 for Brass.

We also wish to establish the thermal conductivity of the heat exchanger tubes. We can write an external function which takes the number entered in reply to the question and which returns the thermal conductivity by means of a table lookup.

Now that we know what a rule base looks like in source form, I will describe the operation of the run-time system. To understand the internal operation of this program it is necessary to know how the knowledge base is laid out in main memory. The storage, which is taken from the PASCAL heap, consists of two types of records known as box records and arrow records. Figure 8.5 shows the umbrella example as it is physically laid out. These record types are each of a fixed size and, as you will remember, all the text strings in the source are held on disk as a separate file and are only loaded into main memory when they are wanted for display. The box records contain only pointers to the text file.

There is also an array of pointers which points to all the goals in the model. This is used to get initial access to the trees which form the model.

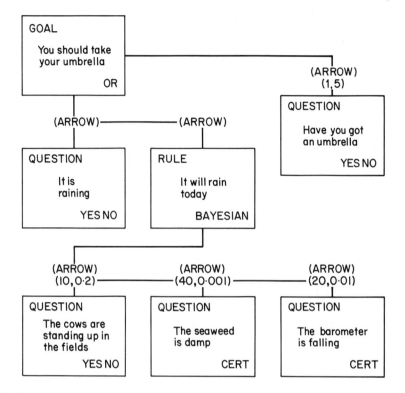

Fig. 8.5

Each box record contains two real numbers; the current probability and the *a priori* probability of the hypothesis which it represents. It also contains two pointers. The first of these points to the beginning of a chain of arrow records which connects it to its contributory factors. The second points to another chain of arrow records which themselves point to the blocking factors for this rule. The record also contains two record numbers which point to associated text on the text file for the model and some Boolean flags which indicate the current status of the box such as 'blocked', 'answered' etc.

Each arrow record contains two pointers. The first of these pointers points to the next arrow record in the chain of which it is a member. The other pointer points to the appropriate contributory factor or blocking factor. The arrow record also contains space for two numbers. These can contain the LS and LN constants or if required the blocking range constants which are associated with the arrow.

The basic method of operation is first to search the tree until it encounters an unanswered question. The question is displayed and the reply is entered into its current probability field. The probabilities of all boxes in the tree are then updated. This will continue until either the user aborts the process or until no more questions can be found.

There are a number of subsidiary functions which the system can perform. These are invoked by the user by entering a control character when a question is displayed rather than directly answering the question. These control characters are all alphabetic except for the 'Help' request which is a question mark. Invoking help will cause a list of all the control codes to be displayed.

I do not intend to examine all these codes in detail, merely to show some of the salient features so as to give an idea of the type of thing which is needed. There are a number of housekeeping operations which can be used such as 'Quit' and 'Backup' (i.e. repeat the previous question). The system normally investigates the goals in the model one by one, in the order in which they occur on the goal list. However each time the system changes goal it informs the user and allows him to override its choice if he so wishes. There is a control code which causes the present goal to be abandoned and returns the system to this goal selection level thus allowing the user to select goals to investigate at will.

There is an explanation facility. This consists of tracing the path from the current question back to the goal from which the search for this question started. The display produced by this trace is couched in an English format of which the following is an example.

The current question is whether or not the seaweed is damp.
The truth of the statement the seaweed is damp strongly confirms and the falsity of this statement strongly denies the assertion that it will rain.
It will rain is one of the factors which must be true for the statement you should take your umbrella to be true.
You should take your umbrella is the current goal.

This type of explanation facility is included in most of the current expert systems and much is made of it in the literature. It is alleged to make the system more user friendly and understandable to the user. Although it can look good in a demonstration we find that users quickly tire of it in daily use and find its explanations shallow. There seem to be two reasons for this. One of these is that a human being giving an explanation would skip over the more obvious steps and only explain them if the hearer showed signs of having difficulty in following. The other reason is that humans do not appear to think in terms of rules most of the time. The explanation wanted is not 'I have a rule which says that if your seaweed is damp then it is likely to rain'; the inquirer wants to know why the computer thinks that damp seaweed should indicate rain. Nevertheless this facility as it stands is essential for debugging your model, and the type of need which it tries to fill for the user is a real one. However we all have some way to go before this need is satisfactorily filled.

There are control codes which enable the user to examine any or all of the goals, rules or questions in the model at any time. This feature displays the current value and status of any box in the model. This is very useful when debugging a model.

There is also a facility which can display in graphic form how near the system is to reaching a decision. At the beginning of a session the only thing which we can say with certainty about a goal hypothesis is that its probability lies between zero and one. As the questions pertinent to this goal are answered the upper and lower bounds on the probability will change. The lower bound will increase and the upper bound will decrease. When all the relevant questions have been answered the upper bound of this goal probability will meet the lower bound and we will be left with a single probability figure for this goal.

The appropriate control code causes the current upper and lower bounds of all the goal probabilities to be displayed. This display is in the form of a bar chart. In most cases the aim of the user is not to establish accurately the probability of all the goal statements in the model. He more likely wishes to find which are the most likely to be true among a series of possible statements, or which is the most likely to succeed of a series of possible courses of action. The user can look at the bar chart from time to time and can see when he has obtained enough precision for his purposes.

We have now had Micro Expert running for over two years and have seen a wide variety of models running under it produced both by ourselves and by other people. We are now able to draw some conclusions about the strengths and weaknesses of the approach, where it can be improved and which types of problems it is suited to.

We have found that Micro Expert is a good system for anyone who is thinking of starting on an expert system. It is simple in concept and easy to understand. It is powerful enough to enable the user to draw up his first models. It is becoming generally agreed that the way to start on expert systems is to try to do something fairly simple. Micro Expert handles these entry level problems quite well.

We are discovering however that many of the worthwhile problems contain large numbers of rules and that it would be useful to have a more powerful and expressive rules language for this more demanding type of application. The arguments here are similar to those between the proponents of BASIC and PASCAL. BASIC is easy to learn and is fine provided you do not wish to write very big programs. If your programs become very big you will find that the extra facilities of PASCAL are worth the extra effort required to learn how to use them.

The facilities that the various users require from the man-machine interface of an expert system are very varied. We are putting a lot of work into providing comprehensive input/output facilities in our next system. These facilities should enable the model builder to format the screen in any way which suits him and to produce reports in any format he wants both on the screen and on a printer.

We are also working on ways to enable the model builder to define the overall strategies of his models. We need to provide the facility for him to write 'When you know which of A, B or C is the most probable, stop this line of investigation and get on with the next thing'.

As stated above, we are not satisfied with the current explanation facilities. There are several methods which can be used to implement better explanations. However as we have said, a source of much of the weakness lies in the fact that the information which is needed in the model to enable it to do its primary job of deduction or diagnosis is not sufficient to enable good explanations to be produced. Producing good explanations puts a load on the user of writing extra information into his model. We can only provide the facilities to enable him to do this and to control its use. It is up to him whether or not he uses these facilities.

It would be useful to have more advanced facilities for integrating an expert system with other programs. In particular the ability to hang an expert system off another program as a procedure and more easily used ways of integrating to databases would be useful.

Expert systems appear to function reasonably well in spite of the rather shaky mathematical foundations upon which they rest. However if they could be put on a sounder mathematical basis it seems probable that they would use the information in their rule bases in a more intelligent and economical way and that the model builder would be able to express more subtle relationships between the hypotheses in his model. This area should be a target for ongoing research.

In conclusion we have found that the building of Micro Expert has taught us a lot. We have ended up with a modest but generally useful system and the application of the system to a variety of problems, both by us and by others, has enabled us to deduce a great deal about the requirements of potential users of expert systems. We hope that this experience will enable us to make our next system even better.

REFERENCE

Duda, R., Hart, P., Barrett, P. *et al.* (1978) *Development of the PROSPECTOR Consultation System for Mineral Exploration: Final Report*, SRI International, Stanford Research Institute, Palo Alto, Ca.

9

REVEAL: An expert systems support environment

P. L. K. JONES

There are several options available to the developer of a knowledge engineering application. A number of special purpose programming languages oriented towards artificial intelligence applications exist. These include LISP, the most generally favoured language in the United States, and the vehicle for most of the major breatkthroughs in AI technology, by virtue principally of its longevity and wide availability in the university environment.

In Europe, the PROLOG language, originally developed at the University of Marseilles, and subsequently at Edinburgh University, has a wider degree of support, as do other AI oriented tools such as POP-2 and POPLOG. PROLOG, a subset of a predicate calculus programming language, has gained notice in recent years following its selection by ICOT as the starting point for a logic programming language for the Fifth Generation Computer project in Japan.

The use of any of these languages will involve the builder in developing the entire infrastructure of the application from scratch, although it should be said that a complete LISP environment such as is available on dedicated LISP machines will supply very generous library support. The same sort of environment may be expected from the PROLOG workstation expected as the first fruits of the Japanese Fifth Generation Computing initiative.

Clearly, though, building from scratch in a raw programming language will prove a costly exercise in terms both of cash and commitment of time. Therefore, tools have been developed at the next higher level of abstraction from the machine. These fall into two categories – higher level 'knowledge representation' languages, such as ROSIE and OPS-5;

and the so-called expert system shells, such as EMYCIN, AL/X, LOOPS, UNITS and SAGE.

The knowledge representation languages are themselves generally implemented in LISP. This fact alone tends to make them less appropriate for live, 'production' applications, since there is a considerable burden of inefficiency to be borne at runtime. There is a school of thought in the United States that sees their role (and indeed that of LISP) as being a prototyping tool for producing drafts of expert systems, which will then be re-implemented in say BASIC or FORTRAN for runtime efficiency.

The expert system shells, on the other hand, operate at the system rather than the programming level. They contain, essentially invisibly to the user, the data structures and control strategy needed to implement an application. As such, they minimize the programming burden involved in creating an application. But the trade-off lies in the relative inflexibility of such a shell. If the target application is not a good paradigm of the problem for which the shell is designed, there may be grave difficulties in fitting the problem to the architecture of the essentially prespecified answer.

A general problem with all the approaches above is that the tools aim exclusively at knowledge engineering. There are many applications which require the use of the tools of knowledge engineering in their solution, but also need access to the more familiar tools of numeric programming, data management, report generation, graphics and so on. Neither the AI languages nor the shells are particularly well suited to such problems.

The REVEAL system is targeted at just such applications. REVEAL is described as addressing the two technologies of decision support and knowledge engineering. It can be regarded as a decision support system generator in isolation from knowledge engineering applications or as an expert system development vehicle in isolation from decision support systems. But its key strength lies in the synergy of these two technologies allowing it to handle applications requiring both.

If we try to build a taxonomy of computer applications, we might finish up with something along the lines of Fig. 9.1. Here, on the left hand side, we see the large group of applications categorized as Bookkeeping. These are the straightforward commercial applications of computing, historically batch oriented, written in a commercial language such as COBOL or PL/1, and only visible to the end-user in terms of the finished output.

The second block on our chart is labeled Decision support, and refers to those systems which have emerged since the introduction of interactive computing in the late sixties. They are characterized by two

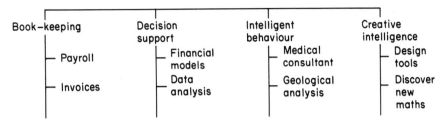

Fig. 9.1   Types of computer applications

things. The accessibility of the computer via terminal interaction means that the end user is in contact with the program itself, rather than its output. And to support the end user, the facilities offered provide primitive data types which ease the programming task. The data types may vary from simple vectors of numbers, as in many financial decision support products, through multi-dimensional data structures, as are available in some of the more recent and powerful systems, right up to the limit of VISICALC paradigms, where the spreadsheet data-structure effectively means that the program *per se* disappears altogether. Also included in this category are the operations research tools of mathematical programming, dynamic programming, simulation, stochastic programming and so on, although clearly these are the proper domain of the management scientist rather than the end user.

The third block on our diagram is labeled Intelligent behaviour, and this encompasses the knowledge based expert systems which have been developed and demonstrated over the last decade. The two examples cited refer to MYCIN (or indeed any of a dozen other medical expert systems now documented) and the PROSPECTOR system developed at SRI for geological analysis.

The final category, here labeled Creative intelligence, essentially refers to the leading edge research in artificial intelligence. The two examples cited refer to the work associated with Professor Douglas Lenat, initially at CMU and more recently at Stanford. Lenat's thesis was concerned with the development of AM, an 'Artificial Mathematician', which given a set of basic pre-numeric mathematical concepts, set out to propose interesting ideas in mathematics, and in so doing 'rediscovered' large parts of number theory. A development of the AM structure, involving self-modifying heuristics, is the EURISKO system, which has been used in a number of areas to carry out exploration of concepts, including the design ('invention') of new three-dimensional VLSI components.

REVEAL is intended to address the two central categories in this taxonomy. Large scale commercial applications are well served by many existing languages and products. And the processing requirements of many of the research-oriented applications in AI mean that they are not likely to be of commercial utility until the next generation of processing power reduces the cost to a level which can be borne out of a production budget.

So the essential design of REVEAL involves adding some of the features associated with specialist AI languages to a decision support system base. These features include the ability to perform logical deduction or inference, and the ability to handle abstract data entities (symbolic programming). The architecture of the system to meet these needs draws upon three strands of research which have been active over the last fifteen or twenty years. The first is the design of effective modeling and decision support systems. The next is the emerging architecture of expert systems. And the third, acting as a bridge between the other two, is fuzzy sets theory.

9.1 REVEAL AS A DECISION SUPPORT TOOL

Professor Ralph Sprague (1980) has suggested that any decision support tool should be analysed on its abilities in three dimensions: those of logic management, data management and dialog management.

To consider REVEAL first along the logic management dimension. REVEAL contains its own programming language. This is designed to be a broad-spectrum tool. At one end of its spectrum of usage, it is suitable for the development of very simple financial or other numerical applications. Fig. 9.2 illustrates its usage to build a financial model of the profit and loss statement for a particular product.

At this level of usage, it is hardly recognizable as a programming language, and is very suitable for direct implementation by the end user of simple descriptive models. However, the language also includes all the data structures and control structures associated with complete high-level languages, and as such is suitable for usage by professional programmers or operations research analysts who need the capability of a powerful algorithmic programming language. Figure 9.3 illustrates the usage of some of the high-level features of the language in embodying De La Loubere's algorithm for the generation of a magic square of odd order.

All models (or programs) so developed in the REVEAL language can be exercised by a range of command driven alternatives. In addition to a simple execute and print, the logic can be repetitively executed under a sensitivity analysis mode. This provides for single or multivariate sensitivity. A very wide range of possible scenarios may thus be set up with a single command. Uniquely, REVEAL allows this potentially huge

```
MODE >inspect

  1 : ! Example P&L model
  2 : ! =================
  3 :
  4 :     price=compound(base.price,price.infl,12)
  5 :     cost =compound(base.cost , cost.infl,12)
  6 :
  7 :     margin=price-cost
  8 :     revenue=volume*price
  9 :     profit=volume*margin
 10 :     net.profit=profit-fixed.exp
 11 :
 12 :     profit%sales=net.profit/revenue * 100
```

<pre>
                        Profit and Loss Projection

                    January February   March   April   May   June
                     -1983   1983   1983   1983   1983   1983

Selling price / unit 10.00   10.12   10.24   10.36   10.48   10.60
Direct cost / unit   7.00   7.10   7.20   7.30   7.40   7.50
                    -------- -------- -------- -------- -------- --------
Unit sales margin   3.00   3.02   3.04   3.06   3.08   3.10
                    -------- -------- -------- -------- -------- --------

Planned sales volume   100   115   110   130   135   140

Gross trading profit $300 $347 $334 $398 $416 $434
 Fixed expenses $150 $150 $150 $160 $165 $170
                    -------- -------- -------- -------- -------- --------
Net operating profit $150 $197 $184 $238 $251 $264
                    ======== ======== ======== ======== ======== ========

Profit as % revenue   15%   17%   16%   18%   18%   18%
</pre>

```
Key assumptions were :

    Selling price inflation of 15% per year
    Direct  cost  inflation of 18% per year
```

Fig. 9.2   A simple profit and loss model

set of possibilities to be scanned at execution time, and thus to limit the output reports to that class of cases meeting some desired criterion. Since the criterion set may itself be generated dynamically by an algorithm, very sophisticated search algorithms may be implemented. Figure 9.4 illustrates a simple case of a sensitivity analysis run on the simple financial model shown in Fig. 9.2.

It also illustrates the goal-seeking or iterative search facility, whereby the required value of an input variable can be computed so as to

```
MODE >execute

..magic square generator
..enter the size of the square >11
..the magic number is    671

    56  69  82  95 108 121   2  15  28  41  54
    55  57  70  83  96 109 111   3  16  29  42
    43  45  58  71  84  97 110 112   4  17  30
    31  44  46  59  72  85  98 100 113   5  18
    19  32  34  47  60  73  86  99 101 114   6
     7  20  33  35  48  61  74  87  89 102 115
   116   8  21  23  36  49  62  75  88  90 103
   104 117   9  22  24  37  50  63  76  78  91
    92 105 118  10  12  25  38  51  64  77  79
    80  93 106 119  11  13  26  39  52  65  67
    68  81  94 107 120   1  14  27  40  53  66


MODE >inspect


 1 :      print('')
 2 :      print(' ..magic square generator')
 3 :      type(' ..enter the size of the square ')
 4 :      imax=tty
 5 :        if imax lt  1 then goto notpos:
 6 :        if imax gt 19 then goto toobig:
 7 :        if int(imax/2)*2 eq imax then goto notodd:
 8 :
 9 :      print(' ..the magic number is ',(1+imax*imax)/2*imax like 'xxxxx')
10 :      print('')
11 :
12 :      repeat i=(1,imax)
13 :        repeat j=(1,imax)
14 :          k=j-i+int(imax-1)/2
15 :          l=2*j-i
16 :          if k ge imax then k=k-imax
17 :                       else do
18 :                              if k lt 0 then k=k+imax
19 :                              enddo
20 :          if l gt imax then l=l-imax
21 :                       else do
22 :                              if l le 0 then l=l+imax
23 :                              enddo
24 :          type(k*imax+l like 'xxxx')
25 :        endrep
26 :        print('')
27 :      endrep
28 :      print('')
29 :
30 :      exit
31 :
32 :      notpos: print('---square side must be positive');exit
33 :      toobig: print('---maximum square side is 19');exit
34 :      notodd: print('---square must have an odd number of rows');exit
```

Fig. 9.3   A REVEAL program

generate some desired value for an output variable. A mix of sensitivity and goal-seeking analysis can be carried on simultaneously, using the stability analysis mode of execution. Here, a variable is taken through a range of values, and at each stage the value of a second variable is computed, so as to stabilize some third variable on a target value.

Any worthwhile modeling application will inevitably accrue data. REVEAL contains its own integral data management facility. All

REVEAL file objects are held in a single host system file, referred to as the REVEAL database. This database is constructed along the relational model of data. Thus multiple datasets, associated with the same or different programs, can be managed at the command level, without the user or builder becoming involved in problems of file or records layout. JOINs and PROJECTions of relations can be created, and logical components of different relations can be compared or moved.

```
MODE >sensitivity
VARY : >price.infl 12% 20% 2%
VARY : >cost.infl  14% 18% 1%
VARY : >
 ..    25 CASES; PROCEED? >no
 ..EDIT? >yes
 ..ENTER CONDITIONS FOR NO REPORT

>if term(net.profit,6) lt 300 then exit

   RESTORE ? >no
```

PRICE.INFL	CURRENT VALUE	.20
COST.INFL	CURRENT VALUE	.14

	January 1983	February 1983	March 1983	April 1983	May 1983	June 1983
NET.PROFIT	150.00	203.77	196.94	260.32	282.40	305.51

PRICE.INFL	CURRENT VALUE	.20
COST.INFL	CURRENT VALUE	.15

	January 1983	February 1983	March 1983	April 1983	May 1983	June 1983
NET.PROFIT	150.00	203.18	195.79	258.27	279.52	301.73

```
MODE >seek price.infl
 ..TARGET : >net.profit jun 350
   RESTORE ? >no
```

VARIABLE	TARGET
.20	290.52
.28	332.30
.31	349.04
.32	349.74
.32	349.99
.32	350.00

Fig. 9.4 Sensitivity analysis: Two variables, edited

In addition to its internal database facilities, REVEAL also provides a full external file I/O capability. Thus external data may be acquired from foreign applications or database, and REVEAL-generated data can be passed to other applications on the same or other machines.

Dialog management encompasses the whole of the man-machine interface. Concerning REVEAL, the first point to make is that the system is entirely self-contained, with its own editor, compiler, file and data management and report generation. This insulates the user from the host operating system, and ensures that applications of REVEAL on different machines will behave in exactly the same way.

The command set is designed as an extensible set of atomic commands. This confers two advantages. Firstly, the novice user can begin useful work in REVEAL with only eight or ten of the hundred plus commands at his disposal, and then acquire further facilities later as his needs grow. Secondly, the atomic nature of the command set supports what is known as the REVEAL command executive. Commands may be grouped together in a command file, which can then be invoked by name. This is obviously useful for automating sets of frequently used facilities. However, further features of the design allow these command files to carry arguments, which may be parsed at runtime. This permits the system builder to configure a complete command vocabulary to the needs of the end user, who is then insulated not only from the host operating system, but from REVEAL itself. For example, complete applications have been developed in REVEAL with the command set translated into a foreign language, without the need to modify the REVEAL system itself.

Nested and recursive command executives can be developed. Whilst recursion is rarely needed in the context of a straightforward decision support system, the facility is essential when we come to the construction of inference engines in a knowledge engineering application. And so, in the limit, the command executive facility of REVEAL offers a powerful programming language in its own right. All REVEAL language features are available at the command, as well as at the programming level of the system.

9.2 FUZZY SETS IN REVEAL

In addition to all the conventional primitive data types of real, scalar and vector, integer, Boolean, character and string, REVEAL recognizes the data type of *Fuzzy Set*. The purpose of this data type is two-fold. On the one hand, it extends the power of the modeling language, and on the other it underlies the formalism used in REVEAL for representing knowledge. But first, what is a fuzzy set?

Classically, a set is defined by its members. So we have the set of all clocks, or the set of all people over six feet in height. Membership of a set is predicated on a two-valued logic – TRUE and FALSE. Thus something is either a clock, or not. And a person is over six feet in height, or not.

But there are many other possible forms of logic – three-valued logic, multi-valued logic, infinite valued logic and so on. One of the class of infinite valued logics is termed *fuzzy logic*, and it admits of the possibility of the truth of a proposition taking on any value in the interval between TRUE and FALSE, which are generally (and arbitrarily) set to be one and zero. Now the sets corresponding to this logic, when defined in terms of their members, are not as crisp as classical sets. Objects may be partly included in a set. Hence these objects are termed fuzzy sets.

Although there were references to concepts analogous to what we now know of as fuzzy sets in the work of Poincaré a hundred years ago, the founding father of the modern approach to fuzzy sets is Professor Lotfi Zadeh, of the University of California, Berkeley. In a seminal paper on the topic published in 1965, he introduced the concept of fuzziness. His motivation at that time was in the area of control systems engineering, and his concern was that the entirely mathematical treatment of the topic was precluding the experience and expertise of practising engineers. This concern was embodied in Zadeh's Principle of Incompatibility:

> As the complexity of a system increases, our ability to make precise and yet significant statements about its behavior diminishes until a threshold is reached beyond which precision and significance (or relevance) become almost mutually exclusive characteristics.

Zadeh essentially was suggesting that human beings can relate to and converse about many important topics, without ever attempting to reduce them to mathematical precision. In fact, fundamental to Zadeh's thesis is the idea that large parts of cognition involve applying labels to more or less fuzzy concepts, and then reasoning with these fuzzy objects. Thus there is a natural relationship between fuzzy sets, as described mathematically, and linguistic variables, as routinely used in human cognition and conversation.

So, whereas classically we can manipulate the concept of a set of people over six feet in height, using linguistic variables we can manipulate the concept of the set of people who are tall. This set does not have a crisp boundary, but we all know perfectly well what the word 'tall' means, and we can converse and discuss such sets, recognizing implicitly that there is a subjective element to the definition of tall in any context.

In Fig. 9.5 we see an example of a fuzzy set, as created in REVEAL. This set represents the concept 'tall' as currently recognized by the person defining it. Thus the mechanics of creating and displaying the primitive data item 'tall' represented as a fuzzy set are extremely simple.

In the example, the fuzzy set has been defined over a *domain* which has its low and high boundaries at four and seven feet. This domain is the extent over which we might expect to be discussing the height of

```
MODE )define tall
 .. LOW BOUNDARY : )4
 ..HIGH BOUNDARY : )7
 .. SET FUNCTION : )grow(5.2, 5.8, 6.4)
 ..QUALIFIER CREATED

MODE )draw tall
```

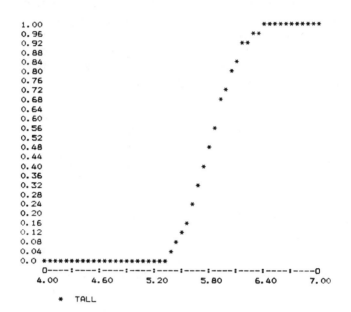

Fig. 9.5   Creating a fuzzy set

adult human beings. All fuzzy sets are supported by such a domain. The characteristic function of the fuzzy set 'tall' has in this case been generated by the intrinsic function GROW, which takes three parameters: the value in the domain for which there is no degree of membership in the set, the value at which there is fifty per cent membership in the set and the value in the domain where there is full membership.

There are a variety of equally simple functions available for the definition of fuzzy sets. If a function is not available within the standard language, then the user may write the required function in REVEAL, and then use it to generate the needed fuzzy sets. And if indeed the fuzzy set may not be representable as a function, then its characteristic (or grade of membership) may be entered numerically.

The question may fairly be asked, 'Who is to define these fuzzy sets, and what reliance is to be placed upon them?' Fuzzy sets are data items. Any computerized simulation depends on the provision of data. (And expert systems are simulations *a fortiori*, although this point is inclined to escape some of the authors widely quoted in the literature.) Thus fuzzy sets represent in an instantiated way the subjective component of the information provided by the builders of a system. They comprise an articulation of perception which creates a communication space for further discussion amongst cooperating builders and users of a system. One of the recognized problems in constructing any knowledge based system is the management of expertise drawn from different sources. A loosely coupled vocabulary of qualifiers (*fuzzy sets*) installed upon a problem context in the REVEAL architecture allows easy and productive comparison of the impact of different subjective judgements on the problem resolution.

Fuzzy sets take the role of adjectives, or qualifiers, in natural language. The role of adverbs, or qualifiers of qualifiers, such as 'very', 'fairly', 'below', 'about' and so on is recognized both in fuzzy sets theory and in REVEAL. Functional operators on fuzzy sets which represent these second level qualifiers ('hedges' as they are known in literature) are available both with default values and as defined by the user. Thus qualifiers may be created from words already existing in a vocabulary. For example, if the qualifier 'low' exists, then it is possible to define 'moderate' as meaning 'quite low but not very low' in exactly those words.

There is a complete calculus of fuzzy logic for operating on fuzzy sets. The set theoretic operations of negation, union, intersection and implication can all be defined in a consistent fashion, and in such a way that all the classical set theoretic identities such as De Morgan's Laws carry over into the fuzzy calculus, with the exception of the law of the excluded middle. In the special case of applying this calculus to sets with a zero degree of fuzziness, we find that it reduces to classical set theory.

In REVEAL, a special named file object called a vocabulary acts as the repository for fuzzy sets. Any vocabulary may be associated with the current problem context, and its elements used in conjunction with the standard programming and control facilities. As a simple example, consider Fig. 9.6. Here we have a relation containing data for a group of companies. Such attributes as industry classification, sales, profits and number of employees are stored, and in REVEAL we can extract a virtual relation under some predicate such as 'sales gt 800', as with many other systems. This returns a set of instances from this small database. But in REVEAL we can also create a relation under a fuzzy predicate, as shown. This retrieves a fuzzy set from the database, where associated with each instance retrieved we find the degree of truth under the fuzzy predicate. This means that we can phrase the query in a fashion much closer to the original need for the enquiry (for surely the user does not really have a crisp boundary at 800 in mind), and in addition be provided with more meaningful information from the database.

```
MODE > relation

                A     B     C     D     E     F     G     H     I

CLASSIFICATN    6     6     12    6     12    6     12    12    6
SALES           200 1,100 1,000  800   500 1,200 1,300  100   400
THOUS. EMPS     3     10    11    9     8     14    12    2     6
PROFITS         40    110   160   120   55    115   200   20    10

MODE > relation : sales gt 800

                B     C     F     G

CLASSIFICATN    6     12    6     12
SALES         1,100 1,000 1,200 1,300
THOUS. EMPS     10    11    14    12
PROFITS         110   160   115   200

MODE > relation :: sales are high or profits/sales are acceptable

                A     B     C     D     E     F     G    ' H

CLASSIFICATN    6     6     12    6     12    6     12    12
SALES           200 1,100 1,000  800   500 1,200 1,300  100
THOUS. EMPS     3     10    11    9     8     14    12    2
PROFITS         40    110   160   120   55    115   200   20
TRUTH           13    49    27    4     1     72    87    13

MODE > relation :: sales are high and profits/sales are acceptable

                C     D     G

CLASSIFICATN    12    6     12
SALES         1,000  800 1,300
THOUS. EMPS     11    9     12
PROFITS         160   120   200
TRUTH           5     3     4
```

Fig. 9.6 Fuzzy relations

Insofar as a fuzzy set is the mapping of some cognitive object into machine processable information, we are dealing with knowledge. Fuzzy sets theory provides us with a method of capturing and manipulating the essentially subjective, vague and ambiguous nature of human cognition and reasoning. And this leads us naturally into the usage of REVEAL for knowledge engineering.

9.3 REVEAL AND KNOWLEDGE ENGINEERING

An expert system is conceived of as possessing at least two architectural components: the knowledge base, and the inference engine. In many systems created in an AI language such as LISP, this distinction is largely conceptual. The actual application consists of source code, and to the untutored eye there is no obvious distinction between knowledge and control. In REVEAL, the distinction is architecturally enforced.

Many formalisms have been employed to represent knowledge. These include procedural representations, predicate logic, Bayesian and semantic networks, and in particular production rule representations.

```
MODE ) input.data

                SMITH      BROWN     DAVIES     ARNOLD   JOHNSON RICHARDS

PHYSICS          .90        .60        .53        .84       .80      .81
CHEMISTRY        .70        .70        .64        .58       .79      .79
MATHS            .95        .65        .81        .64       .80      .96
BIOLOGY          .60        .40        .76        .88       .72      .69
ENGLISH          .10        .60        .63        .25       .39      .42
FRENCH           .05        .10        .29        .71       .60      .28
ECONOMICS        .75        .20        .82        .74       .78      .85
HISTORY          .45        .80        .79        .83       .72      .16
GEOGRAPHY        .30        .70        .75        .68       .59      .42
ART              .60        .05        .20        .75       .40      .80

MODE ) execute
-----------------------------

  ..Candidate's name :       SMITH

  ..Suggested career : RESEARCH

-----------------------------

  ..Candidate's name :       BROWN

  ..Suggested career : TEACHING
  ..Alternate career : ADMINISTRATION

-----------------------------

  ..Candidate's name :       DAVIES

  ..Suggested career : TEACHING
  ..Alternate career : ACCOUNTANCY

-----------------------------

  ..Candidate's name :       ARNOLD

  ..Suggested career : MEDICINE
  ..Alternate career : ADMINISTRATION

-----------------------------

  ..Candidate's name :       JOHNSON

  ..Suggested career : RESEARCH
  ..Alternate career : ACCOUNTANCY

-----------------------------

  ..Candidate's name :       RICHARDS

  ..Suggested career : ACCOUNTANCY
  ..Alternate career : RESEARCH
```

Fig. 9.7   Expert systems

The formalism of fuzzy production rules is the default mechanism employed in REVEAL. There is the concept of a 'policy'. A policy is a collection of zero or more production rules, existing as a named file object in the database. Policies may then be applied to the current problem context under user or program control. It is the structure of this program control which forms the inference engine. Thus there is an absolute distinction between knowledge and control. Moreover, the application of these sets of rules occurs from within the standard REVEAL programming language. In this way, rules may be applied where appropriate, in conjunction with any other numeric or non-numeric algorithmic programming which may be appropriate to the problem.

Consider the example shown in Fig. 9.7. Here we have a table of data, and these data represent the results of some group of candidates in a set of examination topics. The objective is to build a small application which will mimic a career advisor who will, on the basis of these results, make observations as to the suitability of the candidates for various possible career opportunities.

	SMITH	BROWN	DAVIES	ARNOLD.	JOHNSON	RICHARDS
RESEARCH	81				61	63
WRITING						
ADMINISTRATION				65		
TEACHING		85	65	55		
POLITICS						
MEDICINE				65		
LAW						
ACCOUNTANCY			63		57	71
ARCHITECTURE						61

```
  1 :  !Career selection policy
  2 :  !=======================
  3 :
  4 :      If maths is excellent and physics is excellent
            then research is indicated
  5 :
  6 :      If maths is less than average or physics is less than average
            then research is discouraged
  7 :
  8 :
  9 :      If art is more than good and maths is more than average
            then architecture is indicated
 10 :
 11 :      If maths is more than average and economics is more than good
            then accountancy is indicated
 12 :
 13 :      If biology is more than good and the worst.science is more than
            average then medicine is indicated
 14 :
 15 :      If avge.art is less than good and avge.science is less than good
            then teaching is indicated
 16 :
 17 :
 18 :      If english is more than good and maths is more than average
            and worst.science is more than poor then law is indicated
 19 :
 20 :      If english is excellent and worst.art is more than poor
             then writing is indicated
 21 :
 22 :
 23 :      If english is good and economics is good but maths is less
             than average then politics is indicated
 24 :
 25 :
 26 :      If (worst.art is good or worst.science is good)
            and maths is average then administration is indicated
```

Fig. 9.8   Representation of knowledge

Figure 9.7 also shows the execution of such a program. Figure 9.8 indicates the table of data showing the strengths of the various recommendations made, and shows the set of fuzzy rules embodying the 'knowledge' of this career advisor. In Fig. 9.9 we have an illustration of the set of fuzzy sets representing the concepts, 'good', 'poor', 'excellent', etc. used in the rules.

There are a couple of points to be made. Firstly, the rule set is accessible directly through the REVEAL editor, and thus may be modified and extended directly by the end user – in this case the

MODE)draw disgraceful, poor, good, excellent, average

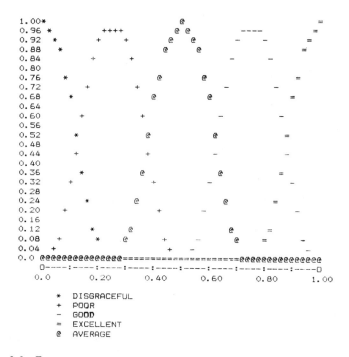

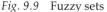

Fig. 9.9 Fuzzy sets

hypothetical career counselor. The language used to represent the rules is of course a formal language, every bit as much as FORTRAN or BASIC. But it is at least superficially close to natural language format, and is designed to be natural in its usage. The system editor checks all new and modified rules automatically to ensure that they meet the constraints, such as they are, of the production language, so that unprocessable rules are not permitted into the system.

```
 1 : !Career counsellor example program
 2 : !===================================
 3 :
 4 : ! The program falls into three parts; for each candidate :
 5 :
 6 : !    1. Compute best, worst and average science and art
 7 : !    2. Apply the selection policy
 8 : !    3. Format a simple  report
 9 :
10 : !Compute averages, etc
11 :
12 : best.science =max(max(max(maths,physics),chemistry),biology)
13 : worst.science=min(min(min(maths,physics),chemistry),biology)
14 : avge.science =avg(physics,biology)
15 :
16 : best.art=max(max(max(english,french),economics),history)
17 : best.art=max(max(best.art,geography),art)
18 :
19 : worst.art=min(min(min(english,french),economics),history)
20 : worst.art=min(min(worst.art,geography),art)
21 :
22 : avge.art=avg(english,art)
23 :
24 : ' Now apply the policy to the raw and computed data
25 :
26 :     apply('SELECT')
27 :
28 : ! Print the summary report of two best options
29 :
30 :     print(30*'-')
31 :     print('')
32 :
33 :     print(' ..Candidate''s name : ',tname(time))
34 :     print('')
35 :
36 :     best=0;secondbest=0;bestptr=0;sbestptr=0
37 :
38 : repeat index=(51,59)
39 :    if series(index,time) ge best then
          do
40 :             secondbest=best
41 :             best=series(index,time)
42 :             sbestptr=bestptr
43 :             bestptr=index
44 :     enddo
45 :                                 else
          do
46 :             if series(index,time) gt secondbest then
                  do
47 :                    secondbest=series(index,time)
48 :                    sbestptr=index
49 :                 enddo
50 :     enddo
51 : endrep
52 :
53 :                      print(' ..Suggested career : ',sname( bestptr)
54 :    if sbestptr gt 0 then print(' ..Alternate career : ',sname(sbestptr)
55 :                      print('')
56 :                      print('')
```

Fig. 9.10 Control program

The application of the rule set occurs from within a REVEAL program, and in this case the control program is shown in Fig. 9.10. In a sense, this example is designed as a paradigm. The three components into which the code falls demonstrate that both before and after applying 'knowledge' to a problem, we may need to be involved in numeric processing of input data (validation, conversion) or in managing data to and from files, to reports and so on.

There are several other formats of rules available in the declarative language of REVEAL. Unconditional assertions may be made. The value of some context variable may be the target of several, perhaps conflicting, rules, and in these cases, the runtime system evaluates the most appropriate output by treating the assertions as fuzzy goals or constraints in a fuzzy optimizing environment. Non-fuzzy rules of course frequently occur, and these too can be handled. Such a rule as 'If function is "marketing" or years.of.service are long, then salary is high' contain both fuzzy and crisp elements.

In the example above, all the rules are just executed once. This, if you like, is the inference engine – so simple as not to justify the name. Typically, knowledge will possess structure, and some more formal method of accessing rules in a context sensitive sequence will be required. The builder (knowledge engineer) is quite free to design and implement any inference strategy desired in the REVEAL language, thus having total flexibility at his disposal in exchange for the work of preparing the code.

Alternatively, there is a suite of functions available in the language for processing a rule set according to many of the standard design approaches to inference engines. A policy of rules can be executed, for example, as a tree structure, coercing the runtime system into either searching for evidence to support some *a priori* hypothesis, or testing all possible hypotheses for some consequent variable on an exhaustive basis, and returning the plausible results along with their degree of confirmation.

9.4 REVEAL IN SUMMARY

REVEAL is a large scale, commercially oriented software product designed to make the techniques of knowledge engineering accessible in an environment which is equally supportive of decision support applications. As such, it is intended to support a very wide range of possible applications and users, from the novice to the skilled system developer. One of the significant design approaches implied in its structure is that there are many applications where the addition of quite small amounts of 'knowledge' to an existing model program using more familiar simulation tools may considerably extend the power of the simulation. It is not necessary to think solely in terms of expert systems being purely knowledge driven, and relying on a knowledge base of hundreds or thousands of rules, although clearly such applications are important, and within the ambit of the system.

Instead, applications containing quite small knowledge bases of some tens of rules can extend the scope of standard modeling or simulation approaches. And this small size brings the construction of such systems out of the realm of the professional and highly skilled knowledge engineer, and back to a more tractable level of complexity.

REVEAL is available on a wide variety of hardware ranges, including IBM, ICL, VAX and IBM PC/XT. Micro to mainframe communication is supported, so distributed applications are quite feasible, particularly since the system is identical in each of its various hardware implementations.

Research into artificial intelligence has been in progress since valve-burning computers were known as electronic brains. For many years, the fruits of this research have been enjoyed only by those involved in the academic environments where such research has flourished. Even today, there is a visible gulf between knowledge engineering and the main stream of operations research and management science activities. One of the primary objectives of the REVEAL system is to bridge that gulf, and to allow the discipline of knowledge engineering to take its place amongst the routine toolkit of those who seek to model reality on the computer.

REFERENCES

Sprague, R.H. (1980) Framework for the development of decision support systems. *M.I.S. Quarterly*, **4:4**.
Zadeh, L.H. (1965) Fuzzy sets. *Information and Control*, **8**, 338–353.

LEARNING

10

Machine learning strategies

RICHARD FORSYTH

With the dramatic rise of expert systems has come a renewed interest in the 'fuel' that drives them: knowledge. For it is specialist knowledge which gives expert systems their power. But extracting knowledge from human experts in symbolic form has proved arduous and labour-intensive (see Wellbank, 1983). So the idea of machine learning is enjoying a renaissance.

10.1 WHAT IS MACHINE LEARNING?

By machine learning, I refer to any automatic improvement in the performance of a computer system over time, as a result of experience. Thus a learning algorithm seeks to do one or more of the following:

(1) Cover a wider range of problems.
(2) Deliver more accurate solutions.
(3) Obtain answers more cheaply.
(4) Simplify codified knowledge.

The last point assumes that simplification of stored knowledge is of value for its own sake, i.e. that clearer expression makes knowledge more accessible to people even it it does not improve the computer's performance.

Machine learning could apply to almost any domain, but in practice most successful systems confine themselves to classification tasks, on which we concentrate here. Even this subset of problems includes a wide variety of important applications, e.g.

(1) Given the weather readings for the last 7 days, predict whether a storm will arise in the North Sea during the next 48 hours.

(2) Given a poker hand and a record of the bidding so far, decide whether to call, fold or raise.
(3) Given a fossilized fragment of Australopithecine jaw, work out whether its owner was male or female.
(4) Given the results from a seismic survey, advise an oil company whether to drill or move on.

10.2 A PARADIGM FOR LEARNING

Any system designed to modify and improve its own performance must include the following major components:

(1) A set of information structures which encode the system's present level of expertise (the 'rules').
(2) A task algorithm (the 'performer') which uses the rules to guide its activity.
(3) A feedback module (the 'critic') which compares actual results with those desired.
(4) A learning mechanism (the 'learner') which uses feedback from the critic to amend the rules.

This is sketched diagrammatically in Fig. 10.1.

Most expert systems have a read-only knowledge base. What we are talking about here is an erasable-programmable knowledge base.

To focus our ideas on a concrete and familiar example, we will draw on a simple concept formation task for illustration through the rest of

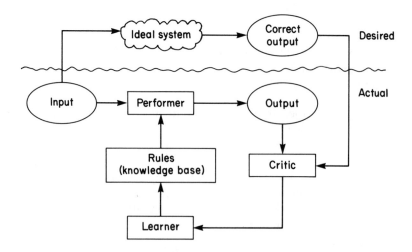

Fig. 10.1

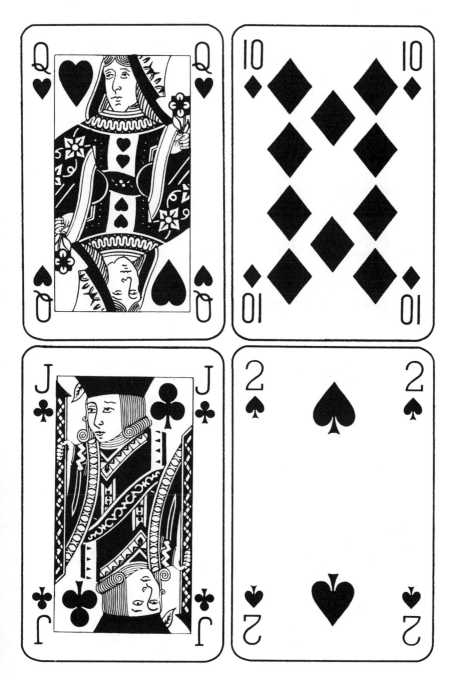

Fig. 10.2

this chapter. We will assume the computer is presented with example hands containing four playing cards, e.g. Queen of Hearts (QH), Ten of Diamonds (TD), Jack of Clubs (JC) and Two of Spades (2S), together with a categorization (T for True in this case) supplied by the teacher. (See Fig. 10.2.) Its task is to discover the rule(s) for distinguishing True from False instances.

10.3 THE DESCRIPTION LANGUAGE

The key to success or failure in such a task is the description language.

The discrimination rules have to be expressed in some form of notation or data structure, and this must be adequate to describe the information in the input that determines the correct response. This is an obvious point, but it is all too easy to struggle in vain to force a computer to learn a concept it has no means of representing. The computer is thoroughly pragmatic: as far as it is concerned, a difference that makes no difference is no difference at all.

Let us return to our playing cards. Suppose the computer is given the following sequence of cases.

AH,	JD,	JC,	2S	:	T
2D,	JH,	AH,	QS	:	F
8C,	TS,	6H,	AC	:	F
3H,	9D,	8D,	7D	:	F
5H,	3C,	TH,	9H	:	T
AD,	3D,	AH,	7H	:	F
JD,	TD,	7S,	2D	:	F

Now what is the rule governing T or F? (Go on: try it yourself, before looking at the answer!)

If the rules are framed rather like search-strings in some text-editors, such as ?D, 3?, 3?, ?? where a question mark (?) is a 'wild' card standing for any rank or suit, then the above rule would represent the concept 'any diamond, a three of something, another three and any other card'. In a real text-editor the sequence would be significant so we would presumably have to add 'in that order'.

However we could relax the ordering constraint so that the pattern shown would match 3C, 3H, JD, AS as well as JD, 3C, 3H, AS which extends the language somewhat.

But it does not extend it far enough to cope with the rule I had in mind, namely

IF   there are no red cards THEN F
ELSE IF there are no black cards THEN F

ELSE IF the lowest red card is higher in rank than the lowest
black one THEN T
ELSE   F;

which you saw at a glance, no doubt.

If you think that rather unfair on a mere machine, try extending the
rule for, say, two hearts, which is easy enough:

?H, ?H, ??, ??

to capture the concept of a pair, i.e. any two cards with equal rank. In
this language even such a simple concept as 'two of a kind' cannot be
expressed by a single pattern. It would require several, as in

2?,   2?,   ??,   ??
3?,   3?,   ??,   ??
4?,   4?,   ??,   ??
etc.

which is clumsy.

So before starting to build a learning system, it is vital to ensure that
the proposed rule description language is capable of expressing the kind
of concepts which will be needed, and that is harder than it sounds.

10.4 FEATURE VECTORS

One neat trick is to use the same representation for the input as for the
rules.

It is handy if you can get away with it, since it saves translation from
data format to rule format. A particularly simple format received
considerable attention in the early days of statistical pattern recognition.

If your data is a one-dimensional array of numbers, each of which
measures an aspect of the input, a[i], i=1 . . N,

e.g. $1, 7, 2, 0, -8, -19, 77, 4 \ldots$

then this vector can be multiplied by an array of weights, w[i], i=1 . . N,

e.g. $0, -1, -2, 0, 0, 1, 1, 0 \ldots$

and the resultant sum of products compared to a threshold (typically
zero). If the sum exceeds the threshold the machine classes the input as
a positive example, otherwise it classes the input as a negative example.
This is the basis of the PERCEPTRON, whose learning algorithm works
by re-adjusting the weightings after an erroneous response, as follows:

IF the sum of products was greater than threshold and the answer should have been No,

THEN subtract the a[i] values from the corresponding w[i] values;

IF the sum was less than threshold and the answer should have been Yes,

THEN add the a[i]s to the w[i]s;

IF the answer was right, leave well alone.

The weights can start, within reason, from any random set of values, and will converge towards a near-optimal set.

In effect, the weighting vector w[i] expresses the system's knowledge: it indicates the importance of each input feature in the discrimination task. The algorithm is simple, elegant and efficient, as long as the two classes are 'linearly separable' and the training set is not very noisy. It can also be extended to handle more than two categories.

Unfortunately many real-life classification problems are not linearly separable. In practice is is almost impossible to find a set of features which are truly independent. The feature vector approach breaks down even on apparently trivial problems like 'there is a heart to the left of a black card'.

10.5 MORE POWERFUL LANGUAGES

Structural learning – where the relationships between elements are important as well as the attributes of those elements – precludes the use of feature vectors in their basic form.

Most structural learning systems employ some form of predicate calculus representation, often extended in certain respects (e.g. Michalski, 1981). A language for our card-hand domain would need functions like

  left-of (a,b) right-of (a,b)
  rank (a)   suit (b)

as well as logical and comparison operators

  AND, OR, NOT
  $<, =, >, <>, <=, >=$

but even they might not suffice. For instance we could say

  rank (C1) = rank (C2) OR
  rank (C1) = rank (C3) OR
  rank (C1) = rank (C4) OR
  rank (C2) = rank (C3) OR

rank (C2) = rank (C4) OR
rank (C3) = rank (C4)

to express the notion of a pair; but how could we encode 'there is a diamond of lower value than any heart or spade?'

The choice of a compact, expressive notation is far from easy. And remember: playing cards are a 'toy' problem area.

10.6 LEARNING BY SEARCHING

Assuming that we can solve the non-trivial problem of devising a good description language, how do we automate the generation of accurate descriptions in it?

One way of looking at the problem is as a search through the space of all possible descriptions for those few which are both true and useful in the current context. The number of possible descriptions is astronomical, and the more expressive the language, the more explosive is this combinatorial problem.

Clearly some way has to be found of guiding the search and thereby ignoring the vast majority of potential descriptions (concepts) which are irrelevant to the purpose in hand.

A number of methods have proved successful with noise-free training instances (e.g. Langley, 1977; Mitchell, 1979). We shall restrict ourselves here to discussing four specific example systems that can deal with noisy data.

All of them learn classification rules by examining a series of correctly classified training instances – the training set. The aim is that these rules can later be applied to fresh data of the same kind that was absent from the training set. Correct classification is at the heart of many AI systems, such as intelligent controllers, diagnostic systems, advice givers, robot sensors and the like.

10.7 ID3

Quinlan's Interactive Dichotomizer 3 (Quinlan, 1979) is not very robust in the face of noisy data, though it could in principle be improved in this respect if it did not always seek a 'perfect' rule. The program works as follows.

(1) Select at random a subset of size W from the training instances (the 'window').
(2) Apply the CLS algorithm to form a rule for the current window.
(3) Scan the entire database, not just the window, to find exceptions to the latest rule.

(4) If there are exceptions, insert some of them into the window and repeat from step 2; otherwise halt and display the rule.

The CLS algorithm (Hunt *et al.*, 1966) repeatedly partitions the training instances according to the variable with the greatest discriminatory power. Quinlan used an information-theoretic measure of entropy for this purpose. Each subset as defined by the most discriminatory variable is partitioned again (unless it contains only one class of data) on the next most discriminatory, and so on. Partitioning stops when a subset contains only one kind of data. This process produces a decision tree.

ID3 trees performed well on a series of King-Rook/King-Knight chess endgame problems. ID3 can cope with a little noise, but not much, so chess is a suitable domain for it. Really noisy data leads it to grow very bushy decision trees which fit the training set but do not generalize well to new examples. Another limitation of ID3 is that it uses feature vectors to describe the data (though not the rules).

A more serious weakness is the poverty of the description language. Rules are decision trees of a particular kind in which each node is a test and typically has two branches, one for True and one for False. The tests can only be a simple comparison of one variable with one constant, e.g. rainfall > 10, otherwise the search would become unmanageable. But this excludes compound tests of any kind, using logical or arithmetic operators. It even precludes comparing one variable with another, as in rainfall > mintemp, which is a grave limitation. These restrictions place the onus firmly on the user to devise a very effective set of descriptors, incorporating within them whatever preliminary calculations need to be performed.

ID3 forms the basis for a product commercially available as 'Expert-Ease' in the UK.

10.8 INDUCE

Dietterich and Michalski (1981) have produced a structural learning program called INDUCE which uses a method known as the Beam Search.

(1) Set H to contain a randomly chosen subset of size W of the training instances.
(2) Generalize each example/concept in H as little as possible (i.e. make minimal generalizations).
(3) Prune implausible hypotheses according to a measure of size and performance – i.e. keep those which are simple and cover many examples, drop those which are complex and cover few examples – retaining the best W rules only.

(4) If any description in H covers all (or enough of) the examples, print it out.

(Steps 2 to 4 are repeated until H is empty or enough concepts have been printed.)

This method has reasonable noise immunity, and can be used for a variety of tasks. It is the successor to a highly successful program used to learn diagnoses of soybean diseases, and represents a continuation of leading-edge machine learning research by Michalski and his associates.

The effectiveness of INDUCE depends crucially on the adequacy of the description language ('annotated predicate calculus') and on the performance criterion which decides which rules deserve to be kept. This latter function cannot, in general, be specified in advance. It must be tuned by the user since different situations call for different trade-offs between the complexity and power of rules.

Another significant factor is the method of generalization. This is no simple matter. A rule (or example) such as

$$suit (C1) = diamond \text{ AND } rank (C1) = 8 \text{ AND}$$
$$suit (C2) = club \text{ AND } rank (C2) = Queen$$

may be generalized in several ways.

(1) AND becomes OR, e.g.
   suit (C1) = diamond AND rank (C1) = 8 OR
   suit (C2) = club AND rank (C2) = Queen.
(2) Drop conditions, e.g.
   suit (C1) = diamond AND rank (C1) = 8 AND
   suit (C2) = club.
(3) Extend range, e.g.
   suit (C1) = diamond AND rank (C1) > 7 AND
   suit (C2) = club AND rank (C2) = Queen.
(4) Weaken or relax condition, e.g.
   colour (C1) = red AND rank (C1) = 8 AND
   colour (C2) = black AND rank (C2) = Queen.

Each method of generalization can be applied in several ways. For example, AND could be replaced by OR in a total of 7 ways (any one, any two or all three ANDs). Michalski reduces the number of options by only making a single alteration at any one time. Even so the number of single-change possibilities to be considered at each step in a realistic task is very large, and if too many possibilities are pruned an optimal rule may never be found.

In practice other constraints (such as only allowing rules of a certain syntactic form) have to be introduced to keep the problem manageable.

10.9 HOLLAND'S GENETIC ALGORITHMS

John Holland's theoretical treatment of adaptation (1975) was largely ignored by the AI community at first, but recently some workers (e.g. Smith, 1980) have used his ideas as the basis for very effective learning systems. The basic algorithm has a biological flavour. It is deliberately modeled on what Darwin and Mendel, among others, have taught us about the process of evolution – a well-tried technique, surely, after 3600 million years of field testing!

(1) Randomly generate an initial population of M rule-structures.
(2) Compute and save the performance score of each rule (e). If the overall average is good enough, stop and display the rules.
(3) For each rule calculate its selection probability $p = e/E$ where e is its individual score and E is the total score of all M rules.
(4) Generate the next population of rules by selecting via the selection probability distribution and applying genetic operators.
(5) Repeat from Step (2).

Thus the expected number of 'offspring' of any rule in the next generation is proportional to its measured success in the task being learnt – survival of the fittest.

The genetic operators employed in Step (4) are crossover, mutation and inversion. Crossover is a kind of mating in which, for instance, rules (A,B,C,D) and (a,b,c,d) might produce descendants (A,B,C,d) and (a,b,c,D) in the following generation. Holland argued that this algorithm, and its derivatives, search the rule-space in a very economical manner, and Smith's results confirm his predictions in practice. The main problem is that the crossover operator requires rules to be equal-length strings containing position-independent components. This makes it difficult to devise a workable description language, and extremely difficult to devise one that is also intelligible to people.

The inversion operator is rather like an internal crossover with reordering. Mutation, which is merely included to ensure all descriptions are potentially producible, consists of making a random transcription error. (These methods are described in more detail in Chapter 11 of this volume.)

We turn next to a learning method which also owes its inspiration to Darwin, but which uses a slightly less restrictive description language, based on Boolean algebra.

10.10 BEAGLE

BEAGLE (Biological Evolutionary Algorithm Generating Logical Expressions) is a computer package for producing decision rules by induction from a database (Forsyth, 1981). As such it attacks the problem, frequently side-stepped, of where the rules in a rule-based system come from.

BEAGLE works on the principle of 'naturalistic selection' whereby rules that fit the data badly are killed off and replaced by mutations of better rules or by new rules created by mating two better adapted rules. The rules are Boolean expressions represented by tree structures.

The software consists of two PASCAL programs, namely HERB (Heuristic Evolutionary Rule Breeder) and LEAF (Logical Evaluator And Forecaster). Together they perform the task of classifying samples into one of two or more categories on the basis of the values of a number of variables or features. HERB creates or modifies rules which LEAF then uses (see Fig. 10.2.).

HERB requires three input files: a datafile, a payoff file and an old rule file (possibly empty). It produces as output a new rule file which is at

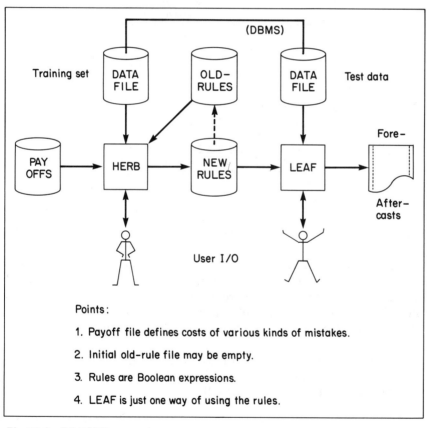

Fig. 10.3   BEAGLE synopsis

least as good as the old one. The datafile contains the training set for which correct category membership is known. The user also has to furnish a payoff matrix which defines the value or cost of each classification or mis-classification (see Fig. 10.3).

A rule is represented as a fully bracketed expression ended by a dollar sign,

e.g. ((£4 GE 20) OL (£7 LT £8)) $

which states that variable 4 (£4) should equal or exceed 20 or that variable 7 should be less than variable 8 to give a true result. (Odd names like OL for OR were chosen to avoid a clash with PASCAL predefined symbols.)

Computer decision		Actual class	
		Lived	Died
−1	No	−1	+1
0	Maybe	0	0
+1	Yes	+1	−1

Sample rule:

((6l LESS #14) LE #6) $

Value of variable #14 (urinary output) subtracted from 61 is less than or equal to value of variable #6 (mean arterial pressure).

Fig. 10.4   Sample BEAGLE payoff matrix

LEAF is simpler. It takes a datafile in the same format as the training set and runs a rule file on it. It can be asked to produce, among other things, an ordering of cases by rule consensus from most likely Yes to most likely No. Note that rules produced by HERB do not require extensive calculation and could in principle be applied by a person. LEAF is merely a convenience.

The BEAGLE learning algorithm consists of repeating the following procedure for a number of generations, where each generation is one run through the training data, as follows:

(1) Evaluate each rule on every sample according to the payoff matrix, with a bonus to shorter rules.

(2) Rank the rules in descending order of merit and remove the bottom half.

(3) Replace 'dead' rules by applying the MATE procedure to a pair of rules randomly chosen from the top half, thus combining parts of good rules.

(4) Mutate a few randomly chosen rules (but not the top one) and apply procedure TIDY to all new rules – ready for the next generation.

The TIDY procedure merely cuts down syntactic redundancies such as double negatives, constant expressions and so forth, leaving the pruned rule-tree with the same value but expressed more succinctly.

Tests on hospital admissions (classing heart patients as deaths or survivors) and on athletic physique (classing Olympic athletes as sprinters or long-distance runners) have been carried out. It appears from the trials that the method works better than a standard discriminant analysis technique based on linear functions, and is quite robust in the presence of noisy data. In addition the rather naive Neo-Darwinian theory embodied in the program behaved in a gratifyingly lifelike fashion.

What typically happened was the appearance, and subsequent disappearance, of dominant 'species' of rule. Each type flourished for a while until quite suddenly supplanted by a new and superior line – usually a mutation of one of its own offspring. When this happened the extinction of the more primitive form was rapid and complete. Indeed the value of systems like BEAGLE may in the long run be as tools for helping biologists refine their theories and test their consequences.

At present I am working on a more user-friendly commercial version of BEAGLE which can be 'bolted on' to a database package. The aim is to produce a database that learns.

10.11 EURISKO

Our brief survey has omitted the most important discovery program of all, Lenat's EURISKO (1983). We cannot end without mentioning it, though there are several reasons why a detailed treatment is impracticable here.

In the first place EURISKO is a bit too subtle for a two-page summary. One cannot point to a single algorithm and say: this is the essence of the method. That would not do it justice even as an abstract.

Secondly, EURISKO is a moving target. It is a research program rather than a product. It changes almost every day (that is the whole point) and Lenat himself lends a hand in the learning process by inserting, deleting and modifying its heuristic rules. So it is only semi-automatic. This makes it more effective, but less easy to describe.

The main reason, however, is that EURISKO owes its success not so much to the clever algorithms it employs for learning as to the richness of its representation language. Every concept in the system, including the rules, is represented as a 'unit'. Each unit has a number of 'slots'.

To those of us reared on traditional programming languages the unit is a data structure akin to the record, with the slots being its fields. But units are exceptionally flexible. A unit may have any number of slots and new slots may be added or deleted during processing. Slots may contain all kinds of data (strings, dates, numbers, functions etc.) since LISP structures are self-typing and EURISKO is written in LISP. Moreover, new slot types may be created by the system as part of the learning process. Several rules are devoted to the question of when to create a new type of slot.

Above all, the whole system is self-referential; so it should come as no surprise that each slot type is described by its own unit. This is EURISKO's most notable feature. Because all data objects, including procedural units (i.e. heuristic rules), are described in terms of units and slots, reasoning and meta-reasoning are all of a piece. There is nothing to prevent a rule applying to and altering another rule, or indeed itself. Thus EURISKO could begin with a rule such as

> *Rule 10*
> IF   a rule has fired only once,
> THEN generalize it

(where IF and THEN would be slots).

On turning its attention to this (i.e. firing Rule 10 for the first time), the system would start looking for rules that had fired once only. Rule 10 itself would be one candidate, which might lead to the creation of

> *Rule 20*
> IF   a rule has fired less than 5 times,
> THEN generalize it.

This is somewhat more general, and may in its turn apply to itself or to Rule 10 its progenitor.

This process could go on indefinitely, which is why I characterize EURISKO as an introspective system, but each rule has a 'worth' slot that dictates how much processing time it should receive. Only rules which directly or indirectly pay off will be generalized or specialized in several ways.

To conclude, EURISKO has made at least two important contributions to machine learning. It has achieved some noteworthy successes, such as the design of a novel 3D VLSI AND/OR gate; and it has pioneered the development of the most sophisticated description language used to date. But whereas you might get a program based on ID3 or INDUCE up and running on your personal computer, you would be well advised to steer clear of EURISKO as a model for your own systems – unless you happen to have a roomful of dedicated LISP machines and plenty of time on your hands.

REFERENCES

Dietterich, T. and Michalski, R. (1981) 'Inductive learning of structural descriptions'. *Artificial Intelligence*, **16**, 257–294.

Forsyth, R. (1981) BEAGLE: a Darwinian approach to pattern recognition. *Kybernetes*, **10**.

Holland, J. (1975) *Adaptation in Natural and Artificial Systems*, University of Michigan Press, Ann Arbor, Michigan.

Hunt, E., Marin, J. and Stone, P.T. (1966) *Experiments in Induction*, Academic Press, New York.

Langley, P. (1977) Rediscovering physics with BACON-3. *Proceedings of the Fifth International Joint Conference on Artificial Intelligence*.

Lenat, D. (1983) The nature of heuristics III. *Artificial Intelligence*, **19**, 189–249.

Michalski, R., Stepp, R. and Diday, E. (1981) A recent advance in data analysis. *Progress in Pattern Recognition*, North-Holland, Amsterdam.

Mitchell, T. (1979) An analysis of generalization as a search problem. *Proceedings of the Sixth International Joint Conference on Artificial Intelligence*.

Quinlan, J. (1979) *Induction over Large Databases*: Report HPP-79 14, Stanford University, Palo Alto, Ca.

Smith, S. (1980) *A Learning System Based on Genetic Adaptive Algorithms*, Ph.D. Thesis, University of Pittsburgh, Pa.

Wellbank, M. (1983) *A Review of Knowledge Acquisition Techniques for Expert Systems*, British Telecom Research, Ipswich, England.

11

Adaptive learning systems

STEPHEN F. SMITH

11.1 INTRODUCTION

With the advancements that have occurred in the field of expert systems over the last several years, it has become apparent that domain specific knowledge is the fundamental ingredient of expert problem solving abilities. Systems equipped with the appropriate knowledge have been shown to demonstrate expert level performance in such diverse problem domains as medical diagnosis (Shortliffe, 1976), computer configuration (McDermott, 1980), chemical analysis (Buchanan, 1969), and mineral exploration (Duda, 1978). Despite this success, however, the current state of expert system technology suffers from some serious limitations:

- The construction of an expert system still remains pretty much of an art. While tools and methodologies have emerged to provide considerable aid in this activity (c.f. Hayes-Roth, 1983), the process of eliciting, representing, and refining the knowledge utilized by the domain expert remains ill-defined and time consuming.
- Application of this technology is still restricted to fairly narrow, self-contained problem domains, and performance typically degrades rather sharply as the system approaches the boundaries of its knowledge. There is little ability to adapt or reorganize knowledge as performance requirements change over time.

Perhaps the most potential for providing long term solutions to these problems lies in the area of machine learning. Current research into methodologies for operationalizing advice (Mostow, 1981), learning by analogy (Carbonell, 1983), generalization (Mitchell, 1982), and discovery (Lenat, 1983) suggests a wide range of promising approaches to easing the present knowledge acquisition bottleneck and increasing the flexibility of future expert systems. This chapter advocates a particular approach to these problems, considering an adaptive learning strategy that offers several opportunities for acquiring, refining, and reorganizing system knowledge in response to observed performance.

As suggested by Mitchell (1982), the learning process can be formulated as a search. Given a particular language for expressing knowledge, the task of the learning mechanism is to explore the resulting representation space for points (descriptions) that lead to good performance when applied by the system's reasoning apparatus. The manner in which this search is conducted will ultimately determine the general effectiveness of the learning mechanism. We can identify a few critical factors:

- The size of the underlying search space, for cognitive tasks of practical significance, prohibits a systematic consideration of all alternatives. The learning mechanism must possess heuristic methods for reducing the scope of the search.
- This reduction in focus must not affect the reachability of good points in the space. In particular, the search must have the freedom to move beyond the confines of any pre-conceived notions of the problem at hand.

This latter point argues against excessive reliance of the learning mechanism on domain specific criteria and assumptions. While there have been successes in tailoring a system's learning methods to the problem at hand (e.g. Buchanan, 1978), such approaches run the risk of imposing a kind of *tunnel vision* with respect to the underlying search space. More generally, the effort expended in devising such methods provides little leverage for resolving the larger problems identified above, as the methods are generally not transferable to other domains.*

Given the inherent limitations of relying on domain specific strategies for exploration in the representation space, the problem becomes one of finding a domain independent search technique powerful enough to effectively and efficiently operate in such a space. This is a tall order, requiring a mechanism that exhibits a synergistic balance in its *exploitation* of knowledge structures that have led to good performance in the past and its *exploration* of new structures in the space. One example of such a mechanism can be found in nature where, despite the extreme immensity of possibilities, the evolutionary process rapidly yields structures (organisms) that are highly adapted to the specific environ-

---

*It should be emphasized that we are not arguing here against the use of domain specific knowledge, but addressing the manner in which it should be employed. The point is that such knowledge should serve as *grist* for the learning mechanism's *mill* rather than the basis for its construction.

mental niches in which they exist. Indeed, some of the earliest efforts in the area of machine learning (e.g. Friedberg, 1958; Fogel, 1966) sought to exploit models of this process in the construction of computer based learning systems. These efforts, however, did not produce the useful learning behavior that had been expected, and the evolutionary search paradigm was largely abandoned.

The fatal flaw in these early efforts lies in the fact that the computational processes employed did not accurately reflect the phenomenon being modeled. The assumption that evolution is a process driven solely by random mutation (a view, incidentally, that is still maintained in some biological circles today) is simply not the case. It is a considerably more sophisticated process that efficiently detects and exploits regularities in the structures (organisms) that are generated over time. Recent work (Holland, 1975) has yielded a theory that elucidates some of these basic properties and places the resulting process within a computational framework. Equipped with this more reasonable model of adaptation, this chapter re-examines the applicability of the evolutionary metaphor to the design and construction of general purpose learning systems.

The remainder of this chapter is organized as follows. Section 11.2 introduces a general class of adaptive search strategies and examines their essential properties. An application of the methodology is examined in Section 11.3 in the context of a system that learns control heuristics to govern the application of a set of problem solving operators. Performance results obtained by the system in attempting to learn to make appropriate bet decisions in the game of draw poker are presented to demonstrate the viability of the approach. In Section 11.4, some alternative paradigms for genetic-based learning are identified and discussed. Some general observations are made in Section 11.5.

11.2 GENETIC ADAPTIVE ALGORITHMS

This section introduces a class of adaptive search strategies that have emerged as a central component of a recent theory of adaptation put forth by Holland (1975). These so called *genetic algorithms* are motivated by standard models of heredity and evolution in the field of population genetics, and embody abstractions of the mechanisms of adaptation present in natural systems. Principal among these mechanisms are:

- A focus of attention based on the observed performance of generated structures.
- A collection of search operators that exploit coadapted sets of structural components (i.e. structure configurations that collectively contribute to good performance) in the generation of new structures for testing.

By extracting these processes from the specific context of genetics, the algorithms are made applicable to a wide range of problems encountered in adaptive system design.

11.2.1 Overview

A genetic algorithm simulates the dynamics of population genetics by maintaining a knowledge base (population) of structures (individuals) that evolves over time in response to the observed performance (fitness) of its structures in their operational environment. Each structure is presented to the algorithm as a sequence of its constituent components (its genotype) and is manipulated as such by the search operators. A specific interpretation of the structure (e.g. as a collection of parameter settings, a condition/action rule, etc.) yields a unique point in the space of alternative solutions to the problem at hand (the phenotype), which can then be subjected to an evaluation process and assigned a measure of utility. The search proceeds by repeatedly selecting structures from the current knowledge base on the basis of the associated utility measures derived via interpretation, and applying idealized *genetic*

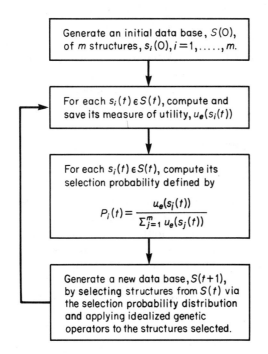

Generate an initial data base, $S(0)$, of m structures, $s_i(0), i = 1, \ldots, m$.

For each $s_i(t) \in S(t)$, compute and save its measure of utility, $u_e(s_i(t))$

For each $s_i(t) \in S(t)$, compute its selection probability defined by

$$P_i(t) = \frac{u_e(s_i(t))}{\sum_{j=1}^{m} u_e(s_j(t))}$$

Generate a new data base, $S(t+1)$, by selecting structures from $S(t)$ via the selection probability distribution and applying idealized genetic operators to the structures selected.

Fig. 11.1   Basic paradigm

operators to these structures to produce new structures (offspring) for evaluation. The basic paradigm is made more precise in Fig. 11.1.

To gain a feeling for the behavior of this search strategy, consider the selection probabilities defined in step 3 of Fig. 11.1. We see that if m structures are selected to participate in the generation of new structures at time t, the expected number of new structures to be derived from any given structure in the current knowledge base is

$$m \times \frac{u_c(s_i(t))}{\sum_{j=1}^{m} u_c(s_j(t))} = \frac{u_c(s_i(t))}{1/m \sum_{j=1}^{m} u_c(s_j(t))} = \frac{u_c(s_i(t))}{\bar{u}_c(S(t))}$$

where $\bar{u}_c$ denotes the average utility of its argument. Thus, the probabilities impose a selective bias toward above average performing structures relative to the rest of the structures in the knowledge base. In the absence of any other mechanisms, such a selective pressure would cause the best performing structure in the initial knowledge base to occupy a larger and larger proportion of the knowledge base over time.

Mere propagation of the best structures through the knowledge base, however, does nothing to further the search for better performing structures. It is the genetic search operators that fulfill this role, transforming the structures selected from the current knowledge base into new, untested structures. While these operators perform simplistic syntactic transformations on the selected structures, they will be shown in Section 11.2.3 to have subtle and highly parallel effects when utilized in conjunction with the above selection procedure.

11.2.2 The search operators

The principal means for generating new structures is the *crossover* operator. It takes two selected structures as input, randomly selects a breakpoint (i.e. a component boundary) on the structures, and exchanges the sequences of components falling to the right of the break point. For example, if two structures consisting of the component sequences c_1,c_2,c_3,c_4,c_5 and c_1',c_2',c_3',c_4',c_5' are crossed between the second and third positions, the new structures generated are c_1,c_2,c_3',c_4',c_5' and c_1',c_2',c_3,c_4,c_5. Specific decisions as to whether both resulting structures are to be entered into the knowledge base, whether the precursors are to be retained, and which other structures, if any, are to be purged define a range of alternative implementations.

The crossover operator draws only on the information present in the structures of the current knowledge base in generating new structures for testing. If specific information is missing, due to storage limitations or loss incurred during the selection of process of a previous iteration, then crossover is unable to produce new structures that contain it. A *mutation* operator, which arbitrarily alters one or more components of a selected structure, provides the means for introducing new information into the knowledge base. However, in contrast to the early computational models of evolutionary processes, mutation functions solely as a background operator within a genetic algorithm (i.e. its probability of application is very low). Its presence ensures the reachability of all points in the search space.

A third operator, *inversion*, alters the linkages amongst the components of a structure. It takes a single selected structure, randomly selects two distinct breakpoints on the structure, and inverts the sequence of components falling between the breakpoints. For example, an inversion of the structure c_1, c_2, c_3, c_4, c_5 with breakpoints between the first and second positions and the fourth and fifth positions yields the structure c_1, c_4, c_3, c_2, c_5. Note that the inversion operator does not produce a different structure but an alternative representation of the same structure (i.e. a reordering of its constituent components). The importance of such representational changes will become evident below.

11.2.3 The source of power

The power of the adaptive search strategies described above lies not in the testing of individual structures but in the efficient exploitation of the wealth of information that the testing of structures provides with regards to the interactions amongst the components comprising these structures. Specific configurations of component values observed to contribute to good performance (e.g. a specific pair of parameter settings, a specific group of rule conditions, etc.) are preserved and propagated through the structures in the knowledge base in a highly parallel fashion. This, in turn, forms the basis for subsequent exploitation of larger and larger such configurations. Intuitively, we can view these structural configurations as the regularities in the space that emerge as individual structures are generated and tested. Once encountered, they serve as *building blocks* in the generation of new structures. Let us characterize more precisely this source of power. To simplify the analysis, we will restrict our attention to problem spaces wherein structures are composed of a fixed set of l components, each identified by its position in the structure and reflecting the presence or absence of a specific attribute. Thus, for example, the sequence 1,0,1, . . . ,1 suffices to describe the structure that possesses the first attribute, doesn't possess the second attribute, possesses the third attribute, and so on.

Given these representational conventions, we can formally character-ize the search as one which efficiently focuses its exploration in parti-tions of the underlying l-dimensional space that have been associated with good performance. A specific partition (or hyperplane) of the space is defined by binding values to k of the l structural components ($1 \leqslant k \leqslant l$). For example, the partition designated by 1,□,0□, . . . □ (read □ as 'unbound') isolates all structures that possess a *present* value for attribute one and an *absent* value for attribute three. In evaluating a structure that lies in a particular partition j of the space, information is also acquired about the utility of the region of the search space delineated by that partition. Stated another way, the structure evaluation also constitutes an evaluation of the specific configuration of component values that serve to *define* partition j (e.g. the configuration of attribute one present and attribute three absent in the above example). Note that a single structure is a member of 2^l-1 distinct partitions of the space (i.e. $\sum_{k=1}^{l} \binom{l}{k}$). Accordingly, the measure of utility derived in evaluating a given structure in the knowledge base actually yields information as to the utility of the specific configuration of component values embodied by each of the 2^l-1 partitions to which it belongs.

With this in mind, it is interesting to consider structures in the knowledge base that belong to common partitions of the space. To this end, let $S_j(t)$ denote the subset of structures in the knowledge base at time t that belong to partition j, and $m_j(t)$ the number of structures in $S_j(t)$. Appealing once again to the selection probabilities defined in Fig. 11.1, the expected number of new structures to be derived from structures in $S_j(t)$ can be shown to be

$$\sum_{s \varepsilon S_j(t)} \frac{u_e(s))}{\bar{u}_e(S(t))} = m_j(t) \times \frac{\bar{u}_e(S_j(t))}{\bar{u}_e(S(t))}$$

If the resulting structures also belong to partition j, then

$$n_{m_j}(t+1) = m_j(t) \times \frac{\bar{u}_e(S_j(t))}{\bar{u}_e(S(t))}.$$

This indicates that the number of structures belonging to a given partition of the space will increase or decrease over time at a rate directly proportional to the observed performance of the structures belonging to that partition. Thus, we see that the generation of new structures is constantly focused toward the most promising regions of the search space, and, further, that this exploration occurs in an implicitly parallel fashion. Note that for a knowledge base containing m structures, the above sampling rate is approached simultaneously for somewhere between 2^l-1 and $m(2^l-1)$ distinct partitions of the space.

Achievement of the above sampling rate with respect to a given partition j is of course dependent on the specific configuration of component values that defines the partition passing unchanged from the precursor to the new structure. Hence, it is necessary to examine the disruptive effects of the genetic operators. The crossover operator will disrupt a given structural configuration if the selected breakpoint falls between two or more of the configuration's component values. The probability of this occurring is directly proportional to the length of the smallest sequence of components containing the configuration, which we will call the *defining segment* of the corresponding partition. For example, the probability of disruption by crossover associated with the partition $\square,0,\square,1,1,\square, \ldots ,\square$ (having the defining segment $0,\square,1,1$) is $3/(l-1)$. Thus, crossover tends to preserve the above sampling rate with respect to partitions whose defining segments are small relative to l, and tends to be disruptive with respect to partitions having large defining segments. But, as structures belonging to specific, high performance partitions with small defining segments begin to dominate the knowledge base over time, there is an effective reduction in the defining segments of other partitions, lessening the disruptive effects of crossover on the rate at which they are sampled. The mutation operator has a negligible effect on the sampling rates, given its background role in the search.

The search may still encounter difficulties, however, if the essential partitions (i.e. the primitive building blocks) possess long defining segments. The problem here is a representational one, stemming from an inappropriate ordering of the structural components. In these situations, the inversion operator provides the means for increasing the productivity of the search. By altering the order of the components in a structure, its application tends to reduce the length of long defining segments which, in turn, provides greater opportunities for exploitation via crossover.*

To summarize, the power of a genetic algorithm derives from its ability to exploit, in a near-optimal fashion, information about the utility of an exponential number of structural configurations without the

*Note that the representational conventions we have adopted for the purpose of this analysis place some constraints on the simultaneous use of crossover and inversion within the search. Specifically, it is necessary to maintain knowledge of the location of each component in a given structure to ensure that crossover is always applied to similarly represented structures. Different representational assumptions can lead to a more natural coexistence of these operators (c.f. Smith, 1980).

computational burden of explicit calculation and storage. This leads to a focused exploration of the search space wherein attention is concentrated in regions that contain structures of above average utility. The knowledge base, nonetheless, is widely distributed over the space, insulating the search from susceptibility to stagnation at a local optimum. The reader is referred to Holland (1975) for a much more comprehensive presentation of the algorithm and their properties.

11.3 APPLYING THE METHODOLOGY TO LEARN PROBLEM SOLVING HEURISTICS

The analysis of the last section argues well for the use of genetic search as a general purpose learning mechanism. This section demonstrates the viability of the technique by considering its application to a complex learning task. Specifically, we will describe the design and performance of a prototype learning system implementation called LS-1 (Smith, 1980, 1983). LS-1 learns a set of heuristics, represented as production rules, to govern the application of a set of operators in performing a particular problem solving task. This is accomplished through the accumulation of experience in the task domain, with a genetic algorithm constituting the system's sole means of improving its problem solving performance. LS-1 provides a good example of the power of genetic search in that learning problem solving heuristics requires the effective manipulation of fairly complex symbolic structures.

11.3.1 The LS-1 learning paradigm

Functionally, the LS-1 system is composed of three interacting components:

- The problem solving component – an inference engine for applying alternative sets of control heuristics to instances of the task under consideration.
- The critic – a mechanism for evaluating the performance of a given set of heuristics in solving instances of the task.
- The learning component – a genetic search strategy responsible for generating new sets of heuristics in response to the performance assessments provided by the critic.

The organization of these components is depicted schematically in Fig. 11.2.

In operation, the system maintains a knowledge base of m structures, each a candidate set of control heuristics (or rule set) for solving the task at hand. On a given cycle through the learning loop, each candidate rule

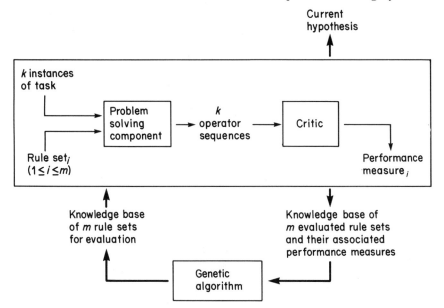

Fig. 11.2   The LS-1 learning paradigm

set is applied by the problem solving component to k instances of the task. The critic analyses the k operator sequences generated by the rule set during this proficiency test as well as characteristics of the rule set under evaluation, and assigns a performance measure indicative of the relative *worth* of the rule set as a potential solution to the task. Once all structures in the knowledge base have been evaluated in this manner, the genetic algorithm is invoked to generate a new knowledge base of structures for testing, and the cycle is repeated. The knowledge base of structures, together with the associated performance measures, is viewed as LS-1's internal memory, representing the sum of the system's experience in the task domain at any point in time. Externally, LS-1's current hypothesis as to a solution to the task under consideration is the rule set that has received the highest performance rating thus far in the search. LS-1's progress in the task domain is monitored by considering the (potentially discontinuous) sequence of hypotheses generated over time.

As alluded to above, the domain of structures to be searched within the LS-1 learning paradigm differs in some rather significant ways from the simple representation used to illustrate the properties of genetic search in Section 11.2. While a given structure (rule set) in the LS-1 knowledge base can certainly be viewed, at the lowest level, as a sequence of symbols over a small alphabet (e.g. a binary sequence), these symbols also combine to form meaningful symbolic components (e.g. patterns, actions, productions, etc.) at higher levels. Moreover, these higher level components need not possess any positional dependencies with respect to the overall structure. At the rule level, for example, components have the same interpretation regardless of their physical location in the structure. To effectively exploit regularities in the space at all levels of abstraction, the learning strategy must be cognizant of these representational characteristics. Accordingly, the genetic algorithm employed in LS-1 utilizes a revised set of operators that enables the manipulation of structures at various levels of granularity. The theoretical implications of these changes, while beyond the scope of this chapter, are explored by Smith, (1980) and shown to result in properties analogous to those of the basic algorithms.

11.3.2 Representing problem solving heuristics

The use of a genetic algorithm as the means for manipulating knowledge structures in response to observed performance places specific demands on the form of the representation language. Given that the genetic search operators transform structures without regard to any specific interpretation, it is essential that the productions exhibit a syntactic simplicity if repeated application of the operators is to consistently produce valid points in the search space. This requirement must be balanced against the desire for a representation expressive enough to describe all effective problem solving behaviors in the task domain. The LS-1 knowledge representation is the result of an attempt to reconcile these seemingly conflicting objectives.

Broadly speaking, the LS-1 problem solving component is organized as a domain independent production rule interpreter into which task specific primitives must be injected for application in a given domain. It is instantiated in a particular problem solving domain by supplying an appropriate set of state variables and problem solving operators. The state variables provide the system with a characterization of the domain and the operators constitute the system's repertoire of alternatives in reacting to the current state. Problem solving heuristics are encoded as a set of simple productions which, when enabled, invoke operators and enter messages into working memory in response to perceived state variable and working memory configurations.

The individual productions adhere to a simple, uniform syntax. Each antecedent consists of a fixed number of elementary patterns, one sensitive to each of the state variables supplied to the system and a prespecified number attending to the messages that appear in working memory. Each consequent consists of a message, to be posted in working memory if the production is activated, and the designation of an operator to be applied to the current state. A production may be intended solely for internal communication purposes (see below) in which case a special *noop* operator is specified. The stylized form of an LS-1 production is illustrated in Fig. 11.3.

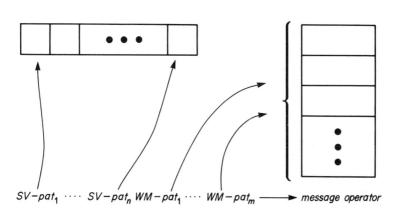

Fig. 11.3   The stylized form of an LS-1 production

All information perceived by the productions (i.e. both the values characterizing the external processing state and the messages in working memory) is presented in binary form. This enables the use of a syntactically simplistic yet fairly powerful pattern matching language. Specifically, each pattern appearing in a production is expressed as a string over the alphabet $\{0,1,\#\}$, where 0's and 1's serve as pattern constants and # will match either symbol. Thus, for example, the pattern #1#0 will match any of the inputs 0100, 0110, 1100, and 1110. Additional expressive power is provided through a pattern *prefix*, which can be optionally used to either complement the associated pattern (i.e. the set of inputs that the pattern previously matched becomes exactly the set that now fails to match) or simply instruct the matcher to disregard the associated pattern. The latter provides a convenient facility for restricting a production's context to a specific portion of the processing state.

The net effect of adopting the above representational conventions is an encoding of heuristics as fixed length sequences of simple components that are easily transformable into new heuristics via syntactic manipulations. (Recall that a given set of productions is viewed as a single structure in the LS-1 knowledge base). However, this is not accomplished without imposing some limitations on the recognition capabilities of individual productions. While the patterns expressible in the above language characterize a large range of potentially useful subsets of values, there are other situations (subsets) that cannot be recognized in this manner. These deficiencies are balanced by incorporating a non-standard control regime that promotes cooperative recognition of more complex aspects of the current state by distinct productions. Specifically, the conflict resolution step is removed from the basic recognize/select/act cycle of typical rule interpreters and all instantiations found during the recognition phase of a given cycle are activated. Global synchronization is postponed to the end of the cycle, at which time the messages generated by activated productions are deposited into working memory, and the suggested problem solving operators, if any, are applied to the current external state. The messages posted in working memory persist for the duration of the next cycle only. Hence, a particular state description might trigger several productions whose activations result solely in the placement of messages in working memory. These messages can then be detected by another production on the next cycle, leading to the application of a specific operator. By adopting this parallel architecture, the system is made computationally complete with respect to the domain primitives that have been provided.*

There is a need to coordinate external problem solving activity if the operators suggested for application during any given cycle are not mutually exclusive in their effects. In such cases, a *default resolution mechanism* is employed which probabilistically selects one of the conflicting operators based on the number of activated productions suggesting each alternative. This nondeterministic behavior is viewed as reflecting the system's current uncertainty with respect to the current problem solving state. The stronger the bias toward the application of a particular operator in a given context (i.e. the larger the percentage of activated productions suggesting its application as opposed to a competing operator) the less uncertain the system is about how to respond.

---

*Conflict resolution is typically seen as a necessary precondition for learning in that it coordinates the interactions amongst productions, and allows the productions themselves to possess a fair degree of autonomy (McDermott, 1978). Note, however, that this perspective is predicated on a view of learning as the incremental addition of new rules. Within LS-1, rule sets are shaped over time as integrated structures.

11.3.3 The issue of credit apportionment

Critical to the success of any learning system is an ability to effectively apportion credit to those units of knowledge that have led to good performance in its operational environment, and, likewise, to assign blame to those units that prove to be ill conceived. Attempts to improve performance will flounder without this global focus of attention. In the context of LS-1, the credit assignment issue becomes one of providing an adequate mechanism for assessing the relative worth of each rule set generated as a potential solution to the task to be learned. As we have seen from the analysis of Section 11.2.3, a genetic learning strategy is particularly adept at isolating those characteristics of a structure actually responsible for good performance and exploiting them in the generation of new structures. However, the degree to which these search properties can actually be exercised within a particular problem solving domain will ultimately depend on the discriminatory power of the performance measures that are provided. Thus, the level of intelligence achievable by LS-1 within a specific domain is always bounded by the quality of its evaluation function.

The evaluation function provided by the LS-1 critic draws on both task specific and domain independent sources of knowledge in assessing the performance of the rule sets generated by the genetic algorithm. The former sources produce measures relating directly to the external behavior generated in the rule set's proficiency test, and are given primary emphasis in the derivation of the composite measure of utility. The latter sources produce measures that reflect general characteristics of rule set which appear to contribute to good performance regardless of the specific domain. These sources have a less influential effect on the overall utility measure but serve to supply a finer level of discrimination. These two types of knowledge sources are considered in turn below.

To evaluate problem solving performance in a given domain, the LS-1 critic necessarily requires a means for analysing the correctness (or partial correctness) of the k operator sequences produced by the rule set during its proficiency test. The nature and scope of this knowledge will obviously vary from one domain to the next and is somewhat a function of the designer's ingenuity. Indeed, the critic is the component of the system wherein any amount of domain specific knowledge can be usefully injected. The only constraint imposed is that the knowledge relate to functional (observable) aspects of performance in the intended domain, and not structural characteristics of the target problem solving knowledge. To utilize domain specific knowledge of the latter form would introduce potentially narrow bounds on the learning mechanism's search, particularly in not well understood domains where a learning system could perhaps provide the most benefit.

The domain independent measures utilized by the LS-1 critic can be grouped into three broad categories.

- Structural properties of the rules – There appear to be discernible characteristics of the rules that are *conducive* to good performance. Within the LS-1 critic, the assessment of such characteristics is made via measures reflecting the potential for communication between rules' messages and working memory patterns, the level of specificity in the rules' patterns, and the presence of specific deficiencies (e.g. uninstantiable productions, infinite loops, etc.).
- Dynamic properties of the rules – Other general indications of a rule set's overall utility as a potential solution can be obtained by examining the trace of its execution during the proficiency test. Measures indicating the amount of reliance on the default resolution mechanism in selecting problem solving operators as well as percentage of rules actually participating in the problem solving process are derived in this manner.
- Efficiency concerns – Here the number of productions in the rule set is used to emphasize the generation of concise rule sets.

The incorporation of these measures increases the discriminatory power of the LS-1 critic, and makes differentiation possible even in situations where little or no external performance is observed (a distinct possibility given the domain independent nature of the learning strategy).

11.3.4 Some experimental results

The operational characteristics of LS-1 have been observed in two distinct and unrelated problem solving domains, both of which have been addressed in the context of other efforts in learning system construction:

(1) Learning to perform a simple maze walking task – This problem domain was the subject of an earlier genetic learning system (see Section 11.4) and was considered to enable a comparison of the two distinct paradigms.
(2) Learning to make the bet decision in the game of draw poker – This problem domain was the focus of Waterman's classic AI study in machine learning (Waterman, 1970).

In both of these domains, LS-1 has demonstrated an ability to significantly improve its performance over time. We will concentrate here on the experiments conducted in the more challenging poker betting domain, as the results provide an interesting contrast to those obtained by Waterman with the use of a more domain specific learning strategy. A detailed account of both sets of experiments is given by Smith (1980).

In brief, the poker betting problem addressed by Waterman is described as follows. The system engages an opponent in a standard game of draw poker with the goal of making bet decisions that maximize its profits. Each time it is the system's turn to bet, it must therefore infer the most appropriate bet decision to make, given the current state of the poker game. The system perceives the current state of the game through the values of a collection of state variables and is provided with a fixed set of betting alternatives from which to select its response. The general scenario, including the specific set of primitives supplied to the system, is depicted in Fig. 11.4. For purposes of evaluation in the experiments to be described below, the objective was to generate the correct bet decisions in each of ten consecutive rounds of play.

In determining the correctness or incorrectness of a given bet decision, Waterman's system employed a deductive procedure based on

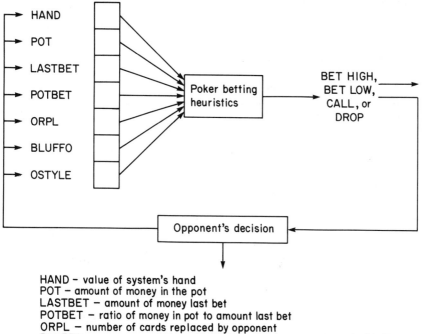

HAND – value of system's hand
POT – amount of money in the pot
LASTBET – amount of money last bet
POTBET – ratio of money in pot to amount last bet
ORPL – number of cards replaced by opponent
BLUFFO – a measure of the probability that the opponent can be bluffed
OSTYLE – a measure of the conservativeness of the opponent's playing style

Fig. 11.4   Waterman's poker betting domain

an *axiomatization* of the game of poker. This same procedure was embedded in the LS-1 critic to serve as the primary basis for assessing performance in the domain. Specifically, a measure indicating *the percentage of agreement with the axioms in the bet decisions generated* was defined and incorporated into the evaluation function. A second measure relating to performance, *the number of successfully completed rounds of play*, was also utilized to ensure that premature *drop* decisions (i.e. drops issued before cards have been replaced) would not be assessed as appropriate by the critic.

LS-1 was pitted against P[built-in], a poker betting program hand crafted by Waterman and judged to perform at roughly the same level as an experienced human poker player (Waterman, 1970). An internal knowledge base of 50 rule sets was maintained by the system, generated at the outset by randomly selecting conditions and operators for the individual productions of each structure.* Running for 2 DEC10 cpu hours, LS-1's operation versus P[built-in] was observed over an interval of 4,200 rule set evaluations (approximately 85 cycles through the learning loop). As indicated by the performance results depicted in Table 11.1, LS-1 achieved the performance objective within this time frame. A set of productions was generated that successfully completed 10 consecutive rounds of play in which there was total agreement with the poker axioms as to the bet decisions generated.[†]

Table 11.1 Performance results in experiment 1

Number of evaluations performed	500	1000	2000	3000	4200
Performance rating of current hypothesis (scale: 0.0–1.0)	0.461	0.490	0.562	0.748	0.893
Percentage of agreement with the poker axioms	71.4	80	76.1	85.7	100
Number of successfully completed rounds	3	4	7	8	10

An examination of these performance results led to the discovery that the heuristics used by P[built-in], while appropriate within Waterman's

---

*The decision to start LS-1 from *scratch* in these experiments was motivated by a desire to provide a direct comparison with Waterman's results. One could certainly envision initializing the system at a higher level of expertise.
[†]The results presented here actually represent averages over several distinct runs of LS-1, reflecting the concern that successful performance in a single run might be simply a consequence of stochastic factors (e.g. the random number seed).

paradigm, were not designed for such an extended game of poker (i.e. 42 000 rounds of play). Generally speaking, P[built-in] incorrectly judged LS-1 to be an extremely conservative player over time, and, with this misconception, could be easily bluffed into dropping. LS-1 responded to its opponent in precisely the right manner, generating rule sets that exhibited an overriding tendency to bet.

To test LS-1 against a more formidable opponent, adjustments were made to P[built-in] to eliminate the above misconception and a second experiment was conducted. The results obtained in this case are presented in Table 11.2. We once again observe a steady and significant improvement in the hypotheses generated by LS-1 as the poker game progressed. Within 4000 evaluations, a rule set was generated that successfully completed 9 of 10 rounds of play while generating bet decisions that agreed with those deduced by the critic 82% of the time.

The relative success of LS-1 in the poker betting domain can be gauged by comparing these results to those obtained with Waterman's system. Waterman subjected his *trained* learning system to a proficiency test consisting of 50 rounds of poker against a human opponent, also measuring performance in terms of the percentage of agreement with the axioms in the bet decisions generated. Agreement of 86% was achieved by his system in this test (Waterman, 1970). Thus, while LS-1 rule sets were subjected to a shorter proficiency test (i.e. 10 rounds), the levels of performance achieved by the two systems are comparable. This becomes particularly significant when we examine the domain specific dependencies inherent in the methods employed by Waterman's system in manipulating its set of productions. The creation of new productions was driven by an *a priori* supplied *decision matrix*, specifying for each possible bet decision, the reason why each state variable is relevant to that decision if, in fact, the variables are relevant. This knowledge was used directly in formulating the predicates of each new production's antecedent. In contrast, this knowledge was neither required by nor supplied to LS-1.

Table 11.2 Performance results in experiment 2

Number of evaluations performed	500	1000	2000	3000	4000
Performance rating of current hypothesis (scale: 0.0–1.0)	0.414	0.483	0.619	0.689	0.740
Percentage of agreement with the poker axioms	58.75	73.03	89.9	75.1	81.93
Number of successfully completed rounds	3	4	6	8	9

11.4 ALTERNATIVE GENETIC-BASED LEARNING PARADIGMS

The performance results obtained with LS-1 clearly demonstrate the potential of an adaptive learning strategy. Nonetheless, the approach taken in LS-1, in manipulating a knowledge base of alternative sets of productions, illustrates just one point in the spectrum of possible opportunities for genetic based learning approaches. Constraining the scope and form of the knowledge to be manipulated by the system gives rise to a variety of useful learning mechanisms. This section, in reviewing some other work that has been done with genetic search strategies, identifies some of these alternative learning paradigms.

The initial arena for investigating properties of genetic search algorithms was the domain of function optimization. DeJong provided the first definitive experimental study (DeJong, 1975), exploring the tradeoffs among many variants of the class of genetic search algorithms and contrasting their performance with that of more traditional function optimization techniques. Genetic search strategies were demonstrated to be superior in non-linear and multi-dimensional optimization problems. Analysis of the operational characteristics of the algorithms was continued in (DeJong, 1980; Brindle, 1981). A recent study (Grefenstette, 1983) took the experimentation one step further, employing a genetic algorithm itself to explore the space of possible implementations. The results obtained, interestingly enough, verified many of the conclusions reached in the earlier work. Some initial steps toward a formal characterization of the classes of functions most amenable to solution via genetic search strategies were taken by Bethke (1981).

Function optimization represents the simplest form of genetic based learning. Yet, the ability to effectively optimize the settings of a large collection of interacting parameters has many useful applications that have a direct bearing on current expert system technology. One such application can be found in rule based systems that exploit measures of belief (and disbelief) in the rules to reason plausibly under uncertainty. These measures are typically subjective estimates provided by the domain expert and, as such, the task of maintaining consistency among beliefs quickly becomes unmanageable as the size of the rule base increases. The problem is further compounded when the estimates of multiple experts are considered. A genetic adaptive strategy offers a straightforward approach to fine tuning these belief measures as the system accumulates experience in the domain.

An alternative genetic based paradigm for learning rule knowledge has been pursued by Holland and Booker (Holland, 1978, 1980, 1983; Booker 1982). This work has led to the construction of a class of systems that improve performance through the creation and refinement of rule constructs called *classifiers*, similar in many respects to the representation described in Section 11.3.2. However, the paradigm differs from the approach taken in LS-1 in the manner in which the genetic search strategy is employed. These systems operate with a knowledge base of *individual* classifiers, and the genetic algorithm assumes a somewhat different role of maintaining diversity in the classifiers that are generated over time. Accordingly, classifiers attending to different types of behaviors (e.g. designating the application of mutually exclusive problem solving operators) are kept physically separated in the knowledge base and each set of classifiers is manipulated independently by the genetic algorithm. To provide a basis for selection, a measure of *strength* is associated with each classifier in the knowledge base, reflecting the extent to which its use has led to the achievement of system goals in the past. These strength measures are shaped by a sophisticated apportionment of credit strategy (termed the *bucket brigade algorithm*) as the system engages in specific cognitive tasks. As new classifiers are generated by the genetic learning strategy, they supplant those classifiers in the knowledge base having the lowest associated measures of strength. Experimental studies with these classifier systems in various cognitive domains (e.g. the maze walking problem mentioned in Section 11.3.4) have also demonstrated robust learning capabilities.

11.5 SUMMARY

This chapter has focused on the applicability of a particular class of adaptive search strategies called genetic algorithms to the problems surrounding the acquisition of knowledge in present day expert systems. Let us briefly reiterate the main points that have been made. We began by arguing that a general learning ability requires a search technique that is capable of moving beyond any pre-conceived notions of the problem domain, and, hence, must not be based on domain specific assumptions. Noting the efficiency of adaptive search in natural systems, the genetic algorithms, which abstract the essential mechanisms of this process, were suggested as likely candidates. A formal analysis of their properties provided some insight into the power of the approach, indicating a highly parallel and broad based search through the system's representation space. We then turned attention to the particular application of learning problem solving heuristics to examine the operational characteristics of the technique in a complex learning task. The design of LS-1, a genetic based learning system implementation, was presented, and experimental results obtained by LS-1 in attempting to learn heuristics for making bet decisions in the game of draw poker were reported. Within this problem domain, LS-1 demonstrated an ability to improve its performance rapidly over time, and achieved a level of competence comparable to that achieved by a previous learning system based on more domain specific methods. Finally, we explored some alternative learning paradigms in which genetic adaptive strategies have been exploited, suggesting the wide range of opportunities offered by this approach.

ACKNOWLEDGEMENTS

This work was supported in part by the Computer Science Department at the University of Pittsburgh, and the Robotics Institute at Carnegie-Mellon University.

REFERENCES

Bethke, A.D. (1981) *Genetic Algorithms as Function Optimizers*. PhD thesis, Dept. of Computer and Communication Sciences, University of Michigan.

Booker, L.B. (1982) *Intelligent Behavior as an Adaptation to the Task Environment*. PhD thesis, Dept. of Computer and Communication Sciences, University of Michigan.

Brindle, A. (1981) *Genetic Algorithms for Function Optimization*. PhD thesis, Dept. of Computing Science, University of Alberta.

Buchanan, B.G., Sutherland, G. and Feigenbaum, E.A. (1969) Heuristic DENDRAL: a program for generating explanatory hypotheses in organic chemistry. *Machine Intelligence*, **4**, 209–254.

Buchanan, G.B., and Mitchell, T.M. (1978) Model-directed learning of production rules. In *Pattern-Directed Inference Systems* (eds. D. A. Waterman and F. Hayes-Roth), Academic Press, New York.

Carbonell, J.G. (1983) Learning by analogy: formulating and generalizing plans from past experience. In *Machine Learning* (eds. R. S. Michalski, J. G. Carbonell and T.M. Mitchell) Tioga Publishing Co., Palo Alto, California.

DeJong, K.A. (1975) *Analysis of the Behavior of a Class of Genetic Adaptive Systems*. PhD thesis, Dept. of Computer and Communication Sciences, University of Michigan.

DeJong, K.A. (1980) Adaptive system design: a genetic approach. *IEEE Transactions on Systems, Man and Cybernetics*, **10**(9), September, 566–574.

Duda, R.O., Hart, P.E., Barrett, J.G. *et al* (1978) *Development of the PROSPECTOR Consultation System for Mineral Exploration: Final Report*. Technical Report, SRI International.

Fogel, L.J., Owens, A.J., and Walsh, M.J. (1966) *Artificial Intelligence Through Simulated Evolution*, Wiley, New York.

Friedberg, R.M. (1958) A learning machine, Part 1. *IBM Journal of Research and Development*, **2**, 2–13.

Grefenstette, J.G. (1983) *Optimization of Genetic Search Algorithms*, Technical Report CS-83–14, Vanderbilt University.

Hayes-Roth, F., Waterman, D.A., and Lenat, D.B. (eds.) (1983) *Building Expert Systems*, Academic Press, Reading, Mass.

Holland, J.H. (1975) *Adaptation in Natural and Artificial Systems*, University of Michigan Press, Ann Arbor, Michigan.

Holland, J.H., (1978) Cognitive systems based on adaptive algorithms. In *Pattern-Directed Inference Systems* (eds. D. A. Waterman and F. Hayes-Roth) Academic Press, New York.

Holland, J.H. (1980) Adaptive algorithms for discovering and using general patterns in growing knowledge bases. *International Journal on Policy Analysis and Information Systems*, **4**(2), 217–240.

Holland, J.H. (1983) Escaping brittleness. In *Proceedings 2nd International Workshop on Machine Learning*, July, University of Illinois.

Lenat, D.B. (1983) The role of heuristics in learning by discovery: three case studies. In *Machine Learning, An Artificial Intelligence Approach* (eds. R. S. Michalski, J.G. Carbonell and T.M. Mitchell) Tioga Publishing Co., Palo Alto, California.

McDermott, J., and Forgy, C.L. (1978) Production system conflict resolution strategies. In *Pattern-Directed Inference Systems* (eds. D. A. Waterman and F. Hayes-Roth), Academic Press, New York.

McDermott, J. (1980) *RI: A Rule-Based Configurer of Computer Systems*. Technical Report CMU-CS-80–119, Carnegie-Mellon University, Pa..

Mitchell, T.M. (1982) Generalization as search, *Artificial Intelligence*, **18**, 203–226.

Mostow, D.J. (1981) *Mechanical Transformation of Task Heuristics into Operational Procedures*. PhD thesis, Computer Science Dept., Carnegie-Mellon University , Pa.

Shortliffe, E.H. (1976) *MYCIN: Computer-Based Medical Consultations*, American Elsevier, New York.

Smith, S.F. (1980) *A Learning System based on Genetic Adaptive Algorithms*. PhD thesis, Dept. of Computer Science, University of Pittsburgh.

Smith, S.F. (1983) Flexible learning of problem solving heuristics through adaptive search. In *Proceedings 8th International Joint Conference on Artificial Intelligence*. August, William Kaufman Inc., Los Altos, California.

Waterman, D.A. (1970) Generalization learning techniques for automating the learning of heuristics. *Artificial Intelligence*, **1**, 121–170.

12

Automating knowledge acquisition

ROY RADA

12.1 INTRODUCTION

The meaning of AI is different to different people, but the standard approach clearly views *search* and *knowledge representation* as key issues. No searching or problem solving algorithm can be efficient on all search spaces or problems. A key challenge to AI is to classify search algorithms and search spaces and then to demonstrate which search algorithms perform well on which search spaces. For the majority of problems of interest to people, the algorithms that solve those problems seem to require large amounts of knowledge that are specific to the problems. The proper representation of this knowledge is critical to the success of an AI program. Applications of AI, particularly through *expert systems*, to science, medicine, and education help illustrate the enormous impact that AI is having in the skilled professions.

A major bottleneck in the development of expert systems occurs during the knowledge acquisition phase. Domain expertise, in fields such as medicine and law, cannot currently be easily entered into the computer. In this chapter a medical expert system is used to illustrate an approach to automated knowledge refinement. Medical students are given large amounts of information in the first two years of their training. In the ensuing years these students are expected to learn how to structure and use this information by observing more experienced practitioners (Elstein *et al.*, 1978). Formal instruction in problem-solving methodologies has not been common, in part because of a limited ability to describe such methodologies. The creation of computerized medical expert systems has tended to require explicit entry by a physician of rules for solving problems. The science of how to do this is little developed. The way one person creates these rules tends to vary so much from the way that another person would create the rules that extension of a computerized expert system by other than its creator is uncommon. From the thesis of how the student becomes expert and the antithesis of how the computer becomes expert, a new goal is derived – to try to create computer systems that can digest large amounts of factual information and then structure that information for efficient problem-solving strategies.

What is it about a problem that allows it to be solved? At a meta-level, what is there about a problem-solver that allows him to improve his problem-solving ability through experience? The answer to both these questions is that the space of alternatives to be searched must be constrained in such a way that examination of a small part of the space gives very useful information about unexplored parts of the space. The space of alternatives that defines a problem should be seen by the problem solver as having continuity or predictability. The theme of this chapter is that with the notion of continuity, better methods of knowledge acquisition can be demonstrated. More specifically, the problem of augmenting the knowledge used in medical diagnosis is addressed. A set of rules for the interpretation of computerized tomograms of the brain has been extracted from the neuroradiology literature. Methods of refining these rules so that they more accurately interpret images are being explored in the context of the continuity of the space of possible rules.

This chapter is divided into four main parts: (1) Overview of AI, (2) Continuity, (3) Learning survey, and (4) Another approach to knowledge refinement. Part (1) emphasizes the role of search and search spaces and serves as an introduction to the definition of continuity that appears in part (2). Part (3) reviews key points of many learning projects. In part (4) the work of others and the role of continuity are put together in the design of new knowledge acquisition methods. The fourth part has itself three main divisions; first a domain of application in interpretation of radiological images is described, then a simple weight improvement scheme is presented, and finally a more ambitious rule-refiner is proposed.

12.2 OVERVIEW OF AI

12.2.1 Search

Problem-solving can be viewed as searching. One common way to deal with search uses *rules*, *data*, and *control* (Nilsson, 1980). The rules operate on the data, and the control operates on the rules. In the Traveling Salesman Problem, for instance, the data is the set of tours and their costs in a weighted graph, the rules are ways to proceed from tour to tour, and the control decides what rule to apply and when.

Since a major objective of AI is to relate problem-solving methods and problems, both the methods and problems must be characterized. Problem-solving classes can often be distinguished by their degree of reliance on: (1) chaining in a production-rule system, (2) matching, and (3) generate-and-test. A very simple production-rule system has two rules: 'IF a THEN b' and 'IF b THEN c'. Given the fact a an algorithm can *chain* forward to b and then to c. If c is the solution, the algorithm halts. Conversely, in a backward chain a goal, such as c, is given, and the search goes backward to b and then a. If a is known to be true, then the backward search halts. The appropriateness of forward or backward chaining depends, of course, on the problem. *Matching* techniques are frequently an important part of a problem-solving strategy. In forward-chaining, for instance, an 'IF a THEN b' rule is activated only if a exists in the data. The match between the a in the data and the a in the rule may not have to be exact, and various deductive and inductive methods may be used to try to ascertain whether or not an adequate match exists. In the *generate-and-test* approach, the problem is viewed as a search space, and an element in the search space is generated and then tested. Based on the results of the test, another element is generated and then tested, etc. Depending on the constraints that the generate mechanism employs, various categories of generate-and-test algorithms arise. When the elements of the search space are connected by a tree structure, a 'depth-first' generation mechanism goes from the root to a leaf as quickly as possible.

The Traveling Salesman Problem can, in principle, be solved by an exhaustive search, but, in practice heuristics or problem-specific rules of thumb must be found to expedite the search process. In fact, some (Rich, 1983) would define the discipline of AI as: 'The study of techniques for solving exponentially hard problems in polynomial time by exploiting knowledge about the problem domain.' This exploitation involves characterizing the problem or search space. In general, a problem is solvable to the extent that examination of part of its search space gives significant information about the nature of the remainder of the search space. A variety of questions can be asked about a search space in the effort to characterize it. Is the problem neatly decomposable into smaller problems; does consistent, exact information about the problem exist, and should a human be expected to interact with the computer in the process of solving the problem?

12.2.2 Knowledge representation

Knowledge may be declarative or procedural. In a declarative representation most of the knowledge is represented as a static collection of facts accompanied by a small set of general procedures for manipulating the facts. Procedural representations embody knowledge in executable code that acts-out the meaning of the knowledge. In most domains there is need for both kinds of information. Declarative representations can be further classified according to the amount of structure. The first-order predicate calculus (FOPC) is considered less structured than semantic nets.

First-order predicate calculus is an adequate system for representing any knowledge which people know how to formalize. Furthermore, FOPC is the standard language of logicians. Algorithms exist for converting any FOPC expression into a canonical form, such as the conjunctive normal form. Methods of performing deduction within FOPC have been thoroughly characterized, and a number of amendments to FOPC have been made to facilitate the storing of information. Some of these amendments permit inconsistent deductions or probabilistic deductions to be made.

Semantic nets were originally designed as a way to represent the meanings of English words. In a semantic net, information is represented as a set of nodes connected to each other by a set of labeled arcs, which represent relationships among the nodes. For instance, one might have the three nodes 'boy', 'person', and 'arm' and connect them with the arcs 'is-a' and 'is-part-of'. One can readily imagine creating arbitrarily complex semantic nets, but for practical reasons one typically wants to circumscribe the set of possible nodes and arcs. Information is extracted from a semantic net by a graph-like traversal. Conceptual dependency diagrams are one variant of semantic nets that include a small-set of arc types, such as 'ingest' and 'grasp'. Conceptual dependency diagrams have been principally used in programs for natural language processing.

12.2.3 Expert systems

Two of the oldest and most famous expert programs in AI are DENDRAL and MACSYMA (see *Handbook of AI*, Vol. 2, 1982). DENDRAL accepts a mass spectrogram of a chemical and determines the molecular structure of the chemical. MACSYMA assists scientists in solving mathematical problems. Both DENDRAL and MACSYMA are massive programs that evolved over years. Both are often used by professionals in the field for whom the programs were intended to be

helpful. The design principles behind both projects are rather complicated, as at the time of the inception of the projects, the AI principles
that were appropriate were being first developed.

In the past decade numerous programs have been written to incorporate a skilled professional's expertise into software. One progam diagnoses a patient's infectious disease as well as, if not better than, a
physician. Another program looks for signs of important minerals in
seismic data, and a third provides intelligent computer instruction in a
variety of courses. The conclusion has been reached that only a few
hundred rules are typically adequate to represent the knowledge that is
crucial to an expert's successful performance within his domain of
expertise. Surprisingly, the areas of human activity which depend most
on common sense are the areas where AI research has been least
successful.

12.2.4 Learning and creativity

Shortly after electronic computers became available, experimentation
began with computers that learn. Current learning research focuses on
the transference of human expertise from a professional to a computer.
In many learning experiments a computer studies a set of examples and
determines a concept which underlies the examples. Learning programs
must search among alternative conceptualizations and store in their
knowledge-base only the most useful alternatives.

Programs have been written whose goal is to discover interesting
conjectures (Lenat, 1982). It seems inevitable that machines will be
designed which will try to find interesting problems and solve them.
Robots are being built which have significant sensory and motor contact
with the world. Eventually, the focus of AI may be on the development
of machines which have an active, creative role in society.

12.3 CONTINUITY

12.3.1 Continuity in learning

When learning is viewed in its broad context as a part of intelligent
behavior that characterizes many living systems, the role of *influence* and
continuity in learning become apparent. In this chapter the major AI
approaches to learning are discussed in terms of the influence and
continuity that each has. Whether the mechanism of learning is as crude
as memorization or as broad as induction the role of selective growth in
spreading influence can be seen. Whether the learning method depends
on numbers and the PERCEPTRON algorithm, on symbols plus single-

concepts in version spaces, or symbols plus many-concepts in a discovery system, some parts of the learning structure must be augmented and some parts removed as learning proceeds. In order that this augmenting and removing process proceeds gracefully, the system should have the property of continuity. AI learning systems often use a single representational scheme for the learning examples and the learned concepts. Progress from examples to concepts may then involve addition or deletion of a few symbols in a way that permits smooth or gradual transition from examples to concepts and from one concept to another.

12.3.2 Influence

A retrospective view suggests that the function of living things is to have *influence*. An organism can extend its influence by:

(1) Staying alive – maintaining the self.
(2) Begetting a family.
(3) Sharing or communicating with others.
(4) Creating a system or 'machine' that has influence.

The fourth method of influencing is simultaneously the loftiest, most challenging, and least attainable. Scientists regularly engage in the third form of influence when they publish articles, lecture, and confer with colleagues. Staying alive and begetting a family are objectives that people have in common with all living systems.

For a system to spread its influence it must generate new twists on the information that it transmits. Simply transmitting someone else's information does not constitute perpetuation. One can not know in advance, however, exactly what twists will be successful in the world. Accordingly, some amount of trial and error is needed. Intelligent organisms try to minimize the error by making trials whose probability of success is high, and the best known criterion of success in a highly interactive world is that what is good now is likely to be similar to what will be good in the near future. The probabilistic argument is more formally and powerfully elaborated by Conrad (1979).

12.3.3 The measure NIV

In the trial and error process of perpetuation an organism confronts the problem of 'what trial to generate next'. Problems may always be viewed as search spaces, and one convenient formalization of a search space SS is as a quadruple of S, O, I, G (Banerji, 1982 and *Handbook of AI*, 1981). S is a set of states, O is a set of operators that go from one state to another, I is a set of initial states, and G is a set of goal states. The problem is to choose the operators that lead from I to G. The search process typically relies on a heuristic evaluation function f.

The continuity in a search space depends on the degree to which similar states in S have similar f values. The similarity of two states in S is inversely proportional to the number of operations O required to go between the two states. The similarity in f values of two states, when the range of f is numeric, can simply be the closeness of two numbers.

To characterize the predictability of f on SS a measure NIV (which is an acronym for *Number of Inversions*) is created (Rada, 1983). Predictability is often related to computational complexity, but NIV directly characterizes relationships within the search space. NIV on (SS, f) tells the degree to which similar states have similar f values. The following terms are introduced: equivalence classes of states, heuristic-predictions, and inversions. The equivalence class S_i is defined to be

$\{\ s\ |\ s \in S$ and s can be reached from I by a sequence of i operations $\}$

The heuristic-prediction function h on $s \in S_i$ is

$$h(s) = \max\ \{\ f(w)\ |\ w \in S_{i+1} \text{ and 1 move connects } s \text{ to } w\ \}.$$

The ordering imposed by h on S_i is compared to the ordering imposed by f on S_i, and to quantify this comparison, inversions are used. Let a_1, . . ., a_n be a permutation of the set $\{1, . . ., n\}$. If $i < j$ and $a_i > a_j$, then the pair (a_i,a_j) is called an inversion of the permutation (Knuth, 1973). For example, the permutation 2, 4, 1, 3 has the three inversions $(2,1)$, $(4,1)$, $(4,3)$.

To determine $\text{NIV}_k(S_i,f)$ the following three steps are performed:

(1) Order all $s \in S_i$ so that $f(s_1) \leq f(s_2) \leq . . . \leq f(s_m)$.
(2) Compute h for each s and create the sequence $h(s_1), h(s_2), . . ., h(s_m)$, where $f(s_j) \leq f(s_{j+1})$. If $f(s_j) = f(s_{j+1})$, then $h(s_j) \leq h(s_{j+1})$.
(3) $\text{NIV}_k(S_i,f)$ = number of inversions in the sequence $h(s_1), . . ., h(s_k)$. $\text{NIV}_k(S_i,f)$ depends on k, S_i, S_{i+1}, and f.

Rule-based planning systems, like STRIPS and DCOMP (Nilsson, 1980), fit the framework of this paper. For a simple example, denote the registers of a computer by r_i and the contents of r_i by c_i. The S of SS is $\{(r_1,c_1), (r_2,c_2), (r_3,c_3), (r_4,c_4)\}$, where $c_i \in \{0, a, b\}$. The initial state is $\{(r_1,a), (r_2,b), (r_3,0), (r_4,0)\}$. One exchange problem E_1 has the goal of $\{(r_1,0), (r_2,0), (r_3,a), (r_4,b)\}$. Another exchange problem E_2 has the goal of $\{(r_1,b), (r_2,a), (r_3,0), (r_4,0)\}$. The operator is the assignment rule described by Nilsson (1980):

rule: assign (r_i,a,r_j,b)
precondition: (r_i,a), (r_j, b)

delete: (r_i, a)
assert: (r_i, b)

The heuristic $f(s)$ tells the number of registers in s whose contents are the same as the corresponding registers in the goal. Both E_1 and E_2 can be solved in four steps. E_2 seems harder because it requires one step from a higher-valued state to a lower-valued state. Application of NIV to E_1 and E_2 reveals that NIV is much higher for E_2 than E_1. This supports the hypothesis that NIV distinguishes problems by their difficulty.

12.4 LEARNING SURVEY

12.4.1 Environment

In most learning experiments the environment is isolated. It gives examples or rules to the learning machine, but the machine does not compete with other machines in the environment. Any influence that occurs must be within the much smaller context of the learning machine itself. In other words, at the micro-level of the learning machine's internal parts there may be seen to occur an evolutionary struggle which pits program fragments against each other. At the macro-level of the learning machine's interaction with the environment, matters are so constrained that influence can only indirectly be seen to be occurring.

12.4.2 Optimal strategy

Holland (1975) has studied strategies for learning in a variety of contexts. For many purposes, learning can be viewed as a search for an optimum of a function. If the function maps slot-machine gambling strategies to the losses that the strategy would incur for a particular set of slot-machines, then one wants to learn which strategy minimizes the losses.

As long as the slot-machines can be assumed to behave as random variables, the strategy which minimizes losses is one which gives progressively more trials to the slot-machines that are giving better rewards. The strategy is basically a reproduction-with-change plus selection-of-the-fit one. Exponentially more trials are awarded to the slot-machines that are manifesting higher payback.

The best strategy has the form of an evolutionary process where a population of trials is made, feedback is obtained, the trials which did well are repeated, and the trials which did poorly are unlikely to be repeated. There must continue to be sampling of slot-machines that have had poor payback thus far but which might, nevertheless, have high payback in the long run.

An analysis of this situation with the influence measure, discussed earlier, reveals that a subpopulation of trials that first represents less than half of the total population comes with time to dominate the population. After some time almost all trials are being awarded to the best performing slot-machines, and from that time onward influence stops being a prevalent property of this slot-machine game. Still unusual trials are occasionally generated from the trials that otherwise go to the seemingly best slot-machines. If these wayward trials happen upon a slot-machine that is starting to give more reward than had been expected, then perhaps those trials could come to dominate the population of trials. Those new trials would be viewed as descendants of the trials that were dominating at the earlier time, and thus the dominant subpopulation would continue to give rise to the dominant subpopulation.

12.4.3 Memorization

Memorization may be viewed as a kind of learning. Memorization alone would, however, be woefully inadequate for almost all interesting learning problems. Memorization can be embellished with various devices to make it more powerful. One such device is selective forgetting. Samual (1959) tried a memorization approach to assessing board positions and to prevent memory from becoming too encumbered implemented a selective forgetting scheme.

In selective forgetting, items of memory, whose value to the machine is considered to be below some threshold value, are erased. New items are added to memory that are given a chance to prove themselves to be useful. In other words, items that have high fitness are maintained and, in a sense, they perpetuate themselves. This perpetuation or influence is limited in that components of the memory are not copies with changes in the memory. New items come from the outside. Thus, most fundamentally, a memorization scheme allows the environment to successfully influence the learning machine but does not allow the learning machine to monitor influence within itself.

12.4.4 Knowledge debugging

Intermediate in complexity between learning by memorization and learning by example is learning by debugging. Here the learning machine is told what it should know but must convert this knowledge from its input form to a form which permits the machine to perform effectively against the environment based on the knowledge it has received. In other words, the input must be made operational.

Mostow (1982) has built a computer program to accept advice which the program then operationalizes. A variety of routines are considered for application to the input in order that the appropriate routines for transforming the input can be found. The routines which are chosen have, in effect, an opportunity to spread their influence, as part of the routine is now copied in place of the input advice. The influence that occurs is, however, of only a limited sort. A more robust system would also be learning what operationalizers are good to have. This might be determined on the basis of the performance of existing operationalizers, such that those which were having good influence would be utilized to produce new operationalizers. In this way influence as discussed earlier in this paper might more robustly exist.

Davis's (1982) TEIRESIAS system allows a person to interact with MYCIN and to direct improvements to the knowledge-base. TEIRESIAS can trace through the rule-base of MYCIN to answer questions like HOW and WHY which help the human expert debug the knowledge-base. Furthermore, TEIRESIAS creates meta-level knowledge about the rules so that it can more directly guide the knowledge refinement process.

12.4.5 Learning concepts

(a) PERCEPTRONS

The PERCEPTRON recognizes classes of patterns. A PERCEPTRON Ψ may be viewed as a linear threshold function.

$$\Psi(x) = \text{yes}, \qquad \text{if } a_1\omega_1(x) + \ldots + a_j\omega_j(x) \geq \Delta.$$
$$ = \text{no}, \qquad \text{otherwise}$$

The a_i are integers and act as coefficients of the ω_i. The ω are binary-valued predicates which operate in some simple way on patterns.

The interest in PERCEPTRONs was based on the learning rather than classification abilities of PERCEPTRONs. Say that we have two sets of patterns F+ and F−. Also assume that there exist a_j for $1 \leq i \leq j$, such that the linear threshold function $a_1\omega_1(x) + \ldots + a_j\omega_j(x) \geq \Delta$ is true when $x \in$ F+ and false when $x \in$ F−. The PERCEPTRON convergence theorem (Minsky and Papert, 1972) says that a PERCEPTRON can: (1) start with an arbitrary set of a's, (2) follow a simple learning algorithm, and (3) converge in a finite number of steps to the desired a's.

The PERCEPTRON learns by making small changes in its coefficients a. Consider $(a_1, \ldots, a_j) = \mathbf{A}$ a vector and place all possible $\mathbf{A}$ on the axes of a j-dimensional space. A small change in $\mathbf{A}$ leads to a small change in $a_1\omega_1(x) + \ldots + a_j\omega_j(x)$. The search of the PERCEPTRON may be viewed as going along the surface of a function G where $G(\mathbf{A}) = \mathbf{A} \times \mathbf{A}^* / |\mathbf{A}|$, and $\mathbf{A}^*$ is a vector of coefficients which correctly identifies the patterns in F+. The PERCEPTRON moves along G(**A**) in the direction of larger values of G(**A**) (Minsky and Papert, 1972). The surface of G is smooth.

If continuity of a discrete function means that small changes in the domain tend to be associated with small changes in the range, then the PERCEPTRON learning algorithm can be viewed as searching a 'continuous' discrete function. The continuity of G(**A**) is, however, not a sufficient condition for convergence of the learning algorithm. That G(**A**) is unimodal and that the learning algorithm follows an upward gradient are the sufficient conditions. The PERCEPTRON learning algorithm depends on a continuous, unimodal function or search space. These characteristics of a search space might also be important for an algorithm that learns the ω's.

(b) Data-driven learning
Data-driven methods of learning single concepts include Mitchell's (1977) version spaces and Langley's (1977) BACON. In the version space approach, most specific and most general concepts define the upper and lower bounds of a partially ordered search space. Learning examples cause 'specific' descriptors to be generalized and 'general' descriptors to be specialized. In this process, the useful descriptors retain much of their original character. The final, most concise description is likely to contain parts of descriptions that existed from the beginning, and those influential descriptors give the version space approach an influence characteristic. In BACON features are propagated with alteration through a feature space. When a set of features converges to a constant value, BACON concludes that a concept has been discovered. The operators which manipulate the features have influence on the system and cause finally one characteristic of the feature space to dominate.

(c) Model-driven learning
Michalski (1983) describes a model-driven method for learning single concepts. The model includes a kind of evolutionary mechanism for generating and testing hypotheses. Influence, as a notion, is based on the evolutionary paradigm, and it is thus natural that a learning technique based on that paradigm would manifest influence.

The Michalski (1983) learning algorithm has 4 basic steps: (1) select an initial population of hypotheses, (2) generate new hypotheses by generalizing existing ones, (3) select the best hypotheses and use again in step (2) and (4) review the results of each step (3) to decide whether or not the iteration process should stop. The (2) + (3) loop is a reproduction-with-change + selection-of-fit loop and causes a subpopulation of hypotheses to spread its influence more successfully than others.

Swartout's (1983) XPLAIN system was originally devised to explain the action of the Digitalis Therapy Adviser. In the process of building an adequate model of digitalis therapy, Swartout realized that he could also generate the specific rules that were needed for advising about therapy. The model has a variety of components to assure that smooth transitions occur during the creation of therapy rules.

(d) Heuristic-driven learning

In Lenat's (1983) AM system, concepts are generated and refined in a way that can be viewed as evolutionary. Existing structures are massaged by heuristics that both amend the basics of structures and add fitness information to structures. Based on the fitness of a structure it may or may not become grist for expansion into other structures.

Structures or concepts that perpetuate themselves at one point have an opportunity to continue to do so. These concepts include both the mathematics specific ones, such as 'number', and the heuristic concepts, such as 'generate extreme examples'. When something new is created it carries with it information from both types of concepts. Some of the concepts are inevitably more useful than others and spread their influence more. As meta-heuristics are to be developed, the opportunities for differential influence increase.

12.5 ANOTHER APPROACH TO KNOWLEDGE REFINEMENT

12.5.1 A radiology expert

Several papers have been written about the use of computers for diagnosis of X-ray images. A group at Ohio State has been extending its Artificial Intelligence in Medicine work to the interpretation of radio-nuclear scans of the liver (Chandrasekar *et al.*, 1980). A group in England (Innocent *et al.*, 1983) is developing rules for automated interpretation of CT (Computer Tomography) brain images. In general, the medical and computer community is placing more energy into the development of systems that can facilitate the interpretation of radiological data. This trend is encouraged by, among other things, the growing use of digital radiographic imaging machines.

By studying several textbooks of neuroradiology, such as Ramsey (1981) and Valk (1980), about 200 rules for interpretation of brain CTs were produced. The rules that derived from a text varied with the nature of the text. A summary of the results of that study can be found in Rada and Ackerman's paper (1983). Some books emphasize data from the patient history; some focus on the anatomical location of a lesion. In any case, the width of the tree of rules was far greater than its depth. The conclusion of Lenat (1983), that expertise seems to depend on a bushy but not deep rule tree, was supported by the CT data.

An Expert Tomographer (ET) was developed to process the rules for CT interpretation. The ET has a structure similar in several ways to that of MYCIN (Shortliffe, 1976). It depends on probabilistic, rule-based knowledge. Certainty factors are propagated in the same manner as they are in EMYCIN (van Melle, 1979). The differences include the fact that ET forward-chains rather than backward-chains and that variable thresholds are used. Each proposition that occurs as an antecedent in a rule has a threshold assigned to it. A fact or proposition must have a certainty greater than that in the threshold in order for the rule with that fact in its antecedent to fire. The weight attached to the proposition in the consequent part of the rule is used to attenuate the conclusion (see Winston, 1984 for an explanation that uses similar terminology).

12.5.2 Weight adjustment

(a) Method

The rules first developed for ET did not interact meaningfully. Of the several problems, one of the simpler ones stemmed from the propagation of certainties. What had seemed as a reasonable threshold and attenuation for a rule in the middle of a deductive sequence proved on implementation to prevent the flow of information. Exactly what needed to be done was unclear. The manipulation of weights so as to improve performance seemed straightforward but very tedious.

The elaboration of an algorithm for the systematic correction of the weights (thresholds and attenuations) was begun. One obvious strategy included raising the attenuations (the number by which the certainty of the conclusion was multiplied) when a proposition was concluded without enough certainty and lowering the attenuations when a proposition was concluded with too much certainty. This logic can be extended to the cases where a rule either failed to fire or fired at the wrong time. The amount by which a rule's weight was to be changed would depend on the past performance of that rule.

The weight adjusting or learning algorithm (LEARNER) depends on a Learning Set (LS). Each element of LS is an ordered pair (I,D) where I is a set of initial propositions and their associated certainties and D is a set of conclusions and their certainties. Symbolically, I or D is {(proposition$_1$, certainty$_1$), . . . , (proposition$_m$, certainty$_m$)}.

In addition to LS, LEARNER depends on a set of rules (RULES). RULES must be such that LS can be correctly handled once the weights are properly adjusted. This is the same kind of assumption that is necessary for the PERCEPTRON – namely, that the feature detectors are adequate (Minsky and Papert, 1972).

The goal of LEARNER is to have RULES produce the same D for a given I as is indicated by LS. Each proposition in RULES is marked by a special first word that specifies some category, which for ET includes HISTORY, CT, and DIAGNOSIS. LS shouldn't have to specify the intermediate conclusions which RULES might make, so only those conclusions of RULES which begin with DIAGNOSIS are compared to the D in LS.

LEARNER has a Credit Assignment (CA) and Weight Adjustment (WA) phase. Each phase reads an element S_i from LS. RULES are then applied to the I_i of S_i; the propositions that are produced, which have DIAGNOSIS at their beginning, are placed in a group called $CONC_i$. To compare $CONC_i$ and D_i the DIAGNOSIS propositions are first divided into three categories:

(1) Those that occur in $CONC_i$ and D_i.
(2) Those that occur in D_i but not $CONC_i$.
(3) Those that occur in $CONC_i$ but not D_i.

Propositions in (1) are further divided into three categories:

(i)   Perfect are those that have the same certainty in $CONC_i$ and D_i.
(ii)   TooMuch are those that have more certainty in $CONC_i$ than in D_i.
(iii) TooLittle are those that have less certainty in $CONC_i$ than in D_i.

Each rule has a property list with the following identifiers: Perfect, TooMuch, TooLittle, NeedPath, and WrongPath. For a given S_i, CA determines the sequences of rules that lead to each proposition in $CONC_i$. For cases (i), (ii), and (iii) each of those rules has its Perfect, TooMuch, or TooLittle property, respectively, augmented with S_i. For a proposition in D_i but not in $CONC_i$, CA determines what path would lead from I_i to D_i. Those rules, which didn't fire but should have, have atom S_i concatenated to their NeedPath property. When a proposition from $CONC_i$, is not in D_i, then CA notes that on the WrongPath property of all those rules that were on the path to $CONC_i$.

WA changes the weights to improve the performance of RULES on LS. For case (1,i) no adjustments are necessary. For case (1,ii) the attenuations of those rules that lead from I_i to D_i should be lowered (and perhaps the thresholds lowered to accommodate the lowered attenuations). The extent to which each attenuation in each rule for a proposition p that was on the path from I_i to D_i is lowered is proportional to both (a) the difference between the certainty in $CONC_i$ and D_i and (b) an algebraic assessment of the history stored on p. One assessment on p

is |TooMuch| + |WrongPath| − |TooLittle| − |Perfect|. Case (1,iii) is handled similarly to case (1,ii).

For case (2) WA wants to increase the likelihood that a path which didn't fire will fire. WA first determines the path that should fire and what if any initial sequence of rules in it did fire. The threshold of the rule that should next be activated is lowered so that the rule is more likely to fire next time. In case (3) a proposition was concluded which shouldn't have. Accordingly, the rule which produced that proposition has its threshold raised so that the rule won't fire next time.

(b) Results

Initial testing of LEARNER revealed that learning sets could easily be arranged which couldn't possibly be correctly identified by the rules. As a simple example, one can't expect an $S_1 = \{\ \{(a,0.7)\}, \{(b,0.6)\}\ \}$ and an $S_2 = \{\ \{(a,0.4)\}, \{(b,0.8)\}\ \}$ to both be handled by the same set of rules. More subtle difficulties can occur any time that two different sets of initial propositions in LS are not disjoint.

Another insight that dawns on one after some experimentation with the weights is that all the significant weights can be located in the rules that are at the first level. A first level rule is one for which the antecedents are propositions provided in the I of an S in LS. A significant weight is a threshold other than -1 or an attenuation other than 1. LEARNER manipulates weights throughout RULES because people like to codify their knowledge in rules with weights at many levels.

Forty rules from the set of 200 mentioned earlier were extracted for an experiment. All the rules dealt with cerebral infarcts. An LS was created that tested all the major cases of LEARNER. LEARNER is implemented in about 500 lines of LISP. After three cycles of CA and WA, RULES worked perfectly on LS.

Producing the LS by hand-picking examples is difficult work. The intent is, however, that LS would be automatically generated from the cases in the hospital. Many CT images of the brain and their correct diagnosis have been stored on the computer. LEARNER could be amended so as to read such files and automatically produce LSs.

This author is currently investigating the role of continuity in the search spaces that arise during knowledge acquisition for expert systems. To facilitate refinement of the learning algorithm, a search space SS is formalized and NIV is applied. A set R of rules with thresholds and attenuations (weights) on the propositions in each rule is chosen. This weighted, rule-base is the initial state of SS. The weights are restricted to a small set, and the set S of states includes all possible weight assignments to R. A learning set LS of associated 'fact' propositions and 'conclusion' propositions indirectly defines the goal state; a goal state performs optimally on LS. Each application of an operator in the O of SS changes exactly one weight.

From the SS and NIV framework one can quantitatively assess the performance of a learning algorithm and the characteristics of the weighted rule-space. Investigations confirm that a desirable representation for a search space provides a low NIV. Other important issues, such as the ordering of examples in the learning set and the step-size of the learning algorithm, are fruitfully approached in the precise contexts of NIV.

12.5.3 Genetic algorithm, heuristics, and frames

A PERCEPTRON-like algorithm can work well when the propositions or feature-detectors of the rules are guaranteed to be able to distinguish the patterns in the learning set. Often, however, the selection of this set of propositions is a very difficult task. Attempts to automate the acquisition of these propositions include the early work of Samuel (1967). The search space for learning propositions does not seem to be unimodal but does seem smooth. Holland's (1975, 1983) genetic algorithm is designed to handle smooth but multi-modal search spaces. The major obstacle to implementation of learning schemes with the genetic algorithm is the representation problem. The algorithm only works well when a representation has been found such that many substrings are meaningful.

Heuristics and frames are fundamental components of Lenat's (1982) discovery systems. Lenat feels that the key to success of his representation is that the primitives allow many different combinations to be useful. This is a similar requirement to that for Holland's system. Lenat's system has discovered many interesting concepts and powerful plans. Holland's system has a robust mathematical basis. Both Lenat and Holland feel that the time is ripe for the combination of some of the better features of the work that each has championed.

While the genetic algorithm is designed to work on strings, this author applies it to a frame-oriented representation. Each frame corresponds to a rule of the ET system. Now, however, each proposition is replaced by a hierarchy of slots. There are slots for data from the Computed Tomography Image (CT), for data from the patient History (HX), and for the Diagnosis (DX). Within a slot there are subslots. For instance, CT includes Location (LOC), Density (DEN), and Shape; HX includes Onset and Duration; and DX includes Vascular, Infectious, and Neoplastic. Within the subslots there may be sub-subslots. For instance, LOC includes artery, lobe, and ventricular space; and DEN includes hypodense, isodense, and hyperdense.

The author has been collecting and organizing a large number of terms for the slot hierarchies. Also the rules of ET are being translated into frames. A *genetic+heuristic* algorithm is being implemented to partially automate improvement of the frames. Application of the genetic algorithm requires that the frames be assigned credit in proportion to the value of their performance. For this the 'bucket-brigade', credit-assignment method (Holland, 1983) is used. The genetic algorithm deals with large populations in which many individual members (or frames, in our case) should differ from one another in small ways. Accordingly, each of the previous 200 rules is expanded into several frames that are small variants on one another.

To illustrate the operation of the proposition-learner consider a rough sketch of two frames in Fig. 12.1. Assume that both of these frames have high CR values. Then the genetic algorithm might copy them and cross them. One possible crossover would occur between the duration

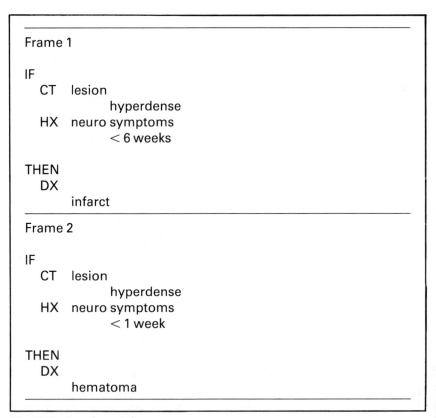

Fig. 12.1   Two frames for crossover

components of the history. The effect of the crossover would be to create a descendant of frame 1 that had duration of '1 week' and a descendant of frame 2 that had duration of '6 weeks'.

The beneficial effects of this particular crossover could have been achieved in other ways. Medical science has determined that an X-ray image of a blood clot is initially hyperdense but that over a period of about 2 weeks it becomes isodense. A program with such knowledge could change frame 1 so that hyperdensity was expected only during the first week rather than during the first 6 weeks. When such knowledge is available to the computer, it ought to take advantage of it. The genetic algorithm is designed for cases where such knowledge is not available. On the other hand, a system can try to take advantage of both methods – the genetic and knowledge – when the situation is appropriate.

Another alternative to the genetic algorithm is analogical reasoning. In analogical reasoning two events are studied in order to extract from one event information that might be useful in the other event. In the illustration, one could view the genetic algorithm as extracting information from frame 2 and transferring it to frame 1. In a sense the genetic algorithm reasons by analogy. The genetic algorithm doesn't have particular knowledge to let it know that the exchange it made is better than some other exchange. The genetic algorithm is appropriate for situations where less is known about exactly what exchanges might be useful.

For the radiology experiment the author proposes to use a combination of analogical reasoning and genetic algorithm in trying to refine the slots. Several hundred frames, a body of hierarchically organized terms, and some neuroradiology-specific heuristics will be encoded into a program that uses a genetic algorithm plus heuristics to produce a better set of frames. Initially, frames will not contain the weights (thresholds, attenuations, and certainty factors) discussed in the previous section. The ET would first be trained to output the correct diagnostic categories and later to identify the relative certainties of each.

12.6 DISCUSSION

The AI learning programs discussed in this chapter frequently use, what Dietterich *et al.* (1982) call, the 'single-representation trick'. This means that the input from the environment, the representation of this input in the machine, and the final conceptualization of the machine are all based on the same symbols and syntax. For instance, both Mitchell's version space and Dietterich's INDUCE use the first-order predicate calculus (FOPC) with a few predicates and atoms to represent input, associations, and output. This single-representation trick facilitates continuity.

The operations of the AI learning programs often generalize or specialize some concept. This can be accomplished by adding or deleting symbols from an FOPC expression. This addition and deletion process is constrained by the mechanisms of the learning program so that the resulting concepts typically represent a concept which is very close to the concept that was represented by the parent concept. The FOPC expression is itself a structure, and the interpretation imposed on that expression is, in a sense, the function. In the AI systems discussed in this paper the structure-function relationship tends to facilitate continuity.

Many fields have developed over centuries a wisdom as to how to compartmentalize, label, relate, and test that are now the identifying mark of that field. Take, for instance, the paradigm of mathematics: axiom, inference rule, lemma, theorem, and conjecture. Or the paradigm of medicine: disease, therapy, double-blind study, and morbidity. Artificial intelligence is a much younger discipline than either mathematics or medicine and its paradigm is much more in flux and without clear definition. This fluidity makes the comparison of results across experiments in AI difficult.

The AI methodology typically involves the selection of some well-circumscribed domain and the application of some principles to the development of a program to operate intelligently in that domain. The principles involved are usually interesting and intuitively appealing. Usually the program shows some success in its task and the principles are considered to be vindicated. There should be new work that defines intelligence rigorously and tries to find necessary and sufficient conditions for intelligence. In this chapter intelligence is related to *influence*, where influence is a kind of selective growth. A necessary, but hard to achieve, condition for influence is *continuity*. With a precise definition of continuity the researcher can investigate principles of intelligence and obtain quantifiable results that facilitate comparison across experiments. In science such comparisons are critical, for the results of one set of experiments must be used to constrain the parameter space of another set of experiments.

One of the barriers to the wider applicability of expert systems is the paucity of techniques for facilitating the refinement of knowledge. In this chapter a method LEARNER is developed for the adjustment of weights in a probabilistic, rule-based expert system. The method has roots in the PERCEPTRON work but differs from that work in two major ways. For one, multiple levels of rules are handled. For another, heuristics in several forms are stressed. The weights placed into the rules at the beginning encode what experts think the weights should be. The LEARNER program only slowly changes weights from their original form. Heuristics are also incorporated in the way that weights are changed – account is taken of the history of each rule along several dimensions.

To facilitate automated knowledge acquisition considerations of continuity may guide the choice of representation for search spaces and of algorithms for search. The rule-base that has been developed for interpretation of computerized axial tomograms needs refinement. The refinement can occur at several levels including the weights on the rules and the propositions in the rules. The space of rules that has to be searched in order to improve the system seems to be a smooth space. Classical algorithms like the PERCEPTRON and genetic algorithm have been shown to work well on smooth spaces. Their difficulty is that they do not typically accommodate much domain specific knowledge. This author has proposed two methods of knowledge acquisition or refinement for a medical expert system that take advantage of strengths of the classical algorithms, while including some of the knowledge-dependency that is important for practical success.

REFERENCES

Banerji, R. (1982) Theory of problem solving: a branch of artificial intelligence. *Proceedings of the IEEE*, **70:12**, 1428–1448.

Chandrasekar, B., Mittal, S. and Smith, J. (1980) RADEX – towards a computer-based radiology consultant. In *Pattern Recognition in Practice* (eds Gelsema and Kanel) North Holland, Amsterdam.

Conrad, M. (1979) Bootstrapping on the adaptive landscape. *BioSystems*, **11**, 167–182.

Davis, R. and Lenat, D. (1982) *Knowledge-Based Systems in Artificial Intelligence*, McGraw-Hill, New York.

Dietterich, T., London, B., Clarkson, K. and Dromey, G. (1982) Learning and inductive inference. In *Handbook of Artificial Intelligence*, Vol. 3 (eds P. Cohen and E. Feigenbaum) William Kaufman, Los Altos, Ca., 323–512.

Elstein, A., Shulman, L. and Sprafka, S. (1978) *Medical Problem Solving: an Analysis of Clinical Reasoning*, Harvard University Press, Cambridge, Mass.

Handbook of Artificial Intelligence, Vol 1 (1981) (eds A. Barr and E. Feigenbaum) *Vol 2* (1982) (eds A. Barr and E. Feigenbaum) *Vol 3* (eds P. Cohen and E. Feigenbaum) William Kaufmann, Inc, Los Altos, Ca.

Holland, J. (1975) *Adaptation in Natural and Artificial Systems*, University of Michigan Press, Ann Arbor, Michigan.

Holland, J. (1983) Escaping brittleness. *Proceedings of the International Machine Learning Workshop*, 92–96.

Innocent, P., Teather, D., Wills, K. and Du Boulay, G. (1983) Operational system for computer assisted diagnosis of cerebral disease. *Proc. MEDINFO '83*, 467.

Knuth, D. (1973) *The Art of Computer Programming, Vol 3, Sorting and Searching*, Addison-Wesley, Reading, Mass.

Langley, P. (1977) Rediscovering physics with BACON.3. *Proceedings of the International Joint Conference on Artificial Intelligence*, 505–507.

Lenat, D. (1982) The nature of heuristics. *Artificial Intelligence*, **19**, 189–249.

Lenat, D. (1983) The role of heuristics in learning by discovery. In *Machine Learning* (eds R. Michalski, J. Carbonell and T. Mitchell) Tioga Publishing, Palo Alto, Ca., 243–306.

Michalski, R. (1983) Theory and methodology of inductive learning. In *Machine Learning* (eds R. Michalski, J. Carbonell and T. Mitchell) Tioga Publishing, Palo Alto, Ca., 83–134.

Minsky, M. and Papert, S. (1972) *PERCEPTRONS*, MIT Press, Massachusetts.

Mitchell, T. (1977) Version spaces: a candidate elimination approach to rule learning. *Proceedings of the International Joint Conference on Artificial Intelligence*, 305–310.

Mostow, D. (1982) Learning by being told. In *Machine Learning* (eds R. Michalski, J. Carbonell and T. Mitchell) Tioga Publishing, Palo Alto, Ca., 367–404.

Nilsson, N. (1980) *Principles of Artificial Intelligence*, Tioga Publishing, Palo Alto, Ca.

Rada, R. (1983) Characterizing search spaces. *Proceedings of the International Joint Conference on Artificial Intelligence*, 780–782.

Rada, R. and Ackerman, L. (1983) Computerized tomography expert. *Proceedings of the Conference on Artificial Intelligence*, 233–241.

Ramsey, R. (1981) *Neuroradiology with Computed Tomography*, W. B. Saunders, Philadelphia.

Rich, E. (1983) *Artificial Intelligence*, McGraw-Hill, New York.

Samuel, A. (1959) Some studies in machine learning using the game of checkers. *IBM J. Res. Devel.*, **3**, 210–229.

Samuel, A. (1967) Some studies in machine learning using the game of checkers, Part II. *IBM J. Res Devel.*, **11**, 601–618.

Shortliffe, E. (1976) *Computer Based Medical Consultations: MYCIN*, American Elsevier, New York.

Swartout, W. (1983) XPLAIN: a system for creating and explaining expert consulting systems. *Artificial Intelligence*, **21:3**, 285–325.

Valk, J. (1980) *Computed Tomography and Cerebral Infarctions*, Raven Press, New York.

van Melle, W. (1979) Domain-independent production-rule system for consultation programs. *Proceedings of the International Joint Conference on Artificial Intelligence*, 923–925.

Winston, P. (1984) *Artificial Intelligence*, Addison-Wesley, Reading, Mass.

13

The knowledge industry

T. STONIER

13.1 THE ECONOMICS OF INFORMATION

13.1.1 History of information as an economic input

There exists no economic activity without an information input. The Paleolithic hunter tracking the spoor of his prey was using information. The mediaeval farmer ploughing his field, or his wife spinning fleece were using information. Often information exists in an accumulated form – embedded in the history of a device such as a plough or a spinning wheel. Even animals can be said to be using information, at times learned from each other. For example, the blue tit, attracted to shiny objects, has learned to pry open the tops of milk bottles standing by the side of the house, then lap up the cream.

In this chapter the term information is used in a very broad sense. At one extreme is an individual datum. The simplest datum is an on-off, zero-one, yes-no, binary piece of information. At the higher level, patterns of information comprise knowledge and patterns of knowledge, wisdom. Information may exist outside of the human brain as, for example, inside a computer or inside the brain of a bird such as the blue tit. Actually, information may exist even in the organized structures of the universe as, for example, in a molecule of DNA. It is not the function of this article to explore that aspect which has been covered elsewhere (Stonier, 1984).

In some ways it is helpful to make an analogy between information and the textile industry. The raw fleece is equivalent to data, it may be spun into yarn which represents information. The yarn, in turn, may be woven into cloth just as patterns of information may be woven into knowledge. A loom can weave strands of yarn into patterns of cloth. Similarly, a computer can weave strands of information into patterns of knowledge. Cloth, in turn, may be tailored into a suit; and knowledge, properly analysed and digested may yield wisdom. In this article the term information covers everything from the simplest datum to wisdom. 'Information' should not be confused with 'intelligence', which analyses information in order to make further use of it. Nor should we confuse the creation or existence of information with the transmission of it via a wide variety of communications devices.

13.1.2 The importance of knowledge as an input into modern productive systems

Information has displaced land, labour and capital as the most important input into modern productive systems. Information reduces the requirement for land, labour and capital, it reduces the requirements for raw materials and energy. It spawns entire new industries. It is sold in its own right, and it is the raw material for the fastest growing sector of the economy – the knowledge industry.

Every machine contains within it a history of innovation and invention. This accumulation of information is as important as the accumulation of capital. Any object or material can be made more valuable by adding information: waste desert land plus information becomes productive crop land. Ignorant labourers plus education become skilled, highly productive operatives. Idle capital plus information becomes revenue-yielding investment. Useless energy like sunshine or ocean waves can be made to perform useful work when you know how. Information can add value not only to other inputs such as land or labour, it can add value to itself. Data may be converted to information by analysing it, cross referring, selecting, sorting, summarizing, or in some other way organizing the data. Information is more valuable than data. It is data transformed into a meaningful guide for specific purposes. Information added to human beings through education, adds value to those human beings. It is for this reason that education is an ever-growing industry which in the long run will absorb a larger share of the gross national product than any other single economic activity and which will absorb a larger share of the labour force than any other employer.

It was the economist, Fritz Machlup, who helped define the knowledge industry and who pointed out that 'education' is the largest of the knowledge industries. Machlup included not only formal educational institutions but also education in the home, the church, and in the armed services. The American sociologist, Daniel Bell, extended Machlup's statistics and amplified his concepts. Bell also emphasized the 'centrality' of knowledge in modern economic systems. More recently Marc Porat updated the pioneering studies of Machlup and Bell. Porat divided the information sector of the economy into two major subgroups: the 'primary information sector' which includes those firms supplying information, either as goods or services to the market (i.e. other firms and consumers), and the 'secondary information sector' which includes all the information services provided for internal consumption by government and private non-information firms. For example, a manufacturing firm still needs to run a large office, and in fact, as a result of the advances in production technology, the offices often absorb a substantially larger share of the labour force than does the factory.

According to Porat (1976) the primary information sector of the United States in 1967 accounted for 25% of its GNP; the secondary sector accounted for an additional 21%. Therefore, the total economic information activity accounted for 46% of the GNP. We are now a decade and a half beyond that point, and information technology (IT) has become formally recognized in its own right. To give an indication of IT growth: in 1967 there were about fifteen thousand computer terminals in use in the USA, by 1980 there were probably in excess of two million. Computer data bases were so scant at that time that on-line searches hardly existed in the 1960s. In 1970–71 there were between one hundred and two hundred thousand of them. By 1980 there were at least two million.

13.1.3 Information as a resource

Information may be sold directly as in electronic data bases or in newspapers; information may also be sold as a wealth creator. This is true when an inventor or an author sells a patent or a copyright or provides a licence for others to manufacture an invention. Owning a good patent can be worth a lot more than owning a whole factory. Therefore, information may generate wealth in its own right.

When information is coupled to people, we find that educated and skilled labour tends to be more productive. Hence, there is a continuous selective pressure favoring the educated and skilled, while the uninformed and unskilled are discriminated against. As a category, the worker with a shovel is displaced by the bulldozer driver, the filing clerk is displaced by the computer programmer.

Universities provide employment and improve human capital. They also produce new ideas and new industries. Silicon Valley, Oxford and Cambridge are all filled with industries whose manpower and ideas emanated directly from the universities. Of interest to information technologists is the basic research in solid state physics which preceded and led to the transistor. The location of the semi-conductor industry in the early 1950s, prior to the Silicon Valley phenomenon, clustered along

Route 128 in Boston. Many of the founders of these new companies were graduates of the Massachusetts Institute of Technology and Harvard who frequently either recruited other staff from local universities or consulted with university experts.

The above should give an indication of some of the aspects of the importance of information and knowledge in driving modern, post-industrial economies. What is needed today is a new field in economics – information economics. It must address itself to questions such as, how do you measure information in economic terms? How do you measure the productivity of people working with information? One can determine fairly easily the percentage of the GNP spent on information, but how does one measure the long term impact on the economy? How does one define the fruits of invention and information? What percentage of the annual growth of the GNP or of the increase in the quality of life (not always the same thing), is attributable to advances in information or education?

13.2 THE RISE OF THE INFORMATION OPERATIVES

Probably the earliest people to make a living as information operatives on a part- or full-time basis were medicine men and priests. In due course they evolved into professional wise men. In ancient Greece, if you were good, you could make a lot of money. Adam Smith calculated how much wealth those most famous of ancient information operatives, the Greek philosophers, made. He came to the conclusion that Socrates, for example, charged ten minae per student and had a hundred such students. Therefore he was making a thousand minae, worth well over three thousand pounds (eighteenth century pounds) for each course of lectures. Another example is Gorgias who made a present to the temple at Delphi of a life-sized statue of himself in solid gold. Plutarch, Plato, Aristotle, all became men of means judging from a variety of accounts.

Today the labour force is dominated by information operatives. That is to say, there are by far more people who make their living working with information than any other single category of worker. Even those working on farms, in factories, or with machinery increasingly need to know more in order to avail themselves of new technology. Information operatives can be categorized into one of the following six categories:

(1) A relatively small group involved with creating new information. This includes scientists, artists, statisticians, architects, designers, that is anybody who either creates new information or is weaving new patterns of knowledge from existing information.

(2) A large group is involved with the transmission of information.

This includes first, telephone operators, postal workers, typists, etc. and second, technical salesmen, journalists and others working in the mass media, and finally a huge industry involving educators of all sorts, including teachers, priests, company training officers, etc.

(3) A third group is involved in information storage and retrieval, including filing clerks, librarians, and of course, computer programmers.

(4) A fourth category includes the professionals: lawyers, doctors, accountants – people who apply information which they have accumulated inside their heads and it is this expertise which they sell.

(5) Then there is a large group of information operatives who are no longer considered part of the labour force, but used to be – students. One must keep in mind that in Britain right up until World War I the average lad of 12, and most of 10, spent at least half his time in the mines and factories, while the girls worked in the factories, shops, and as domestics. They were part of the labour force which now has been diverted to receiving information.

(6) Lastly we have to look at the organization operatives. Modern productive systems involve a complex interaction of land, labour, capital, energy and materials, and a wide range of technology coupled to equally complex transport, communication, and distribution systems. In a modern productive system, from the time a kernel of wheat is planted to the time a slice of bread is put in the family toaster, the product undergoes a complex series of processes and interactions. To get these various aspects organized requires not only producers and consumers but also a wide range of middle men and organization operatives – managers.

Managers possess organizational expertise. They create wealth by making the system work. They create *new* wealth by coupling information to existing organizations or productive systems thereby reducing the costs of production or by creating new products or services. They must weld into a viable organization the producers whether they work in factories, farms, or mines or, for that matter, in the art studio or classroom, with a whole host of other information operatives to get the product out to the ultimate consumer. The tools of their trade are the telephone and the pencil, or an extension of these – the typewriter, word processor, telex and so forth (often run by other information operatives). Organization operatives are among the most highly salaried members of the post-industrial economy because of the important function they have, not merely transmitting information from one individual or group to other individuals or groups, but making complex decisions as to what information goes to whom, where and when. In a large organization managers direct a host of other information operatives who are themselves experts in finance, accounting, legal matters, industrial relations, advertising, public relations, planners and forecasters, research and development scientists and engineers, new product designers, education and training officers, purchasing agents, marketing experts, office managers, data processing personnel etc. Clearly, to weld into a coherent whole such a mix of expertise, itself requires great expertise. It is no wonder that managerial skills are amongst the most important and highly valued information skills in our society.

It must be clear that our education system is often poorly geared to providing the kinds of people needed to run a post-industrial economy. The failure is two-fold. Firstly there is inadequate – or to be more precise, outdated – training which fails to keep up with the rapid increase in information inputs into all forms of employment. The man with the shovel has been displaced by the man who knows how to run a mechanical ditch digger. The woman who is a filing clerk is being displaced by the computer programmer. The tendency is to produce skilled operatives too slow and too late and at the same time keep producing them after they are no longer needed. Take as an example, computer programmers. As high level languages and user friendly systems emerge, the need for professional low level programmers will decline. It is doubtful if the education system as well as the public at large will know when to stop producing programming skills which are no longer needed.

The second flaw is more serious. It is the inability to produce people of sufficiently broad background to be able to understand issues and be able to communicate effectively with experts in other areas. It is probably true to say that the majority of decisions made in Britain and to a lesser extent in many other Western countries, are made by technological illiterates. At the same time most engineers, data processors, scientists, that is, technical experts of all sorts, are humanistic and social illiterates. The upshot is that marketing people cannot communicate with the technical people who cannot communicate with the financial people etc., and top management usually misses opportunities or actually gets steam-rollered into oblivion as new systems emerge totally outside their range of comprehension.

13.3 THE FUTURE OF THE KNOWLEDGE INDUSTRY

13.3.1 From energy machines to information machines

The industrial revolution produced machines which extended the human musculature – devices which lifted things or transported things, spun things and wove things. All these involved machines and machinery carrying out manual operations. In contrast, the electronic revolution involved an extension of the human nervous system. Telephone and radio are an extension of the ear. Film, initially based on sight then coupled to sound, and of course television are extensions of both the eye and the ear. And, finally, the computer is an extension of the brain.

Computers represent a form of machine brain; that is, a device which allows one to do outside of one's head, operations which formerly could only be done internally. We are still in the very early stages of artificial intelligence. On the other hand, we are now making rapid strides in combining information with energy machines.

13.3.2 The coupling of energy and information devices

The robots are evolving! They began in a purely electro-mechanical form – primitive devices which were dedicated to carrying out specific routine tasks. These early electro-mechanical devices could change their performance only by altering the wiring or some other part of their structure.

These earliest electro-mechanical devices are now rapidly being displaced by computer-controlled electro-mechanical devices. With these, it becomes possible to alter the behaviour or performance simply by means of software changes. It is the ability to re-program these second generation robots easily that gives them much greater versatility than the first generation devices. However, they are still primitive. If a second generation robot is programmed to pick up a part, and the part is not there, it will still go through all the motions of picking up such a part even though it is merely empty air.

The third generation robots possess built-in sensors and feed-back devices to assess the environment in which they work. They can respond 'intelligently' to their surroundings. Intelligence refers to the ability to analyse information about the environment and then respond to it appropriately. We are now moving into this third stage of robot evolution where both the sensors and the feed-back mechanisms are becoming more and more sophisticated.

This will lead to the fourth generation of robots: networks of robotized devices connected by, as it were, an artificial neurosystem of sensors and feed-back mechanisms all communicating with each other and utilizing expert systems. Individual robots will now co-operate along an entire assembly line to carry out tasks, including correcting any mistakes that may arise during the process. In the long run this means that each assembly line, and finally each factory itself becomes like a gigantic complex machine. Today, one no longer needs human operators to run individual machines. In the future one will no longer need human operators to run a factory. All that will be needed will be human operators to *maintain* a factory and, where need be, *modify* it.

13.3.3 The emergence of information technology

Information technology is a mix of computers and communications – what the French like to call 'telematique'. It represents a wide spectrum of devices and techniques which manipulate information outside of the human brain. It includes computers and software, peripherals, and a wide spectrum of communication devices ranging from optical fibres to communication satellites.

The range of human activities availing themselves of information technology is growing by leaps and bounds. It is not surprising that IT first manifested itself in those industries noted for information crunching. Banks no longer truck round large sums of money. Instead, they engage in exchanging credit information. Similarly, finance, insurance and many government departments are in the business of collecting, collating, analysing, providing and exchanging information.

Among government departments, the Defence Ministries are, without a doubt, a major user of IT because not only do they have the same problem that any government office does, but from here on in the entire military establishment relies increasingly on IT. Communications and command control, 'smart' ammunition such as the Exocet missiles, submarine warfare, electronic battle fields, etc., all rely increasingly on information technology and increasingly there is an effort to disrupt the enemy's capability to work with information technology.

Another area involving government departments is the health care sector. Here again, the administrative problem involves obtaining and digesting huge quantities of information. But it has now gone well beyond that as computers and expert systems are used to run both diagnostic and operative devices and to provide an increasing back-up for doctors and pharmacists.

13.3.4 Enter the expert systems

Doctors represent only one of the many users of IT which is rapidly entering into the professions. Computer-assisted patient interviewing, whereby the computer utilizes expert systems both to interrogate the patient and to analyse the findings, are beginning to move from the experimental stage to more widespread application. The same is beginning to happen in the legal profession. It will become the norm for most professionals. All high-level information operatives of the future will have available to them some form of intelligent data bases.

As offices begin to automate fully, what is emerging for managers is something referred to as 'the infinite desk'. It means that a manager using computers, facsimile reproduction, two-way video telephones and ultimately, holographic transmission systems, can specify and explore with their counterparts across the world all aspects of a negotiation or other transaction.

Equally dramatic will be the transformation of homes as IT enters the scene not only as control devices for temperature, light, sound etc. but also for entertainment and leisure activities, education, and in many instances for work. The possibility that education will undergo a drastic shift over the next two decades from school-based back to home-based has been discussed elsewhere (Stonier, 1979).

We have alluded above to the emergence of factories which are more like giant complex machines. Actually, fully robotized factory systems will be linked to fully automated office systems. This means that you will be able to obtain products or services without the intervention of human operators. The matter is analogous to direct dialling an international telephone call. You are, in that instance, availing yourself of a fully automated service and need no human operator to intervene in getting your party, perhaps half-way across the world, to answer. Similarly, in the future, via your personal home or office terminal you could order a car direct from a factory, specifying your needs. The factory office computer would acknowledge and confirm. After checking on your bank account it would set into motion the production of your car according to specifications, then make arrangements for delivery. Throughout the process it would check the status of your car and inform you. Upon completion and delivery to your home, it would negotiate with your bank computer for the transfer of funds. There is no need for human intervention except perhaps for the transport of the car to the point of delivery. Companies making such cars will need humans for maintenance and modification of the factory, for supervisory personnel, and for customer relations in case things go wrong. Not much else. The principal need for unskilled labour will be for security staff and lorry drivers. The managers will have to fit such a factory complex into the overall international environment. They will be involved in negotiating purchases of components (often via their computer to the component factory computers), engage in marketing, fix prices, define the product and company image, etc. As in the past, they will need to interact with the public, the government, employees, financial backers, etc.

13.3.5 Expanding intellectual technologies

One of the enormous advantages of the computer is its ability to simulate systems. As our experience and understanding of both various systems and simulation grows, we will simulate ever more complex systems. These will include economic systems using input/output analysis, political systems based on voting patterns – ultimately human history itself.

Among the more sophisticated uses of information technology will be the effort to devise new intellectual methodologies in order to achieve reliable forecasts. Weather forecasting already uses IT extensively, including advanced computers and weather satellites. Weather systems are complex but perhaps not as complex as other systems, e.g. metabolic systems, ecological systems, economic systems, or the political systems which comprise human society.

The reason forecasting is still so inaccurate is that it lacks both a coherent theoretical framework for analysing the future, and a proper method for fleshing out such a theory. Core to the development of the knowledge industry will be the ability to predict business cycles, engage in technological forecasts and accomplish intellectual feats as unlikely to us today as was predicting eclipses in the Middle Ages. Let us consider some aspects of this area of the knowledge industry.

(a) Systems analysis of human societies
This views human society as an evolving system derived from the hominid and primate societies which preceded it. The dominant determinant of primate societal evolution is the environment. Among primate societies today, such ecological pressures are still paramount. With the emergence of technology among the early hominids, the relationship between hominid societies and their environment changed. Weapons, fire, speech, the domestication of plants and animals meant that neither predation nor the variation in food supplies were as important as formerly. By the end of the Neolithic Revolution, cultural evolution began to supersede biological evolution because the two great problems confronting almost all animals – getting enough to eat, and not being eaten – had been largely solved. Instead, relationships with neighbours and enemies became more important.

Since the dawn of humanity, social evolution has been driven by technological evolution. What makes information technology so interesting theoretically is the fact that IT is the most powerful technology invented since the development of human speech (itself an IT). Information technology is a 'meta-technology', i.e. a technology not only in its own right, but a technology which affects large areas of existing technology. A fundamental assumption in the systems analysis of the impact of IT on society is that, from here on in, *IT will drive technological evolution just as technology has been driving social evolution.*

(b) Trend projection

Although this method has severe limitations, it has its place. It can help clarify the nature and extent of change one may reasonably expect. As a rough rule of thumb, *if one wishes to look 25 years into the future, one should look 50 years to the past.* If 1985 is the base year, then to look to advances up to year 2010, one should look back to 1935.

Certain types of technological developments show characteristic S-shaped growth curves. These are typical curves encountered in biological systems such as those exhibited by bacteria growing in a limited medium. The growth of the world's telephone network (like a mold growing over a petri dish) appears to be amenable to that sort of analysis. Plotting the curve from 1935 to 1985 would probably provide a reasonable guide to anticipating growth to 2010.

However, *trend projections do not anticipate the discontinuities.* If, in 1935 one were to look into the future, trend projections of radios would not have predicted that within 25 years most households would have television sets as well. Trend projection of air travel would not have anticipated the emergence of jet planes, much less space travel. And of course, in 1935, the entire world of electronic computers, transistors, integrated circuits, microchips, etc. was non-existent.

(c) History of technology analysis

Computers are an ideal illustration of a discontinuity in technological development. In 1935, calculating machines were all the commercial world knew about. By 1960 no large, self-respecting organization would any longer consider doing its payroll by anything other than a computer. In 1960, however, home computers were unknown, digital watches and pocket calculators virtually undreamed of. By 1985, such devices were commonplace and the talk was of cyrogenic computers, biochips, optical fibres, satellite networks, household robots, and a host of other technological wonders.

Could one have anticipated computers and transistors 50 years ago? The answer is yes, if one knew where to look. By the mid-1930s, Konrad Zuse had clearly defined the concept of general purpose calculators and had started to build working models at home, while R. W. Pohl had already predicted in 1933, that electronic valves in radios would be replaced by small solid-state devices (see Pohl, 1934). If one wants *to anticipate technological discontinuities, one needs to look at basic research,* then envision two things:

(1) The technological possibilities derived from the sciences or other basic technological developments.
(2) The economic or other market forces (such as defense requirements) which transform a discovery or invention into a viable innovation or product.

Whereas trend projection, is useful in anticipating the growth of the global telephone system, trend projection is useless for anticipating the emergence of new technologies. The best way to anticipate the discontinuities, the new technologies of the future, is to identify the individuals and groups engaged in the sort of basic research and development likely to yield commercial innovations over the next 25 years, then to analyse the potential market.

(d)   Expert advice
Some social scientists favour the use of Delphic studies to achieve a consensus on future developments. However, the best people are often unwilling or unable to cooperate. Also the procedure fails to properly weigh the opinions and differentiate between insightful expertise, educated guesses, ignorant folk wisdom, or fanciful speculations. In contrast, in-depth analyses by individuals selected for their expertise and for their creative imagination can be extremely helpful in defining the outlines of future developments. Then, as the concepts mature, it is always helpful to hold a host of meetings ranging from small groups of highly selected experts meeting around a table, to open international conferences and symposia. Such a procedure ought to be one of the prerequisites for creating expert systems.

(e)   Economic impact analysis
To ascertain the full positive impact of IT on the economy, it is not enough to record the direct expenditures on IT – its sales value, or its share of the Gross National Product. The reason IT, and the whole knowledge industry, have grown so remarkably over the past few decades is because their input is so cost-effective. Firms and countries which avail themselves of IT properly, thrive. But how does one measure the value of this IT input?

One approach is that exemplified by Albert Fishlow's study on the growth in productivity of American railroads between 1870 and 1910. Fishlow concluded that it would have cost the consumer an additional $1.3 billion to meet the demands of 1910 traffic loads using the much less efficient technology of 1870. Thus the value of improvements in technology (air brakes, automatic couplers, substituting steel for iron rails, more powerful locomotives and more efficient rolling stock) allowed for trains carrying bigger pay loads, faster. The value of these improvements reduced costs by $1.3 billion.

Using this technique one ought to make in depth studies of insurance, banking and other commercial activities who are large consumers of IT. Specifically, how much would it cost to run the volume of insurance business in 1985 using 1960 technology? How about 1935 technology when the telephone system was still relatively small and computers non-existent? By means of such case studies, one should be able to obtain insights into what the impact is likely to be over the next 25 years.

(f) Input/output analysis

Among the most useful forms of analyses in economics is Leontief's input/output analysis (Leontieff, 1966). If reliable information is available for constructing an input/output matrix, it becomes possible to forecast how changes in one part of the economy affect other parts. The main disadvantage with an input/output matrix is that it is relatively static. One could make it dynamic by making two assumptions:

(1) Technology drives post-industrial economies.
(2) The rate at which technology develops is determined by the quality and quantity of information inputs, including education and IT.

The basis for the first assumption is that post-industrial countries show growth neither in population nor geographic size. Therefore long-term growth in GNP cannot reflect increases either in the labour force or increases in land. Nor, can they reflect external input of capital from other countries, at least not in the long-term. Rather it must be the advances in technology which account for improvement in productivity and in the steady growth of societal wealth.

The economist E. F. Denison (1966), has done an analysis somewhat along the lines suggested above. He considered all the factors he could think of which would increase the growth of an economy. He then assigned a value to them. The sum of these was not equal to the actual growth observed. The difference, the 'residual', he attributed to growth in knowledge. Denison concluded that about half the average annual growth rate in the US between 1929 and 1957 was directly attributable to an increase in the dissemination or creation of information.

If Denison is correct, then half of the growth rate is driven by information. There are good reasons for believing that Denison's assumption substantially *underestimates* the importance of information. This then leads one to postulate that it should be possible to create a dynamic model of the economy which consists of a traditional input/output matrix coupled to a major new external input called 'new information'. This external input drives the system.

(g) The international dimension

Post-industrial economies are transnational. No amount of refined analysis of the economy within any one country can provide an accurate assessment of the future. One of the great tasks of economists must be to create a global input/output table which then, using computers, can provide a world model of the present economy. A number of economists are actually engaged in global modeling and when this work is completed, it will need to be brought into the overall analysis.

Technology is also transnational. This is particularly true for information technology. Most of the IT hardware employed in Britain was obtained from outside the UK. The same can be said for most of the basic research although Britain can claim a remarkable record in spawning ideas. This is, in fact, one of the UK's greatest comparative advantages.

No analysis of the future can make sense if it isn't framed in both a historical and a global matrix. To complete the analysis it becomes necessary to expand input/output analysis to an external output called 'society'. Thus, the dynamic system which needs to be studied is outlined in Fig. 13.1.

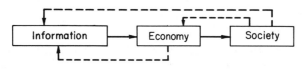

Fig. 13.1

Figure 13.1 represents the theoretical construct which attempts to take input/output analysis beyond the economic dimension by adding the information technology input on the one side, and considering the impact on society on the other.

The dotted lines represent feedback loops. The economy can regulate the growth of information, for example, by funding research and development. Similarly, society can pass laws which regulate the economy, or increase funding for education, thereby increasing the dissemination of information. However, the primary thrust is from left to right because of three unique properties of information technology:

(1) The growth of information and technology is virtually irreversible. It is possible to forget some things and ignore others, but once something becomes known it is almost impossible to unknow it. Similarly, once something has been invented, one can't uninvent it.

(2) The growth of information and technology is exponential: the more is known and the more has been invented, the easier it is to know still more, and invent still more.

(3) There is no foreseeable upper limit to the growth of knowledge or inventions.

No other component of the evolving human societal system has these properties – not the ecological, the economic, the political – that is why the growth of information and technology are the main driving force in human social evolution. New information is the fuel, technology is the steam, and the economy is the locomotive which pulls the train of human progress (and perhaps, occasionally, pushes it backwards).

13.4 CONCLUSIONS AND WARNING

The mechanics of information technology are advancing rapidly. Not only hardware, but software technology is also moving swiftly. Our ability to organize data logically, to devise ever more ingenious algorithms, and to simulate systems with increasing sophistication, reflects our skills at mathematics, programming, and logic. Before long, the limiting factor in creating simple data bases, intelligent data bases, and expert systems will be the limitations in human knowledge and understanding.

Helpful and useful as such systems will be, they could also create serious distortions in our culture. The industrial revolution produced enormous suffering during its inception. Towards the end of the industrial era, although many of the early problems had been solved, it had created a sort of social monster which was largely brawn and very little brain – a global society with a military technology which could destroy our civilization without having developed the political technology to make certain that we wouldn't – a global society in which the affluent sector worried about food surpluses while the poorer sector suffered famines and death from malnutrition.

Expert systems may help. Probably they will. However, we might now be creating a new kind of social monster whose conceit is that all problems may be solved by using the logic and algorithms of a clever chess player. Chess is a zero-sum game. Human existence is not. Devising an expert system to advise a chess player will not lead to fatal errors. Devising an expert system to advise a physician, could. Obviously, we need to create an intellectual technology to help solve human problems including those in economics, politics, belief systems, education, and our culture in general. However we must become increasingly cautious and conservative about compounding complexities.

By applying to highly complex systems which are still poorly understood (e.g. economic systems), new sets of complexities which themselves may also be poorly understood, we are producing new levels of uncertainties, while at the same time creating the delusion of greater accuracy. There is always the danger that people; forever seeking simple solutions, will accept the outputs of machine intelligence with much greater faith than is warranted.

The knowledge industry must therefore address itself with vigor to uncovering the laws of economics, to understanding human society and the human psyche, not only in areas of conflict, but also in cooperation. In particular, we need to make crystal clear what areas of knowledge are reasonably reliable, what areas are unknown, and which parts of human knowledge are in that grey area in between.

Creating valuable, human-serving expert systems is one of the greatest challenges confronting intellectuals and the knowledge industry over the next few decades. Will we have the insights to forge, then use, such tools wisely?

ACKNOWLEDGEMENTS

The author wishes to thank Ms M. Ellison for her patient assistance in producing this manuscript.

Portions of this article were excerpted from the following previous publications:

Stonier, T. (1979) Changes in western society: educational implications. In *World Yearbook of Education 1979: Recurrent Education and Lifelong Learning* (eds T. Schuller and J. Megarry) Kogan Page, London, 31–44.
Stonier, T. (1983) *The Wealth of Information: A Profile of the Post-Industrial Economy*, Thames/Methuen, London.
Stonier, T. (1984) Information and the deep structure of the universe – the need for a new physics. In *Infostorms*, Council for Educational Technology (In press).

REFERENCES

Denison, E.F. (1966) Measuring the contribution of education (and the residual) to economic growth. In *The Residual Factor and Economic Growth*, OECD, 13–55.
Fishlow, A. as cited in N. Rosenberg (1983) *Inside The Black Box*, Cambridge Univ Press.
Leontief, W. (1966) *Input/Output Economics*, Oxford University Press, New York.
Pohl, R.W. (1934) *Mitteilungen der Universitäts bundes Göttingen*, **15** (as cited by E. Braun and S. MacDonald (1978) in *Revolution in Miniature*, Cambridge University Press.)
Porat, M. (1976) *The Information Economy*, Center for Interdisciplinary Research, Stanford University.
Smith, A. (1776) *Inquiry into the Nature and Causes of the Wealth of Nations*, Book 1.
Zuse, K. cited in Evans, C. (1981) *The Making of the Micro*, Victor Gollancz, London.

Bibliography

Specific references can be found at the end of the chapters concerned. This is a general reading list for those who want to delve deeper into the field of expert systems. The books and articles listed here represent essential background reading for anyone seriously interested in knowledge engineering and its applications. The bibliography covers the field of artificial intelligence, with special emphasis on the acquisition, representation and use of knowledge in computer systems.

BARR, A. and FEIGENBAUM, E.A. (eds.) (1981) *The Handbook of Artificial Intelligence, Vol. 1*, Pitman Books, London.

BARR, A. and FEIGENBAUM, E.A. (eds.) (1982) *The Handbook of Artificial Intelligence, Vol. 2*, Pitman Books, London.

COHEN, D. and FEIGENBAUM, E.A. (eds.) (1983) *The Handbook of Artificial Intelligence, Vol. 3*, Pitman Books, London.

DAVIS, R. and LENAT, D. (1981) *Knowledge Based Systems in Artificial Intelligence*, McGraw-Hill, New York.

FEIGENBAUM, E.A. and MCCORDUCK, P. (1984) *The Fifth Generation*, Michael Joseph, London.

FORSYTH, R. (1981) BEAGLE: A Darwinian approach to pattern recognition. *Kybernetes*, **10**.

GRAHAM, N. (1979) *Artificial Intelligence*, Tab Books, Blue Ridge, Pa.

HAYES-ROTH, F., WATERMAN, D. and LENAT, D. (eds.) (1983) *Building Expert Systems*, Addison-Wesley, New York.

HOFSTADTER, D. (1981) *Goedel, Escher, Bach . . .* , Harvester Press, Brighton.

HOLLAND, J.H. (1975) *Adaptation in Natural and Artificial Systems*, University of Michigan Press, Ann Arbor, Michigan.

JAMES, M. (1984) *Artificial Intelligence in Basic*, Newnes Technical Books, Sevenoaks, Kent.

LANGLEY, P. (1981) Data-driven discovery of physical laws. *Cognitive Science*, **5**.

LENAT, D. (1983) EURISKO: A program that learns new heuristics and domain concepts. *Artificial Intelligence*, **21**.

MICHALSKI, R.S., CARBONELL, J.G. and MITCHELL, T.M. (eds.) (1983) *Machine Learning*, Tioga Press, Palo Alto, Ca.

MICHALSKI, R.S. and CHILAUSKY, R.L. (1980) Learning by being told and learning from examples. *International J. Policy Analysis and Information Systems*, **43**, 125–161.

MICHIE, D. (ed.) (1982) *Introductory Readings in Expert Systems*, Gordon and Breach, New York.

MITCHELL, T. (1982) Generalization as search. *Artificial Intelligence*, **18**, 203–226.

NAYLOR, C. (1983) *Build Your Own Expert System*, Sigma Technical Press.

QUINLAN, R. (1982) Semi-autonomous acquisition of pattern-based knowledge. *Machine Intelligence*, **10**.

SAMUEL, A. (1967) Some studies in machine learning using the game of checkers, part II. *IBM Journal of Research and Development*.

SHORTLIFFE, E. (1976) *Computer-Based Medical Consultations: MYCIN*, Elsevier, New York.

WATERMAN, D. and HAYES-ROTH, F. (eds.) (1978) *Pattern-Directed Inference Systems*, Academic Press, New York.

WEISS, S. and KULIKOWSKI, C. (1984) A *Practical Guide to Designing Expert Systems*, Chapman and Hall, London.

WINSTON, P.H. (1977) *Artificial Intelligence*, Addison-Wesley, Reading, Mass.

WINSTON, P.H. (1982) Learning new principles from precedents and examples. *Artificial Intelligence*, **19**.

ZADEH, L. and FUKANAKA, K. (eds.) (1975) *Fuzzy Sets and their Applications to Cognitive Decision Processes*, Academic Press, New York.

Index